ECONOMICS AND THE LAW

ECONOMICS AND THE LAW

FROM POSNER TO POST-MODERNISM

Nicholas Mercuro and Steven G. Medema

PRINCETON UNIVERSITY PRESS   PRINCETON, NEW JERSEY

Copyright © 1997 by Princeton University Press
Published by Princeton University Press, 41 William Street,
Princeton, New Jersey 08540
In the United Kingdom: Princeton University Press,
Chichester, West Sussex
All Rights Reserved

Third printing, and first paperback printing, 1999

Paperback ISBN 0-691-00544-3

The Library of Congress has cataloged the cloth edition
of this book as follows

Mercuro, Nicholas.
Economics and the law: from Posner to
post-modernism / Nicholas Mercuro
and Steven G. Medema.
p.   cm.
Includes bibliographical references and index.
ISBN: 0-691-01174-5 (alk. paper)
1. Law and economics.   I. Medema, Steven G.   II. Title.
K487.E3M468   1997
340′.115—dc21   96-46300   CIP

This book has been composed in Times Roman

The paper used in this publication meets the
minimum requirements of ANSI/NISO Z39.48-1992
(R1997) (*Permanence of Paper*)

http://pup.princeton.edu

Printed in the United States of America

3   5   7   9   10   8   6   4

To Warren J. Samuels

TEACHER, COLLEAGUE, AND FRIEND

Contents

Preface

OVER THE LAST several decades, Law and Economics has developed from a small and rather esoteric branch of research within economics and law to a substantial movement that has helped to both redefine the study of law and expose economics to the important economic implications of the legal environment. For our purposes here, we depart from the usual more narrow definitions given to the field and define Law and Economics broadly to include the application of economic theory (primarily microeconomics and the basic concepts of welfare economics) to examine the formation, structure, processes, and economic impact of law and legal institutions. Given the fact that the law and the economy interact across a variety of fronts, the fundamental insights of Law and Economics have important implications not just for economics and law, but for other contiguous disciplines as well, particularly those branches of political science and sociology that concern themselves with various facets of the law.

The purpose of this book is to present a relatively brief overview of the core elements of the different perspectives on the varied traditions within Law and Economics. Law and Economics is not a homogeneous movement; it reflects several traditions, sometimes competing and sometimes complementary, including the Chicago School of Law and Economics, Public Choice Theory, Institutional and Neoinstitutional Law and Economics, the New Haven School, Modern Civic Republicanism, and Critical Legal Studies.

This book by no means constitutes an exhaustive survey of the contents of each of the schools of thought. In fact, its aim is more modest—to provide the reader with a synoptic, noncritical description of the broad contours of each school of thought. We do not attempt to argue for or against any particular school of thought; rather, we try only to provide a concise overview of just what each school of thought is attempting to convey, recognizing fully that the marketplace of ideas will ultimately serve as the "gatekeeper" that determines which, if any, of these schools of thought will become a permanent part of modern-day jurisprudence.

By offering a noncritical analysis and description, we hope to provide the reader with a fuller understanding of the relationships between the formation, structure, and processes of law and legal institutions and their impact on the performance of the economy. In addition, we also hope to convey a sense of the important elements of and issues between the various schools of thought, and, through this, a sense for both the importance and breadth of the interrelations between law and economy, and an appreciation of the scope of existing legal-economic scholarship.

We have benefited greatly from numerous individuals and institutions in the preparation of this book, and the sum total of these efforts have greatly enhanced its strength. We are grateful to Susan Rose-Ackerman, Peter Boettke, Thráinn Eggertsson, Dub Lane, Bill Lovett, Robin Paul Malloy, Warren J. Samuels, A. Allan Schmid, Mark Tushnet, and Gerald Whitney for their very useful comments and suggestions on various draft portions of the manuscript. Any deficiencies that remain are attributable solely to the authors.

We also gratefully acknowledge the research support given to us over the course of this project. Research support and release time for Medema was provided by the Department of Economics and W. James Smith, Department Chair; Dean Marvin Loflin and the College of Liberal Arts and Sciences; and the Graduate School of the University of Colorado at Denver. Secretarial support was provided by Lynn Ferguson, Hillary Shea, and Diane Watkins of the University of Colorado at Denver Economics Department. The research assistance of Mary Therese Cogeos is gratefully acknowledged. Margaret Henderson of East Lansing, Michigan, and David Tufte and Franklin Lopez of the University of New Orleans Department of Economics and Finance provided invaluable assistance with the preparation of the graphs. Mercuro extends a special thanks to the Chancellor, the Vice-Chancellor, and the Provost of the University of New Orleans for affording him the opportunity to annually teach *The Economics of Legal Relationships* at Tulane Law School; to the Dean of the Law School, John R. Kramer, and the faculty of the Law School for their invitation to teach the course; and, finally, to the many Tulane law students and the students of economics from both the University of Vienna and the Free University of Berlin who, over the years, have asked many probing questions that forced a valuable rethinking and reformulation of many of the ideas contained in this book.

Finally, we would like to thank the staff at Princeton University Press and, in particular, Peter Dougherty, Social Science and Public Affairs Publisher, and his assistant, Michelle McKenna, for their willingness to publish this book and for their suggestions, assistance, and encouragement in seeing this project through to completion. We would also like to thank our production editors, Sterling Bland and Molan Chun Goldstein, and our copyeditor, David E. Anderson, whose efforts greatly enhanced the quality of the final book.

Nicholas Mercuro
Steven G. Medema
November 1, 1996

ECONOMICS AND THE LAW

CHAPTER 1

The Jurisprudential Niche of Law
and Economics

It is somewhat surprising that so conspicuous a
truth as the interaction of economics and law should
have waited so long for recognition—a recognition
by no means universal. Some of those who question
it maintain the independence and self-sufficiency of
law, while others maintain that of economics.
In reality law and economics are ever and everywhere
complementary and mutually determinative.
(Berolzheimer, 1912, p. 23)

INTRODUCTION

The primary purpose of this book is to provide the reader with a concise overview of the dominant schools of thought within Law and Economics and the core ideas they attempt to convey. Today, Law and Economics[1] can be defined as the application of economic theory (primarily microeconomics and the basic concepts of welfare economics) to examine the formation, structure, processes, and economic impact of law and legal institutions. Various schools of thought compete in this rich marketplace of ideas, including the Chicago school, Public Choice Theory, the two institutionalist schools of law and economics (which we shall label "Institutionalism" and "Neoinstitutionalism"), and the New Haven school. In addition to examining these, we provide an overview of the principal contours of both critical legal studies and modern civic republicanism, which, although not traditionally associated with law and economics, place significant emphasis on the interrelations between law and economy and thus may be said to fall under the Law and Economics heading. As implied by the title of this book, we are presenting these schools of thought as competing perspectives or approaches within the marketplace of ideas to the study of the development and the reformulation of law and to the examination of the interrelations of legal and economic processes generally.[2] As such, these ideas are of fundamental importance for those working in the fields of economics, law, political science, and sociology.

It must be underscored from the outset that we are trying only to describe the central ideas that each school of thought is attempting to convey. No attempt is made to critique the schools of thought or the ideas contained therein. We are also well aware of the pitfalls that are to be encountered in trying to describe the essential elements of a particular school of thought when there are continuing, and occasionally acrimonious, disputes within some (and probably all) schools. Our response, in short, is that the benefits of identifying the schools of thought as presented here exceed the costs of expressed misgivings by those few within each school of thought who object to or refuse categorization.

The present significance of the interrelations between law and economics is evidenced by a variety of indicators. First, there is the relatively recent establishment of the American Law and Economics Association, the Canadian Law and Economics Association, and the European Association of Law and Economics. Second, there are now a number of leading publications dedicated to publishing the scholarly contributions to this field, including journals such as the *Journal of Law and Economics*; the *Journal of Legal Studies*; the *Journal of Law, Economics & Organization*; *Public Choice*; *Constitutional Political Economy*; the *International Review of Law and Economics*; and the *European Journal of Law and Economics*. In addition, there are a wide variety of traditional law reviews that now regularly publish Law and Economics articles, and three research annuals—the *Supreme Court Economic Review*, *Research in Law and Economics*, and *The Economics of Legal Relationships*—devoted to Law and Economics. The extent and significance of this literature is reflected in the fact that in 1991 the *Journal of Economic Literature* formally recognized Law and Economics as a separate field within its classification system of the discipline of economics. A third indicator is the existence of a number of programs in law and economics within the major law schools, including Harvard University, Yale University, Columbia University, Stanford University, and the University of California–Berkeley, and the very active working paper series associated with these programs. And finally for the past twenty-three years Henry G. Manne, Dean of the George Mason University School of Law, has organized and hosted the Law and Economics Institutes for Law Professors and for Economists (now held each summer at Dartmouth College); together these two institutes have had over one thousand professors of economics and law as well as judges attend their programs.[3]

THE PRESENT SITUATION IN LEGAL-ECONOMIC SCHOLARSHIP

Although the seeds of contemporary Law and Economics go back at least a century,[4] it has been in the last four decades that it has emerged as a substantial and important body of thought within both economics and law. During this time, Law and Economics has developed within (and in part because of) a somewhat uncertain and unsettled jurisprudence—what may be termed the ambiguous milieu of law. What once existed as prevailing legal doctrine derived from conventional political and legal theory still exists, but law no longer develops in a self-contained, autonomous manner. It has been observed that "[l]aw is now recognized by most teachers of law to be a multidimensional phenomena—historical, philosophic, psychological, social, political, economic and religious" (Packer and Erlich, 1973, p. 56). In addition, commentators such as Lewis Kornhauser (1984, p. 361) have suggested that almost all American legal scholars, judges, and lawyers hold an instrumental view of the law—instrumental in the sense that legal rules are adopted so as to promote some goal, be it equality, justice, fairness, or efficiency.[5]

The study of law is now joined by the ideas and doctrines comprising the several schools of thought that we include under the heading of Law and Economics, as well as by the work of the rights-based theorists,[6] feminist jurisprudential scholars, and critical race theorists, all of whom claim to have something worthwhile to say as to the emergence and development of the law. The outward turn of law thus far has shown no consensus-type movement toward a new and stable foundation for the law (Minow, 1987). We now stand at a point where legal study constitutes a plethora of competing and often mutually exclusive points of view. To use Alan Hunt's (1987, p. 7) metaphor, the glacier that is law has fractured into numerous pieces, and its replacement (if there is to be one) remains to be determined. Perhaps the present situation of the law was best summed up in the comment that "[w]ith the demise of Realism, legal scholarship was left with a plethora of explanatory frameworks, [and] a dearth of criteria for choice among them" (Note, 1982, p. 1676).

The present situation in law and its relationship to economics did not arise in a vacuum. Rather, it is partially the outcome of the development of the *Law* of Law and Economics—in particular, the various evolving perspectives from which one can and should analyze the prevailing *legal relations governing society*—and the development of the *Economics* in Law and Economics—particularly as embodied in the work of neoclassical microeconomists since Alfred Marshall. In the next section, we will examine briefly the path that has led law to its present situation. This will be followed by a brief characterization of the relevant concepts of economic efficiency variously employed by legal-economic scholars.[7] Finally, we will present a description of the underlying logic of Law and Economics.

THE *LAW* IN LAW AND ECONOMICS

The Nature of Common Law

Common law, as it has developed from the English royal courts of centuries past to present-day America, can be said to consist of principles developed gradually by judges as the foundation of their decisions. The history of this common law jurisprudence has at its foundation a search for moorings, for a set of interpretive and adjudicatory principles from which to justify judicial decisions, guide the law's development, and ground its legitimacy and authority. During the Middle Ages, the interpretation of law was profoundly influenced by theological considerations, as law claimed to stand as divine revelation or the will of God. From the time of the Renaissance until the middle of the nineteenth century, this idea received a somewhat more secular cast, as law was said to be grounded in ultimate principles or ideas, such as natural law. Against this metaphysical approach came the positivist scientific attitude toward the law, an attitude born out of the success of the natural sciences in the nineteenth century and the attempts by the social sciences, as well as the law, to apply the methods of the natural sciences.[8] The constant here is that judges of various jurisdictions (from England to America) have added to, and continue to recognize, the authority of this accumulating body of common law.

Sir William Blackstone suggested that the common law can be interpreted as a mass of custom and tradition, manifested in *judge-made maxims*.[9] These so-called maxims of the common law symbolized the broad guidelines which could be considered to underlie and direct legal decision making. As observed by one commentator, "these maxims were the essential core of the common law, woven so closely into the fabric of English life that they could never be ignored with impunity" (Sommerville, 1986, p. 96). This concept of "maxims" points to the enduring idea that the heart of the common law is not comprised of specific decisions as to rules, doctrines, or procedures, but rather of broad notions which are difficult to systematize but nonetheless remain, in some way, woven into the fabric of life. Whereas some commentators observed a surface chaos in these accumulated judicial decisions, classical common law thought continued to argue that it remained an internally coherent, unified body of principles—principles that comprised the substrate of common law. The emphasis on the more malleable principles, as opposed to the less flexible "doctrines" or "rules" of common law, was intended to convey the notion that the common law remained flexible, that is, that the law retained a dynamic character needed in legal decision making in modern society. Indeed, within the United States, at least, the period between the Revolutionary and Civil Wars witnessed a movement "'to frame general doctrines based on a self-conscious consideration of social and economic policies'" that would meet the needs of the time (Duxbury, 1995, p. 9, quoting Horwitz, 1977, p. 2).

Doctrinalism

The second half of the nineteenth century witnessed a positive, scientific movement across many intellectual disciplines, wherein these various disciplines attempted to apply formalistic principles that would give them the status accorded to the natural sciences. The legal manifestation of this more general movement was doctrinalism, which is concerned with the law as it is, apart from reference to the religious, metaphysical, or socioeconomic principles of earlier eras. Law here is not a search for the principles of some natural or divine law, but rather a scientific enterprise which "takes as its starting point a given legal order and distills from it by a predominately inductive method certain fundamental notions, concepts, and distinctions" (Bodenheimer, 1974, p. 95). It is, as Julius Stone (1950, p. 31) has said, primarily concerned with "an analysis of legal terms, and an inquiry into the *logical* interrelations of legal propositions."

It was Christopher Columbus Langdell, Dean of the Harvard Law School, who perhaps came to be most closely associated with this view in American law.[10] Langdell both established the case method within American legal education and promoted the use of this method as necessary for teaching law as a science. He saw law as a set of principles or doctrines that were imbedded in legal cases and revealed through the study of cases over time. Given this, he considered the judicial opinion to occupy a place of preeminence in law, as the corpus of judicial opinions embodied "a handful of permanent, unchanging, and indispensable principles of law" (Posner, 1990, p. 15) that revealed themselves in different guises in different cases. These doctrines, he believed, could only be mastered through the careful and exacting study of cases, and the task of legal reasoning thus became that of discerning the doctrines from the opinions. Because of his emphasis on the evolution of legal doctrine from opinions, Langdell had little use for those areas of law that arose from other sources, such as statutes and the Constitution.

Langdell, says Lawrence M. Friedman (1973, p. 535), believed that law was "a pure, independent science" whose data consisted solely of legal cases. From this body of knowledge it was possible to decide individual cases through the use of syllogistic reasoning from the precedential principles set forth in previous like cases. Inherent within this perspective is the idea that judges neither make nor create law; they interpret and apply it (Cotterrell, 1989, pp. 21–37). In deciding cases, the judge expresses part of the total, immanent wisdom of the law (a wisdom existing only in one's mind) which is assumed to be already existent before the judge's decision. The judge works from within the law and thus from within the repository of the experience of the community over time—a community imbued with its own culture and customs. It is the judge's discernment of the community's culture and customs over time that lends both authority and legitimacy to the common law. Inasmuch as the common law is seen to be residing in the community and not the political arena, the emergent legal order comes to command the highest respect. If instead the judge had *made* the law—that is, had imposed the law on the community as if he were a political ruler or the servant of one—his authority would be undermined. Inasmuch as a judge's authority is based on his being a representative of the community, he is thereby able to *state* the community's law—not *make* the community's law (Cotterrell, 1989, p. 27).

Perhaps nowhere is doctrinalist ethos better characterized than by William W. Fisher, Morton J. Horwitz, and Thomas A. Reed (1993, p. vii), who, in the introduction to their book *American Legal Realism*, say that

> Properly organized, law was like geometry. . . . Each doctrinal field revolved around a few fundamental axioms, derived primarily from empirical observation of how courts had in the past responded to particular sorts of problems. From those axioms, one could and should deduce—through noncontroversial, rationally compelling reasoning processes—a large number of specific rules or corollaries. The legal system of the United States . . . did not yet fully conform to this ideal; much of the scholars' energies were devoted to identifying and urging the repudiation of rules or decisions that disturbed the conceptual order of their respective fields. But once purified of such anomalies and errors, the scholars contended, the law would be "complete" (capable of providing a single right answer to every dispute) and elegant.

This doctrinal method served to legitimate judicial decisions through the logical power of the inductive process and the weight of jurisprudential history. In the process, says Friedman (1973, p. 535),

> the new method severed the cords, already tenuous, that tied the study of law to the main body of American scholarship and American life. Langdell purged from the curriculum whatever touched directly on economic and political questions, whatever was argued, voted on, fought over. He brought into the classroom a worship of common law and of the best common-law judges. Legislation he disdained; illogical decisions he despised. All this he cloaked with the mantle of science. He equated law absolutely with judges' law; and judges' law was narrowed to formalism and abstraction.

Law, under this approach, was self-referential, consisting of a set of objectively inferable rules and procedures logically applied. Law thus became both formal and insular. Jurisprudence consisted only in an established body of legal doctrine, a set of principles in which judicial discretion was minimized, and where ethics, social conditions, politics, ideologies, and the insights of disciplines outside of the law had no proper place.

Friedman (1973, p. 536) suggests that the attraction of Langdell's method was that it served the needs of the profession at that time: "It exalted the prestige of law and legal learning; at the same time it affirmed that legal science stood apart, as an independent entity, distinct from politics, legislation, and the man on the street." The professional belief in the lawyer's monopoly of legal practice was reaffirmed by law's status as a profession that required a rigorous, formal education. The bar association movement, which entrenched the professionalization of the law, arose at the same time as Langdell's movement, and the two fed off each other. Whole subject areas in the present law school curriculum—for example, contracts, torts, and property—have had their boundaries fixed and are distinguished from each other by their respective common law principles. Indeed, today, much of legal education and legal scholarship consists of the exposition and systematization of these general principles and the techniques required to discern and apply them, together with the legal rules, doctrines, and procedures that emanate therefrom.

Moving Away from Doctrinalism

Reaction against doctrinalism gained influence in law already in the late nineteenth century. The early scholarship in this area, which might be classified as "sociological jurisprudence," was contributed by such notable expositors as Oliver Wendell Holmes Jr., Roscoe Pound, and Benjamin Cardozo. Sociological jurisprudence was a reaction against both the formalism of doctrinalism and the traditional concepts of natural or objectively determinable rights.[11] These writers claimed that law cannot be understood without reference to social conditions, and against the idea of the autonomy of law was posited the idea that insights from the other social sciences should be integrated into the law. Judges, they said, should be aware of the social and economic conditions which affect the path of law and which result from the legal decision-making process (Bodenheimer, 1974, pp. 120–21).

Cardozo emphasized the need for judges to be attuned to social realities and, while not rejecting the role of analytic processes in jurisprudence, believed that "considerations of social policy loom large in the art of adjudication" (Bodenheimer, 1974, p. 121). Both judicial decision making and the path of law, he said, are necessarily influenced by subjective elements of instinct, belief, convictions, and views as to social need. Although precedent was important for Cardozo, he believed that when it conflicted with the greater interests of justice or social welfare, the latter should carry the day (Bodenheimer, 1974, p. 121).[12]

Holmes (1923, p. 1), like Cardozo, emphasized the limits of doctrinalism, but went further than Cardozo in discounting the role played by logical reasoning in jurisprudence: "The felt necessities of the time, the prevalent moral and political theories, intuitions of public policy, avowed or unconscious, even the prejudices which judges share with their fellow men, have a good deal more to do than the syllogism in determining the rules by which men should be governed." Law, in his view, expresses the will of the dominant interests in society. Holmes, says Richard A. Posner (1987a, p. 762), "pointed out that law is a tool for achieving social ends, so that to understand law requires an understanding of social conditions"; in addition, Holmes held that judges need to be acquainted with the historical, social, and economic aspects of the law (Bodenheimer, 1974, p. 123).[13] These ideas were echoed by Pound (1954, p. 47), who saw law as "a social institution to satisfy wants" and the history of law as "a continually more efficacious social engineering." These pragmatic and socially attuned conceptions of law set the stage for an even more pronounced move away from the past—Legal Realism.

The Legal Realist Challenge

The most influential of the challenges to doctrinalism was the Legal Realist movement, which reached its zenith in the 1930s. The Realist movement was part of a more general response to formalism and logical reasoning in the early twentieth century, wherein American intellectual life was impacted by "a more empirical, experimental, and relativistic attitude toward the problems and guiding assumptions" of the various scholarly disciplines (Purcell, 1988, p. 359). The Realists, following the work of Holmes, sought to turn law outward to make it attuned to the social realities of the day. In the process, they affected both the process of legal education and the intellectual life of the law (Friedman, 1973, p. 591).[14]

The reverence for the traditions of the law, so central within doctrinalism, held little sway among the Realists. The divergence between the law as written into books as compared with the law as it operates in fact was relentlessly pursued. The Realists rejected the existence of objectively determinable rights; the use of rigid legal rules, categories, and classifications; appeals to the authority of the past—citations, eminent jurists, and classic treatises; and the logic of reasoning from precedent. The Langdellian system in general was thus anathema to the Realists. Karl Llewellyn (1934, p. 7), a leading Legal Realist, suggested that the role of legal rules within the lawmaking process was far less important than generally assumed, and that "[t]he theory that rules decide cases seems for a century to have fooled, not only library-ridden recluses, but judges." In a similar vein, Jerome Frank asserted that, contrary to the logical cloak in which they are enveloped, judicial decisions are largely informed by "emotions, intuitive hunches, prejudices, tempers, and other irrational factors" (Bodenheimer, 1974, p. 125). The judge, rather than the logic of the law, was the central factor in the resolution of legal cases. Law was seen not as a set of rules, but as what judges actually do.[15] The logic of precedent, according to the Realists, was seriously flawed. The use of precedential reasoning was essentially the determination as to whether the decision in an earlier case could be applied in straightforward fashion to the facts of the case at hand. The human factor underlying this form of judicial decision making was apparent to the Realists: Such decisions inevitably entailed a choice as to the relation between the facts of one case and another, a choice that was necessarily determined by subjective value judgments rather than by logic (Mensch, 1990, p. 22). Because decisions rested on the judge's conception of right and wrong, social, political, and economic considerations became important variables. Furthermore, the constant change of law (perhaps most strikingly in response to the industrial revolution) belied the claim that law was certain, fixed, and logical. Against the formalist view of law as a deductive science, then, came the Realist emphasis on developing legal theory through inductive scientific principles (Duxbury, 1995, p. 80).

Along with the idea that law cannot be a logical, self-contained discipline came the prescription that it should cease all pretensions of being so, and that law should become more overtly attuned to the social ends that it necessarily serves. The Realists held a strong instrumentalist conception of law: For them, law was, and had to be seen as, a "working tool" (Friedman, 1973, p. 592). This demanded an understanding of the relationship between law and society and of the way that results—economic, political, and social—followed upon legal decisions. Every legal decision was understood to have social, ethical, political, and economic implications, and the Realists maintained that these should be recognized and explicitly dealt with by judges, not hidden behind a veil of logical reasoning. Thus, the Realists contended that to better understand these implications, it is necessary to explore the interrelations between law and the other social sciences, including sociology, psychology, political science, and economics.

Of particular import for present purposes is the Realist interest in using economics to understand and to guide the development of law.[16] The Realists argued that the importance of the interrelations between law and economics can be seen in the twin facts that legal change is often a function of economic ideas and conditions, which necessitate and/or generate demands for legal change, and that economic change is often governed by legal change.[17] Karl Llewellyn pointed to a number of ways in which law influences economic conditions, including its role in providing a foundation for the economic order, its influence on the operation and outcomes of the competitive market process (particularly through the structure of law pertaining to property, contract, and credit, and through restrictions placed by law on the competitive process), and the influence of taxation, social welfare legislation, and public enterprise on production and distribution.[18]

Given the important interdependencies that they saw between law and economy, it is not surprising that Realists such as Llewellyn considered economic analysis a useful tool for understanding law and legal change and for devising laws that would improve the social condition. Indeed, Samuel Herman went so far as to assert that "[t]he law of a state never rises higher than its economics" (Herman, 1937, p. 831), and expressed the hope that " 'a disciplined judicial economics' might become 'a realistic and tempered instrument for solving the major judicial questions of our time' " (Samuels, 1995, p. 263, quoting Herman, 1937, p. 821). And whereas the Realists found certain aspects of neoclassical economics, such as marginal analysis, useful, it was with the institutional economics of Thorstein Veblen and John R. Commons, rather than with neoclassical economics, that the Realists found a close affinity.[19] From the Realist-Institutionalist project came numerous studies that attempted to probe the linkages between law and economy, and, in the process, to inform legal and economic thinking and decision making.

The Need to Fill the Void

Although Legal Realism largely spelled the end of doctrinalist excesses, it never became established as the dominant view of law. Its sputtering existence (if not its demise) was accompanied by new tension. On the one hand, there was already in the 1940s a renewed belief in the autonomy of law, this time in the form of the legal process movement—a movement that emphasized that certain principles of process were neutral, hence immutable.[20] Thus, with the focus on process, the idea that legal principles can be inferred from the study of judicial opinions, and the accompanying idea that legal education consisted of studying, analyzing, and critiquing authoritative texts—opinions, statutes, and legal rules—was still firmly entrenched in 1960. On the other hand, as described by Edmund Kitch (1983a), it was the Legal Realists who created an environment that was more receptive to the introduction of economics into the law school curriculum.

In the early 1960s, however, this belief in law's autonomy once again began to break down. Posner (1987a, pp. 765–73) suggests several reasons for this. First, this period witnessed the end of political consensus in the United States that was so prominent in the 1950s. As Owen Fiss (1986, p. 2) has put it, the potential "death of law" is derivative of the turmoil of the 1960s, from which came a "rejection of the notion of law as a public ideal" and of "adjudication as the process for interpreting and nurturing a public morality." Second, the "boom" in disciplines complementary to law, such as economics and philosophy, gave rise to efforts by practitioners within these other disciplines to branch out into new areas, especially law. Third, there was a collapse of confidence in the ability of lawyers to solve the major problems of the legal system on their own. Fourth, there was a feeling that there was little new to be said in law, from the traditional autonomous perspective. Fifth, the increasing prestige and authority accorded to scientific modes of inquiry (and thus the relative decline in the prestige and authority accorded to the nonscientific method of legal analysis) pushed legal scholars to adopt more "scientific" modes of analysis. Finally, the increasingly important status of statutes and the Constitution and the lack of adequate tools for interpreting such documents within the traditional legal method caused legal scholars to look elsewhere for interpretive principles.

These and other issues led to a rebirth of the disillusionment with the idea of law as an autonomous discipline, as scholars began to seek other bases on which to ground legal analysis.[21] The result—the setting for which had in fact been established by the Realists (Duxbury, 1995, p. 92)—has been the growth of numerous "law and __" movements over the past thirty years, movements that have sought to bring the insights of economics, Continental philosophy, literary theory, anthropology, feminist studies, Marxism, and so on into legal studies. Each of these projects represents an attempt to turn law outward and has, in its own way, sought to present a basis on which to found law's legitimacy, and, in doing so, to fill the void left by Legal Realism. In the process, legal analysis has become highly politicized and interwoven with the social sciences and humanities (Minow, 1987, p. 79).[22] No longer is law seen to be able to, on its own, generate results that constitute objective truth, and the consensus about how to resolve important legal questions has all but disappeared.

THE *ECONOMICS* IN LAW AND ECONOMICS

Against the idea that law can be understood only through the use of the traditional legal doctrinal concepts based on justice and fairness, economics counters that such understanding can be augmented (supplanted?) by economic concepts, including the criteria of economic efficiency. As such, the *Economics* in Law and Economics is a body of literature that is comprised primarily (but, as will become clear in subsequent chapters, by no means exclusively) of the concepts within neoclassical microeconomics and welfare economics, where the operative organizing concepts are Pareto efficiency in exchange, Pareto efficiency in production, and Kaldor-Hicks efficiency (i.e., wealth maximization). From the outset it must be underscored that not all the schools of thought presented here give equal credence to these various criteria of efficiency, and it certainly is not without dispute across schools of thought (nor within any one school of thought) as to how much emphasis one ought to give to these concepts. Nonetheless, their important place within the Law and Economics literature necessitates an understanding of these concepts. Toward that end, we provide a brief overview of efficiency analysis at this point, and a more extensive discussion in the appendix to this chapter.

The Circular Flow of Economic Activity and the Concept of Efficiency

The intellectual construct that depicts the ideal workings of the *economy* is that of perfect competition. The purely competitive, perfectly functioning market has the following characteristics: (1) many buyers motivated by self-interest and acting to maximize utility; (2) many sellers also motivated by self-interest and acting to maximize profits in atomistic industries or contestable markets; (3) individual buyers and sellers are unable to exert any control over market prices and are thus price takers; (4) prices serve as the guideposts for decision makers in the market to communicate scarcity; (5) products are standardized (i.e., homogeneous); (6) there are no barriers to entry or exit, thus consumers and producers are free to enter or leave all product and factor markets; (7) all buyers and sellers are fully informed as to the terms of all market transactions; (8) resources are held in private property with all rights defined and assigned; and (9) prevailing laws and property rights are fully enforced through the state.

The interrelations and flows inherent in a perfectly competitive economy are best depicted in the standard circular flow diagram (see fig. 1-1). Here the privately owned, scarce factors of production—land, labor, and capital—are allocated through factor markets to firms which, in turn, produce goods and services to satisfy the demands of consumers. In evaluating the outcomes of this process, economists are primarily concerned with allocative efficiency—that is, with (1) the extent to which the allocation of inputs within the productive process results in the production of the combination of outputs that best satisfies the economic wants and desires of the individuals in society, and (2) the extent to which the allocation of these outputs across individuals in society generates the highest possible level of social well-being.

If all factors of production and goods and services pass through perfectly competitive markets, the outcome generated can be shown to be efficient. That is, under the assumptions outlined above and given an initial assignment of rights to resources, the optimal amounts of land, labor, and capital will be allocated to the production of commodities X, Y, Z, . . . Nth good—no more, no less—resulting in the optimal output of each (X*,Y*,Z*, . . . , N*). Such efficient outcomes are said to be *Pareto optimal*, by which is meant that resources cannot be reallocated so as to make one individual better off without making someone else worse off. Formally, this concept is embodied in the first optimality theorem of welfare economics (also known as the duality theorem), which states that, barring major problems with information, public goods, and externalities, a purely competitive, perfectly functioning market will achieve a Pareto-efficient allocation of society's scarce resources.[23] Graphically, this concept is depicted in the supply and demand graphs within figure 1-1 where *all markets have cleared*—the quantity demanded for each commodity and factor of production equals the quantity supplied. This concept deserves closer scrutiny in that it subsumes much and is fundamental to the understanding the concept of efficiency.

From society's perspective, the efficient level of any activity is attained when that activity is engaged in up to the point where marginal social benefit (MSB) is just equal to marginal social cost (MSC). Assuming that the market sector is society's sole means of social control for the allocation of society's scarce resources, all decisions are made by individual consumers and producers attempting to maximize utility and profits, respectively. The effect of this

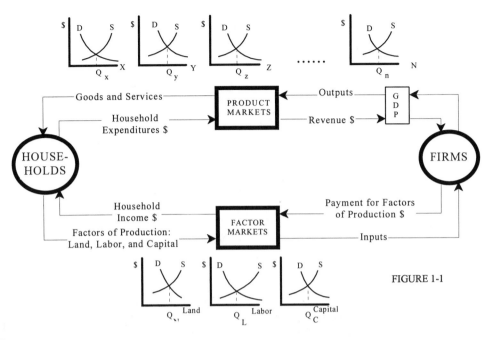

FIGURE 1-1

maximization process is that producers and consumers make their choices based on a weighing of marginal benefits and costs—that is, comparing the additional benefit from engaging in another unit of an activity with the additional cost of doing so. For an efficient outcome to be achieved through the market, it is necessary that the four conditions set forth in table 1-1 be fulfilled for each commodity.[24] These conditions ensure that private calculations of benefits and costs are in line with society's calculations, so that the efficient outcome is achieved. If these conditions are not met, we have a situation of (partial or total) market failure. A brief, but closer, look at each of these four conditions is necessary to fully understand the meanings of efficiency and market failure and their ultimate significance for Law and Economics, and, indeed, all disciplines that assert an interest in the efficient allocation of resources.

- Marginal Social Benefit (MSB) = Marginal Private Benefit (MPB) means that the incremental benefits society acquires by a consumer's individual, private market transaction is not any different than the incremental benefits that consumer acquires in undertaking a particular market transaction; that is, there are no positive or negative externalities in consumption.
- Marginal Private Benefit (MPB) = Product Price (P) means that the price an individual pays for a particular amount of a specified commodity is equal to the marginal benefit of the last unit purchased.

TABLE 1-1

For Good X

MSB = MPB
    MPB = P
        P = MPC
           MPC = MSC

Thus, MSB = MSC yields
Pareto-Efficient Allocation of Resources

• Product Price (P) = Marginal Private Cost (MPC) means that the market price of the commodity is equal to the marginal private cost of producing the good.

• Marginal Private Cost (MPC) = Marginal Social Cost (MSC) means that the incremental cost society incurs by a firm's private production of a commodity is not any different from the incremental cost that the individual firm incurs in undertaking the production of a particular commodity; that is, there are no negative externalities in production.

The satisfaction of these four conditions will ensure that marginal social benefit equals marginal social cost for each and every commodity. In more elementary terms, the market demand curve will reflect MSB and the market supply curve will reflect MSC; thus, the market equilibrium (demand = supply) will be efficient (MSB = MSC). The significance of this condition, and its relation to Pareto optimality, is best illustrated by examining the situation when it does *not* hold.

In figure 1-2, where the marginal social benefits and costs associated with good X are depicted, consider first an allocation of resources such that the quantity X_1 is produced. Notice that, at this point and from it up to X*, marginal social benefit is greater than marginal social cost. Given this, the allocation of additional resources to the production of good X will generate incremental social benefits in excess of the incremental social costs, thus enhancing society's welfare. This increase in net social benefits is available up to X*, beyond which the costs to society of additional units of good X exceed the gains. At X*, then, MSB = MSC and society is said to have achieved a Pareto-efficient allocation of those resources devoted to the production of good X. At any level of output less than X*, where MSB > MSC, and there will be a *persistent underallocation of society's scarce resources* to good X.

Second, consider an allocation of resources to good X which generates an amount X_2 of the good. Here, and at all points between X* and X_2, marginal social cost exceeds marginal social benefit. By reducing the level of resources allocated to the production of good X, and thus the amount of good X produced, the costs saved by society exceed the benefits lost, thereby increasing social welfare until we reach X*, where MSB = MSC. Thus, beyond X*, where

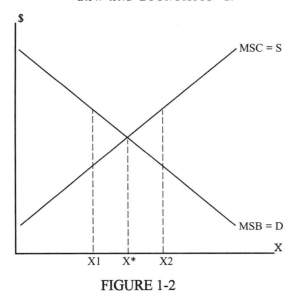

FIGURE 1-2

MSB < MSC, we have a *persistent overallocation of society's scarce resources* to the production of good X.

Finally, let us look at the outcome X* itself. Any reduction in the level of output below X* generates a loss of social benefit in excess of the reduction in social cost, and any increase in output beyond X* generates social costs in excess of social benefits. Thus, it is not possible to move away from X* without making someone worse off. At X*, then, society is said to achieve a Pareto-efficient allocation of resources.

Under the conditions postulated, an exchange will take place only when the parties to the transaction believe they will benefit by going ahead with the transaction. When no additional exchanges can be made, the economy has reached a situation where each individual in it cannot improve his or her situation (i.e., welfare) without diminishing the welfare of another. Once an economy is observed to arrive in this state—when no one can be made better off without someone else being made worse off, a state of Pareto optimality has been attained. By allowing perfectly competitive markets for all goods (X, Y, Z, . . . , Nth good) to clear, society achieves a Pareto-optimal allocation of resources throughout the entire economy. Again, the important point to be underscored is that when supply (S) equals demand (D) for each commodity, all benefits and all costs are accounted for. That is, when MSB = MSC for all commodities in the economy, the outcome is said to be Pareto efficient.

It must be noted that each Pareto-efficient solution is contingent upon an initial and unique assignment of rights to resources within which subsequent market activity can ensue. That is, each initial assignment of rights yields a unique set of supplies and demands, a unique bundle of goods and services produced and consumed, and hence a unique Pareto-efficient allocation of resources—or what may be termed a unique state of *maximum social welfare* (MXSW). Thus, rights assignment #1 (some arbitrary, initial distribution of rights) can be shown to yield a Pareto-efficient allocation of resources MXSW #1; similarly, a different rights assignment #2 (some alternative rights distribution) can be shown to yield an alternative Pareto-efficient allocation of resources MXSW #2; yet another rights assignment #3 can be shown to yield MXSW #3; and so on. Hence, as will become evident in the Edgeworth box analysis (provided in the appendix to this chapter), there are an infinite number of Pareto-efficient states of the economy, each contingent upon the initial assignment of rights, and each of which are noncomparable to each other in terms of efficiency. The only way one could compare these states would be to engage in making interpersonal comparisons of utility—and the positivistic stance of economics was to avoid economic criteria that invoke such comparisons.

Although the attainment of a Pareto-optimal state for the whole economy is predicated upon some initial distribution of rights to assets that exist, the analysis says nothing about the justice or fairness of that initial starting point. Within neoclassical economics, this is an issue of distribution (an ethical problem) as contrasted to efficiency. That is, given the infinite number of Pareto-optimal states, we require additional criteria based on political precepts and/or moral considerations to state a preference for one state of MXSW over another. As stated by Allen V. Kneese (1977, p. 19), "An exchange economy . . . will achieve an *optimum optimorum*—the best of all possible (economic) worlds—if the prevailing income distribution is ethically ideal—a judgement which, in western liberal societies, can be made legitimately only through the political process."

Finally, it must be emphasized that the market sector will fail to generate a Pareto-optimal outcome (i.e., fall short of providing a state of MXSW) if any one of the four conditions is not met. Deviations or departures from the basic structural characteristics of the purely competitive market, the existence of externalities or public goods, the absence of private rights or the failure to perfectly enforce them, or, under some conditions, the existence of open access resources may drive a wedge into any one or more of the four basic equalities. As a consequence, the overall condition for Pareto efficiency (MSB = MSC) will not be met, in which case there exists market failure. All economists recognize that, in reality, there are a variety of factors and forces at work in any market economy that create such inequalities, and, in many respects, it is that recognition together with a desire to find remedies to instances of market failure that constitute the core content of old and new Law and Economics.

The Compensation Principle

It is generally recognized that there are few policies, however creatively structured, whose impact is consistent with someone being made better off and no one being made worse off, as required by the condition of Pareto efficiency. Typically, with the promulgation of a public policy or in the advent of legal change, there are winners and losers. As a consequence the compensation principle was formulated as an alternative to the restrictive Pareto criterion. This principle must be understood in the context of the thrust of the literature that descended from Pareto. Its various formulations were all part of an attempt to see how much can be said about general welfare consequent legal change without resort to interpersonal comparisons (Blaug, 1978, p. 625). The compensation principle is often termed *Kaldor-Hicks efficiency* or, as formulated (and popularized) by Richard Posner, *wealth maximization*. It should also be noted that the compensation principle, beyond being the analytical equivalent to Posner's *wealth maximization*, serves also as the theoretical basis of the economics of benefit-cost analysis.

The compensation principle states that a change from one state of the economy to another (brought on by, for example, a government policy or legal change) that favors some individuals at the expense of others can be said to result in an unambiguous improvement in society's welfare—with almost the same force as the Pareto principle itself—if the gainers could potentially compensate the losers so that the latter will accept the change and the gainers still remain better off. With the potential compensation payments, the gainers are better off and the losers none the worse off.[25] In the simplest of terms, the compensation principle holds that a change constitutes an improvement if the gains to the winners exceed the losses to the losers—a basic benefit-cost concept. An often cited example that provides an intuitive understanding of the principle is that of the discussion in nineteenth-century England regarding the repeal of the Corn Laws. The original Corn Laws prohibited the importation of (cheaper) foreign wheat to England, and thus had the effect of generating artificially high prices for wheat, which benefited farmers at the expense of the bread consumers. It was argued by Nicholas Kaldor (1939) that if those who had benefited from the repeal of the Corn Laws (the consumers) were so much better off that they could have afforded to compensate the farmers for their loss, and yet still be in a better position than before a change in the law, then the repeal of the Corn Laws represented an increase in welfare for the country as a whole, even if the compensation was not actually paid.

The concept of the compensation principle was consciously developed without any requirement that the compensation actually be paid. In an attempt to maintain a positivist stance with respect to evaluating government policy or legal change, the idea was that it would be enough to show that a policy had

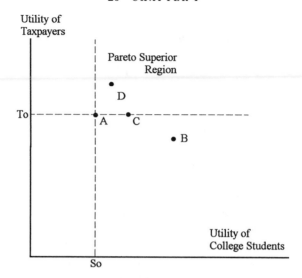

FIGURE 1-3

sufficient gainers to *potentially* compensate the losers. The requirement to actually pay the losers was thought to be purely distributional—within the realm of normative, political decision making, and thus beyond the scope of the more positive thrust of the economic compensation principle as formulated. Simply put, the fact that there exist net gains to be distributed was thought to be proof enough that the change increased economic welfare. Throughout the literature it was clear that if the losers are actually compensated by the gainers, the scheme would essentially revert back to the Pareto principle. However, it likewise was recognized that if the potential compensation was not in fact paid, labeling the change an improvement requires an implicit acceptance of the prevailing distribution of income, inasmuch as the compensation payments are a function of both willingness and ability to pay. Thus, without the actual payments (i.e., the revealing of preferences) we are perilously close to making interpersonal comparisons of utility.

Joe B. Stevens (1993, pp. 48–49) offers a simple example that assists in understanding the compensation principle. The example concerns a proposal to institute a program of tax-funded college scholarships. In figure 1-3, suppose that, before such a program is set in place, the economy is at point A, with the utility of the taxpayers at To and the utility of the college students at So.

Once the tax-funded college scholarships are set up, the outcome of the program would place society at point B: Students would be better off because of the scholarships, but at the same time the taxpayers would be worse off because they have to pay for the scholarships (implicitly assuming higher incomes yield greater utility and lower incomes yield lower utility). How-

after the hypothetical compensation, students are better off and the taxpayers no worse off. One could even conceive of a situation where the taxpayers were even further compensated, taking us to, for example, point D, where both students and taxpayers would be better off than before the program was undertaken.

The concepts of efficiency and the compensation principle, as outlined above, are the operative economic concepts within Law and Economics. Both are used extensively and must be understood in order to grasp the logic underlying Law and Economics, to which we now turn.

THE LOGIC OF LAW AND ECONOMICS

Today, much of the conventional study of the law and what can be said to constitute the law is organized around modern doctrinal principles and concepts that reside in and are derivative of legal and political theory. The perspective that is probably most familiar to law students is to understand the law as being comprised of the totality of constitutional law, tort law, property law, contract law, administrative law, procedural law, criminal law, and so on. From a slightly different vantage point, one can also perceive the law as the total sum of constitutional provisions, prevailing executive orders, statute law, common law, commission and agency rules, and government regulations together with their underlying legal principles and doctrines—principles and doctrines that have withstood both the test of time and legal challenge and critique. These principles and doctrines have been transmitted from generation to generation in varied forms of legal scholarship including restatements, casebooks, law review articles, and classroom lectures.

From the vantage point of Law and Economics, the prevailing legal structure (or simply law) is defined as broadly as possible to include the Constitution, the existing body of statutes, working rules (the internal decision-making rules by which such institutions operate, e.g., bylaws), government regulations, and the current common law doctrines (with the doctrines based on common law principles as described above). The law—perhaps more descriptively, the *legal relations governing society*—together with the rule of law provide the authority for the political and legal institutions and thereby lend legitimacy to their respective decisions. More specifically, the political and legal institutions, together with their respective working rules, organize institution-specific, choice-making processes and thereby channel institutional behavior. Prevailing working rules that structure the political, judicial, and administrative choice-making processes have a direct bearing on the final political, judicial, and administrative decisions made (in sum, the decisions of government). Thus, the law—its principles and doctrines—provides the basis that serves to legitimate (1) the structure of a nation's political and legal institutions, (2) their respective choice-making processes, and ultimately (3) their final decisions. Consequently, it is from the combined political-legal structure and consequent administrative-legislative-judicial behavior that the law emerges.

Let us suggest that, at any one moment in time, a society with a mixed-market economy will be characterized as being comprised of four sectors—a private sector, a public sector, a communal sector, and a sector with open access resources. The scope and character of each of these sectors is contingent upon the extant legal relations governing that society. Each of these four sectors is structured by private property rights, status rights, communal property rights, and open access resources, respectively. That is, the private market sector will be the arena in which exclusive private property rights are defined and assigned, enforced, and subsequently transferred among the parties so as to exhaust gains from trade. The public sector will be made up of the whole array of status rights across the full range of government institutions. Status rights are defined as rights established by the government's pronouncements of eligibility requirements for individuals to use goods, services, or resources. These are undertaken by the government in its role within the modern administrative state in its various capacities, including legislative, agency, commissions, and boards. The status rights are taken to be exclusive and nontransferable.[26] In the public sector, resources are allocated with establishment of status rights—under stipulations set forth within the government regulations. In essence, common-property resources are private property owned by a group of co-owners. Under communal ownership a group of individuals would have the rights to use and transfer the resource. Typically, a management group oversees the manner by which a common property resource can be used and reserves the right to exclude nonmembers. Depending upon the group rules used to manage the resource, communal property can result in an efficient allocation of resources. And finally, the open access sector is that sector wherein rights to commodities or resources will be owned by no one, equally available to all, and thus, will belong to the party to first exercise control over the resource. In this case there are no property rights to the resource. The resulting open-access allocation of the resource would be allocatively efficient only if supply exceeds demand at a zero price. If supply does not exceed demand at a zero price and society nonetheless retains the resource in open access, the resource will be overused. The chosen legal relations governing society—the mix of private, status, communal rights, and open access resources—will directly affect the economic performance of the mixed-market economy, specifically, the economic performance in the economy's private sector, its public sector, its communal sector, and its open-access resource sector.

Altering the *Law*, that is, changing the legal relations governing society in any one or all of the four sectors, or changing the working rules, will ultimately alter economic performance. Thus, the logic underlying Law and Economics suggests the following line of reasoning: Change the legal relations governing society and/or its working rules and you will ultimately and systematically affect economic performance. In symbolic terms:

Δ law and/or working rules $\rightarrow$ Δ incentive structure $\rightarrow$ Δ institutional behavior $\rightarrow$ Δ economic performance.

That is, if there is a change in the law—for example, (1) a change in the definition or assignment of private property rights; or (2) a change in a working rule that alters the manner by which a judicial, administrative, or legislative decision is to be reached; or (3) the altering of a status right (some administrative eligibility requirement); or (4) expanding or diminishing the scope of communal rights—incentives will be altered within the market and/or public and/or communal sectors, which in turn alters the behavior of individuals operating within those sectors, all of which impacts upon the economic performance of the mixed-market economy. In short, Law and Economics can be represented by

Δ Law $\rightarrow$ Δ Economic Performance.

It is again worthwhile to point out that the evaluation of the economy's performance is typically undertaken with the tools of microeconomics and welfare economics—the concepts of Pareto-optimal efficiency in exchange, Pareto-optimal efficiency in production, and Kaldor-Hicks efficiency (i.e., wealth maximization).

As Law and Economics has developed, the predominant concerns have been fourfold. First, some work has been devoted to positive description of the development of the law and legal institutions—for example, looking at the question as to whether law has exhibited an efficiency logic in its development over time. Second, the normative and complementary component to this first line of literature seeks to recommend, based primarily on the efficiency criteria, certain changes in law—those that would tend to promote efficient outcomes. Third, much work has been devoted to efforts to describe what is transpiring in those areas of the law where changes would have direct implications on the allocation and distribution of society's scarce resources—what one may call the economic impact analysis. Here some work relies primarily on the criteria of efficiency to assess outcomes of such legal change, whereas other facets of this research attempt to describe the allocative and distributional impacts of alternative legal structures and working rules. Finally, additional work has gone into the description of what is going on in the decision-making processes where law and economics are intricately intertwined—what may be termed the interrelations between legal and economic processes or the legal-economic nexus. None of the four endeavors has been able to completely overcome the rather formidable task that has been described by Werner Z. Hirsch (1988, p. 6):

Our task would be so much easier if efficiency could be rigorously defended as the only and ultimate objective. Instead we face two all-too-often opposing objectives—efficiency and equity. It must be remembered that the ultimate goal is what economists like to call *social efficiency*, which requires trading off resource-allocation efficiency against distribution of income. . . . Legal rules must be concerned about both efficiency and income distribution. . . . Guidelines given by economic theory require two successive steps—first, income should be redistributed in the most desirable manner; second, resources should be allocated in the most efficient manner, preferably in response to competitive forces. An effort must thus be made to agree on a subjectively preferred income distribution and it must be followed by an effort to attain allocative efficiency. The formulation of prudent legal rules would have to proceed by considering both goals, not just allocative efficiency—a formidable task.

As will become evident in the following chapters, although distribution is often included in the rhetoric of some schools of thought, it is, more often than not, overlooked by much of the work in the economic analysis of law.

CONCLUSION

We have undertaken to write this book based on our belief that, as the schools of thought continue to develop and expand along the four paths of legal-economic analysis described above, in time a new conventional wisdom—a new, more eclectic received doctrine—of law will emerge. It is no longer in dispute that the law has important implications for economic structure, behavior, and performance. It is our contention that, as a consequence, in time there will be a new received doctrine in law, and that this doctrine will incorporate significant features from the body of ideas that has come to comprise Law and Economics. This book will attempt to provide a concise overview of just what each of these schools of thought within the marketplace of ideas is attempting to convey; that is, we will describe the intellectual origins, the respective principles and ideas, and the dominant modes of analysis within each school of thought. In doing so, we hope to provide a fuller understanding of the relationships between the formation, structure, and processes of law and legal institutions and their impact upon the performance of the economy.

> Economists draw on many different forms of
> [efficiency], such as efficient production, efficient
> exchange, Pareto efficiency, national income
> maximization, wealth maximization, and utilitarian
> efficiency. Most economists move easily from
> one form to another, but the subtle shifts in
> significance are lost upon noneconomists.
> *(Cooter, 1982b, p. 1263)*

EFFICIENCY: EDGEWORTH BOX ANALYSIS[1]

Three principle concepts of efficiency are employed within, and are indeed central to the study of, Law and Economics—efficiency in exchange, efficiency in production, and Kaldor-Hicks efficiency. This appendix provides a detailed overview of these three concepts.

Efficiency in Exchange

CONSUMER CHOICE

Consuming units are assumed to derive utility (or satisfaction) from the consumption of goods and services, and to make their consumption choices rationally so as to maximize utility. For present purposes, we assume two individual consumers, A and B, and two goods, X and Y, which the individuals take to be imperfect substitutes. All the analysis, however, generalizes to any number of consumers and goods.

The behavior of individuals A and B is assumed to conform to four axioms:

1. Completeness: an individual either prefers one bundle of X and Y—bundle 'R'—to a different bundle of X and Y—bundle 'S'; prefers bundle 'S' to bundle 'R'; or is indifferent between holding bundle 'R' or bundle 'S'.

2. Transitivity: an individual who prefers bundle 'R' to bundle 'S', and prefers bundle 'S' to bundle 'T', will prefer bundle 'R' to bundle 'T'.

3. Dominance: given bundle 'S' with a specified amount of X and Y, if bundle 'R' contains more of good X and no less of good Y (or contains more of good Y and no less of good X), then the individual will prefer holding bundle 'R' to bundle 'S'.

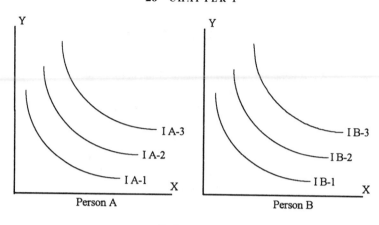

FIGURE A-1

4. Solipsism: an individual's preference ranking is defined over the commodity bundles that he consumes and is not influenced by the commodity bundles allocated to other individuals.

Given these four choice axioms, the relationship between the quantities of goods X and Y consumed and an individual's level of utility can be described with a family of indifference curves. An indifference curve is defined as a locus of points showing combinations of X and Y which yield the same level of utility to the consumer. A family of indifference curves for person A, such as that shown in figure A-1, describes higher ordinal levels of utility as you move to the northeast; IA-3 is associated with a higher level of utility than IA-2, and IA-2 is associated with a higher level of utility than IA-1. In a like manner, a family of indifference curves for person B describes higher ordinal levels of utility as you move to the northeast; IB-3 is associated with a higher level of utility than IB-2, and IB-2 is associated with a higher level of utility than IB-1.

All indifference curves are negatively sloped, do not intersect, are mathematically dense, and are convex to the origin. The convexity property of an indifference curve is a direct corollary of the principle of diminishing marginal rate of substitution. The marginal rate of substitution of good X for good Y (MRS$_{\text{of X for Y}}$) measures the number of units of Y that an individual is, *subjectively*, willing to relinquish per unit of X gained so as to maintain a constant level of satisfaction or utility. An individual's indifference curve for two goods which are imperfect substitutes is convex because as the individual acquires additional units of X (starting at a point such as M in figure A-2 and moving down along an indifference curve), the individual will be willing to give up less and less Y to obtain an additional unit of X while maintaining the same level of utility. That is, as the consumer moves toward N, holding more X

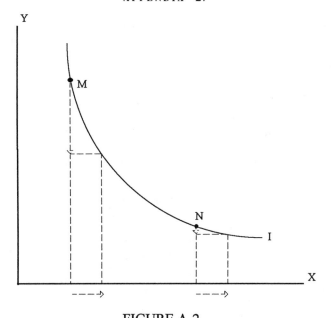

FIGURE A-2

relative to Y (utility constant), the consumer will be more and more reluctant to give up Y to secure an additional unit of X.

A's marginal rate of substitution of X for Y (denoted MRS-A$_{\text{of X for Y}}$) is given by the slope of a line tangent to any point on an indifference curve. As one moves down the indifference curve toward N, the slope of a line tangent to points on the indifference curve becomes smaller and smaller (in absolute value terms), and thus the convex indifference curve is merely the graphical manifestation of the *principle of the diminishing marginal rate of substitution.*

EQUILIBRIUM AND EFFICIENCY IN A PURE EXCHANGE MODEL[2]

Assuming that there exist given amounts of goods X and Y in the economy, Edgeworth box analysis can be used to examine exchange relations in the economy. The given amounts of X and Y determine the dimensions of the Edgeworth box in figure A-3, and the points within the box illustrate all possible allocations of X and Y between persons A and B. Individual B's family of indifference curves is rotated so its origin is now situated in the northeast corner (0_{B}). Consequently, B's utility is enhanced as he comes to rest on inverted utility curves further to the southwest. The origin of individual A's family of indifference curves (0_{A}) is maintained at its initial position in the southwest corner, and A's utility is enhanced as he comes to rest on utility curves further to the northeast.

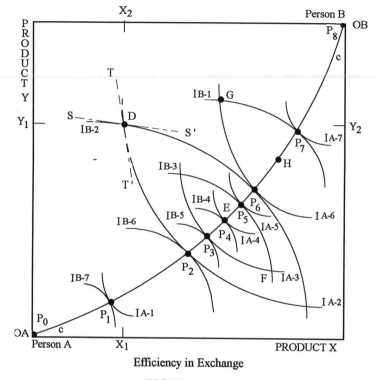

Efficiency in Exchange

FIGURE A-3

Persons A and B are each assumed to start out with an initial endowment of X and Y, such as depicted by point D. Thus, person A is starting out with X1 and Y1 (a lot of Y as compared to X), which places A on indifference curve IA-2. Likewise, person B starts out with X2 and Y2 (a lot of X as compared to Y), which places B on indifference curve IB-2. Given these initial endowments, we can see from the diagram that A prefers all points northeast of IA-2 (since they lie on higher indifference curves and thus make A better off), and, for similar reasons, B prefers all points southwest of IB-2. It is clear, then, that at point D potential *gains from trade* exist. Graphically, the region for realizing this potential is the *trading lens*—the lens-shaped region demarcated by the two indifference curves IA-2 and IB-2 passing through point D. Any point in the area within this lens makes *both* A and B better off than they are at point D. Thus, in a pure exchange model, the individuals will find it advantageous to exchange X for Y or Y for X so as to enhance their respective utilities. Persons A and B can contract and recontract—exchanging X for Y and Y for X, respectively, and, in the process, continuously groping toward higher levels of utility—say, from D, to F, and finally coming to rest at E, a point from which no further gains from trade exist.

The underlying reason for this spontaneous (re)contracting to exhaust the gains from trade lies in the differing subjective $MRS_{of\ X\ for\ Y}$ for persons A and B at point D; that is, at D, person A's $MRS_{of\ X\ for\ Y}$ is high (as graphically depicted by the high slope of TT'), indicating that person A is quite willing to give up a lot of Y for an additional unit of X. Alternatively, at D, person B's $MRS_{of\ X\ for\ Y}$ is low (as graphically depicted by the lower slope of SS'), indicating that person B is simultaneously quite willing to give up a lot of X for an additional unit of Y. Herein lie the potential gains from trade. The individuals contract and recontract, and only fully exhaust the gains from trade once they arrive at a point where their respective marginal rates of substitution are equal—here, point E. As compared to point D, and *given the same amount of X and Y in the economy*, at point E both individuals have increased their utility by consuming bundles of X and Y different than their initial endowment. Person A is now at utility level IA-4 and person B at utility level IB-4. More generally, at E it is said that the economy has attained a *general equilibrium of exchange* where there is no incentive for further trade.

Notice that at this point A's indifference curve is tangent to that of B, indicating that A's $MRS_{of\ X\ for\ Y}$ = B's $MRS_{of\ X\ for\ Y}$. Furthermore, any move away from this point will put either A or B (or both) on a lower indifference curve—that is, it will reduce the utility of one or both of them. Point E is said to be Pareto optimal: There is no movement from this point that can make one person better off without making someone else worse off. All this is brought together in the condition for efficiency in exchange, which states that an exchange equilibrium is Pareto efficient if A's $MRS_{of\ X\ for\ Y}$ = B's $MRS_{of\ X\ for\ Y}$. Thus since, at point E, the marginal rate of substitution between every pair of goods is the same for all parties consuming both goods, *efficiency in exchange* obtains.

Whereas the initial endowments reflected in point D lead to an efficient equilibrium at point E, a different set of endowments will likely generate a different trading lens and, subsequently, a different negotiated equilibrium point (such as that reflected in the movement from point G to point H in fig. A-3). The locus of all tangency points between A's and B's indifference curves—points such as P0, P1, P2, P3, P4, P5, P6, P7, P8—is depicted by curve cc, and is known as the *contract curve*. The exchange equilibrium point on the contract curve that is ultimately realized is partially a product of the distribution of initial endowments between persons A and B, as well as their respective bargaining skills. The contract curve is an *optimal* locus in the sense that if the individuals are located at some point not on the contract curve, one or both individuals can be made better off, and neither suffer a loss, merely by exchanging goods and moving to a point on the contract curve. *Thus, conceptually, a movement from off the contract curve to a point on the contract curve is efficiency enhancing.* Consequently, once on the contract curve, any movement from that point will diminish aggregate utility. If the movement is along the contract curve it must result in benefiting one party at the expense of the other; alternatively, if the movement is off the contract curve, then the utility of both persons will be diminished. Neither such movement can be efficiency enhancing. Being at a point on the contract curve—an exchange equilibrium—constitutes what is termed a *Pareto optimum*.

Formally, a Pareto-optimal state is one from which any change makes at least one individual worse off, regardless of whether or not others are made better off in the process. Alternatively, an economy is not in a Pareto-optimal state if there exists a potential change that will make some people better off and will not make anyone worse off. Consequently, every outcome that is represented by a point on the contract curve is said to be *Pareto optimal*; the contract curve is a locus of Pareto optimality.

THE POINT UTILITY POSSIBILITY FRONTIER

Given the total endowment of X and Y and the family of indifference curves for persons A and B, there exists a point utility possibility frontier that illustrates the utility levels for persons A and B associated with the set of Pareto-optimal outcomes along the contract curve. As such, the frontier lies in a different space—not one of goods X and Y, but in utility space depicting the utility of person A and the utility of person B.

As described above, the contract curve, *cc*, is comprised of the locus of all tangency points between person A's and person B's indifference curves and thus is the locus of Pareto-optimal points such as P0, P1, P2, P3, P4, P5, P6, P7, P8. Let us plot each of these points in utility space, beginning with P0. This point represents a *possible* state of the economy such that there is zero utility for person A and person B attains the highest level of utility possible. At the other extreme, P8 represents zero utility for person B while person A attains the highest level of utility possible. In a like manner each remaining point, P1, P2, P3, and so on, on the contract curve *cc* has a corresponding point in utility space, with more utility for A and less for B as we move northeast along the contract curve, reflecting the fact that, as we do so, A has a larger share of X and Y and B a smaller share.

Several points should be noted regarding the point utility possibility frontier and its relationship to the contract curve:

- All points along the contract curve and all points on the point utility possibility frontier are Pareto-optimal efficient points.
- With respect to point D in the Edgeworth box, all points in the lens are Pareto superior (someone can be made better off and no one made worse off); in a like manner, all points to the northeast of D′ (in utility space) are Pareto superior to D′.

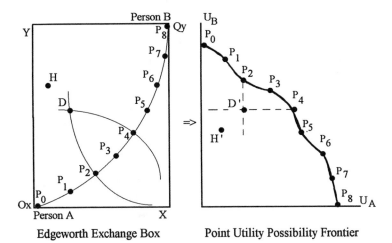

Edgeworth Exchange Box   Point Utility Possibility Frontier

FIGURE A-4

• With respect to point D, all points such as H, to the northwest of D are Pareto inferior (one or both individuals are made worse off); similarly, all points to the southwest of D′ (e.g., H′) are Pareto inferior.

• With respect to any one point on the contract curve or the point utility possibility frontier, say, P5 (in each diagram), all other points along the contract curve or along the point utility possibility frontier are, respectively, Pareto noncomparable.

• With respect to D, all points outside of the lens (exclusive of those to the northwest of D) are Pareto noncomparable; all points to the northwest and southeast of D′ are Pareto noncomparable.

Efficiency in Production

PRODUCER CHOICE

Producing units make choices with respect to the acquisition and use of society's scarce resources and are assumed to produce commodities with the goal of maximizing profits. For our purposes, we assume only two producers—one producing X (Producer X) and the other producing Y (Producer Y)—and two factors of production—labor (L) and capital (K)—which are imperfect substitutes for each other. The analysis generalizes to any number of producers and inputs.

The relationship between the amount of inputs used and the level of output generated by a producer can be described with a family of isoquants. An isoquant is defined as a locus of points showing combinations of labor and

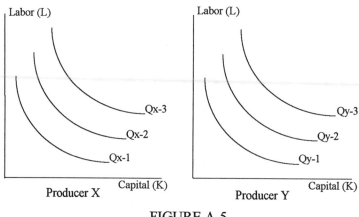

FIGURE A-5

capital inputs that can be used to produce a specified level of output of a particular commodity under the unchanging, prevailing technology. In figure A-5 we show a family of isoquants for each producer depicting cardinally measurable higher levels of output as you move to the northeast. For Producer X, Qx-3 is associated with a higher level of output than Qx-2; likewise, Qx-2 is associated with a higher level of output than Qx-1. Similarly, a family of isoquants for Producer Y depicts higher levels of output as you move to the northeast: Qy-3 is associated with a higher level of output than Qy-2 and Qy-2 is associated with a higher level of output than Qy-1.

All isoquants are negatively sloped in their efficient range, do not intersect, are mathematically dense, and are convex to the origin. The convexity property of the isoquant is a direct corollary of the *principle of diminishing marginal rate of technical substitution.* The marginal rate of technical substitution of capital for labor (MRTS$_{of\ K\ for\ L}$) shows the number of units of labor that can be released (under the prevailing technology) as a result of employing an additional unit of capital while maintaining the same level of output. As we move from N to M along the isoquant depicted in figure A-6, with each additional unit of capital employed the producer would be forced to release less and less labor to maintain the production of two hundred units of X. Alternatively, one can think of the MRTS$_{of\ K\ for\ L}$ as measuring the number of units of labor that must be acquired (under the prevailing technology) for each additional unit of capital released so as to maintain the same level of output. The producer's isoquant is convex because of this technical regularity embodied in the law of variable proportions for factors of production that are imperfect substitutes—that is, to maintain the given level of production it takes progressively larger increases in one input (labor) to compensate for the incremental reduction of the other input (capital). For example, starting at a point such as M, and moving toward N, larger and larger incremental units of

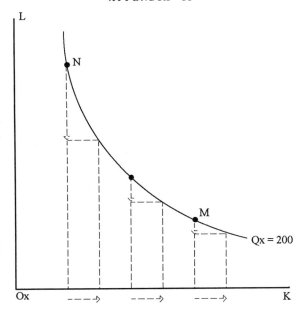

FIGURE A-6

labor would be needed to maintain a constant level of output (Qx = 200) as additional, incremental units of capital are released.

The MRTS$_{of\ K\ for\ L}$ is given by the slope of a line tangent to any point on an isoquant curve. As one moves down the isoquant from N toward M, the slope of a line tangent to points on the isoquant curve gets smaller and smaller (in absolute value terms). Thus, the convex isoquant is merely the graphical manifestation of the *principle of the diminishing marginal rate of technical substitution.*

EQUILIBRIUM AND EFFICIENCY IN PRODUCTION

Assuming there exists a given amount of labor and capital in the economy, an Edgeworth box can be formed (see fig. A-7), the dimensions of which are determined by the given amounts of L and K.[3] The points within the box illustrate all possible allocations of L and K between the production of X and the production of Y. The Producer Y's family of isoquants is rotated so that its origin is now situated in the northeast corner (Oy), and, consequently, the levels of output of Y are higher as he produces on inverted isoquants further to the southwest. Producer X's family of isoquants is maintained at its initial position in the southwest corner (Ox), and the output of X is higher as he produces on isoquants further to the northeast.

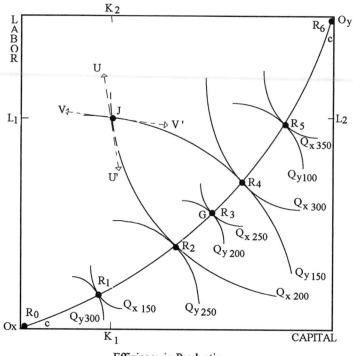

Efficiency in Production

FIGURE A-7

Producers X and Y are each assumed to start out with an initial endowment of L and K such as that depicted by point J, where Producer X is starting out with K1 and L1 (employing a lot of labor as compared to capital) on isoquant Qx-200 and Producer Y is starting out with K2 and L2 (employing a lot of capital as compared to labor) on isoquant Qy-150. These producers will find it advantageous to realign their resource use by exchanging L for K or K for L so as to increase their respective levels of output. It is clear that, at point J, potential gains from trade exist with respect to the realignment of resource use. Graphically, the region for realizing this potential is the *lens*-shaped region demarcated by the two isoquants Qx-200 and Qy-150—those isoquants passing through point J. Any point within this lens enables both producers to increase output relative to point J, and thus they will find it advantageous to exchange L for K or K for L so as to increase their respective outputs. The producers can contract and recontract—continuously groping toward higher levels of their respective outputs—until they reach a point beyond which no further gains from trade are possible, such as point G.

The underlying reason for this spontaneous contracting and recontracting to exhaust the gains from realigning resource use lies in the differing MRTS$_{\text{of K for L}}$ for each producer. At J, Producer X's MRTS$_{\text{of K for L}}$ is high (as graphically depicted by the high slope of UU'), which means that, by using an additional unit of capital, a relatively large amount of labor can be released by Producer X. Alternatively at J, Producer Y's MRTS$_{\text{of K for L}}$ is low (as graphically depicted by the low slope of VV'), and, by using an additional unit of labor, a relatively large amount of capital can be released by Producer Y. Herein lie the potential gains from the realignment of resources use. By shifting labor out of the production of X and into Y and, with the trade, simultaneously shifting capital out of the production of Y and X, *using the economy's same fixed resource base*, both outputs can be increased by moving to point G—here, to Qx-250 and Qy-200. More generally, at G it is said the economy has attained a *general equilibrium of production*.

Notice that, at point G, the producers' isoquants are tangent to each other, indicating that Producer X's MRTS$_{\text{of K for L}}$ = Producer Y's MRTS$_{\text{of K for L}}$. Furthermore, any movement away from point G will result in a reduction in output for one or both producers. That is, point G is said to be Pareto optimal, in that there is no reallocation of inputs that can make one producer better off without making the other worse off. All this is brought together in the condition for efficiency in production, which holds that a production equilibrium is efficient if Producer X's MRTS$_{\text{of K for L}}$ = Producer Y's MRTS$_{\text{of K for L}}$. Thus since, at point G, the MRTS between every pair of inputs is the same for all producers producing both goods, *efficiency in production* obtains.

Whereas the initial endowments reflected in point J lead to an efficient equilibrium at point G, a different set of endowments will likely generate a different trading lens and thus a different negotiated equilibrium point. The locus of all points of tangency between the producers' isoquants—such as R0, R1, R2, R3, R4, R5, R6—is depicted by curve *cc* and is again termed the *contract curve*. The point on the contract curve that is ultimately realized is a product of the distribution of the initial input endowments among the two producers. The contract curve is an *optimal* locus in the sense that if the producers are located at some point not on the contract curve, merely by realigning the use of resources and moving to a point on the contract curve, more of either commodity can be produced while not reducing the other, or the production of both commodities can be increased. *Thus, conceptually, a movement from off the contract curve to a point on the contract curve is efficiency enhancing.* Consequently, once on the contract curve, any movement off it will diminish aggregate output, whereas any movement along the contract curve must result in an increase in the output of one product but at the expense of the other. Neither such movement can be efficiency enhancing. Once again, being at a point on the contract curve—a production equilibrium—constitutes a *Pareto optimum*—efficiency in production.

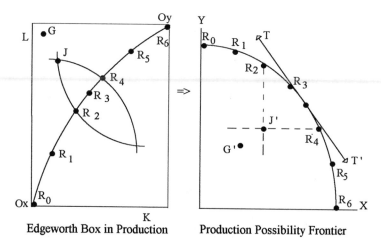

Edgeworth Box in Production   Production Possibility Frontier

FIGURE A-8

THE PRODUCTION POSSIBILITY FRONTIER

Given the total endowment of L and K and the family of isoquants for the production of commodities X and Y, we can construct the *production possibility frontier*. The production possibility frontier (also termed the *transformation curve*) is defined as the locus of points showing the maximum attainable output of one commodity for every possible volume of output of the other commodity, given the fixed resource base of labor and capital and a fixed technology. As such, it shows the maximum combinations of outputs that can be produced given society's resource endowment. The frontier lies in a different space, not one of inputs—labor and capital—but in commodity space for goods X and Y.

As described above, the contract curve is comprised of the locus of all tangency points between the isoquants of Producer X and Producer Y, and thus is the locus of Pareto-optimal points such as R0, R1, R2, R3, R4, R5, R6. Let us plot each of these points in commodity space, beginning with R0. This point represents a *possible* state of the economy such that all of society's scarce resources are devoted to the production of Y and none to X. At the other extreme, R6 represents zero production of good Y and all resources devoted to the production of good X. In like manner each remaining point on the contract curve *cc*—R1, R2, R3, and so on—has a corresponding point in commodity space, with more inputs devoted to the production of good X and less to Y as we move northeastward along the contract curve. The slope of the production possibility frontier (or transformation curve) is termed the *marginal rate of transformation of x into y* (MRT$_{X \text{ into } Y}$) and indicates the number of units by

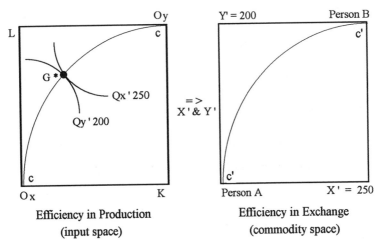

Efficiency in Production
(input space)

Efficiency in Exchange
(commodity space)

FIGURE A-9

which the production of Y must be decreased to expand the output of X by one unit. Thus, the MRT$_{X \text{ into } Y}$ is given by the slope of TT′ at any given point.

Several points should be noted regarding the production possibilities frontier and its relationship to the contract curve:

- All points along the contract curve and all points on the production possibility frontier are Pareto-optimal points.
- With respect to point J, points in the lens are Pareto superior; in a like manner, all points to the northeast of J′ are Pareto superior.
- With respect to point J, all points such as G to the northwest of J are Pareto inferior; similarly, all points to the southwest of J′ (e.g., G′) are Pareto inferior.
- With respect to any one point on the contract curve or on the production possibility frontier, say, R5 (in each diagram), all other points along the contract curve or along the production possibility frontier, respectively, are Pareto noncomparable.

Welfare Economics: Attaining Maximum Social Welfare

TWO LEVELS OF INFINITY

As noted above, given both the level of technology and the resource endowments of labor and capital, a multiplicity (in fact an infinite number) of Pareto-efficient production points along the contract curve in input space exist (see *cc* in fig. A-9). Select any point among the infinite along *cc*, say G*. This point is associated with a particular bundle of commodities X and Y (i.e., X′ = 250 and Y′ = 200). This bundle of X and Y, in turn, yields the dimensions of the adjoining Edgeworth exchange box in commodity space. This Edgeworth box has its own infinite number of Pareto equilibrium points (along $c'c'$). To appreciate the manner by which welfare economics attempts to resolve these two levels of infinity—that is, how it determines the optimal allocation of inputs and outputs for society given the infinite number of efficient production and exchange equilibria—one must understand the three marginal conditions for an economy's attaining a state of *maximum social welfare*.

THE THREE CONDITIONS FOR ATTAINING MAXIMUM SOCIAL WELFARE

The three conditions to attain maximum social welfare are:

1. Marginal Condition for Exchange: For the economy to attain a Pareto-optimal state, the marginal rate of substitution ($MRS_{of\ X\ for\ Y}$) between any pair of consumer commodities must be the same for all individuals who consume both commodities.

2. Marginal Condition for Factor Substitution (Production): For the economy to attain a Pareto-optimal state, the marginal rate of technical substitution ($MRTS_{of\ K\ for\ L}$) between any pair of inputs must be the same for all producers who use both inputs.

It should be clear from the preceding analysis that the inherent gains from trade incentives within a perfectly competitive equilibrium will ensure that the first and second conditions will be met.

3. Marginal Condition for Product Substitution: For the economy to attain a Pareto-optimal state, the marginal rate of transformation ($MRT_{X\ into\ Y}$) must equal the common marginal rate of substitution ($MRS_{of\ X\ for\ Y}$) in exchange for every pair of commodities and for every individual who consumes both—that is, $MRT_{X\ into\ Y} = MRS_{of\ X\ for\ Y}$. This latter condition needs some elaboration.

The third condition states that the MRT must equal the common MRS for both parties for both goods. The underlying market forces take the consumers' preferences as data and respond accordingly. Suppose, following figure A-10, that consumers arrive at an equilibrium at U, where the common $MRS_{of\ X\ for\ Y} = 12/20$ and (for whatever reason) the economy finds itself on the transformation curve producing at point R with a MRT = 10/20. Here, MRS > MRT. The MRS indicates that consumers are willing to give up 12 units of Y to get an additional 20 units of X, whereas the MRT indicates that an additional 20 units of X can be produced at a cost of only 10 units of Y. Given this, consumers will be better off if resources are shifted from the production of Y into the production of X. Market forces will thus *transform* Y into X until MRT = MRS. Similarly, if instead MRS < MRT (as at point S), then consumers will be better off if resources are reallocated from the production of X into the production of Y, and market forces will this time *transform* X

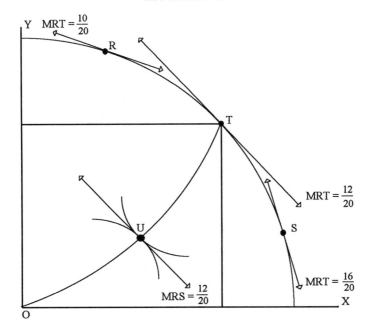

FIGURE A-10

into Y until MRT = MRS. Thus, if MRS is not equal to MRT, it is possible to reallocate society's resources so as to make at least one person better off without making anyone worse off, until MRT is brought into equality with MRS. At this point, no further reallocations can be made without harming at least one party, and thus MRS = MRT is the third condition necessary for the existence of a Pareto-efficient allocation of resources within society.

THE GRAND UTILITY POSSIBILITY FRONTIER

Whereas the point utility possibility frontier shows the maximum attainable utility for A and B given the endowments of goods X and Y in the economic system, the grand utility possibility frontier (GUPF) allows us to illustrate the maximum attainable utilities for A and B when the production of X and Y can vary (subject to the economy's resource constraint). To generate the GUPF, we continue to assume a given technology and a given amount of labor and capital, thereby determining the dimensions of the Edgeworth box in production in figure A-11.

Along the contract curve cc the second marginal condition is fulfilled. Going from input space to commodity space (plotting all the points along cc

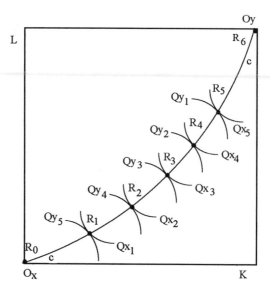

FIGURE A-11

into commodity space) yields the transformation curve (i.e., the production possibility frontier) depicted in figure A-12 (where points R0 → R6 are in a one-to-one relationship in both diagrams).

By selecting any point on the transformation curve, say R4, and drawing horizontal and vertical lines to each axis, one can generate an R4-specific Edgeworth exchange box with dimensions OX4 and OY2, together with its own contract curve *c4c4*. All the points along *c4c4* are Pareto optimal, indicating efficiency in exchange and thus fulfilling the first marginal condition. At point R4 on the transformation curve (Person B's origin), the MRT$_{X \text{ into } Y}$ is given by the slope of the transformation curve; specifically, at R4, MRT$_{X \text{ into } Y}$ = the slope of rr′. Given the selection of point R4, the third marginal condition will be satisfied at a point along the *c4c4* contract curve, R4* where, as indicated, the MRT$_{X \text{ into } Y}$ equals the common MRS$_{\text{of } X \text{ for } Y}$ for persons A and B.

Moving from the interior commodity space to utility space one can now plot the point utility possibility frontier uniquely associated with *point* R4 (hence its name). As we see in figure A-13, plotting *c4c4* into utility space yields the point utility possibility frontier *c4c4*, which includes point R4*, corresponding to R4* in figure A-12. As should be clear from the foregoing analysis, point R4* is the only one along *c4c4* that meets all three marginal conditions for the economy attaining a state of maximum social welfare.

In order to develop the grand utility possibility frontier, it is necessary to

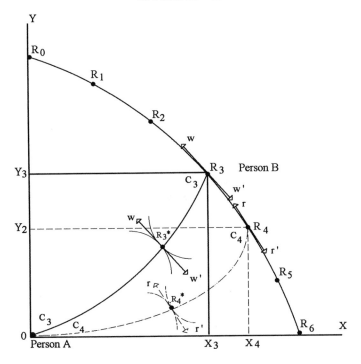

FIGURE A-12

return to figure A-12 and conceptually select another point along the transformation curve, say R3. One can now generate an R3-specific Edgeworth exchange box with dimensions OX3 and OY3 together with its own contract curve $c3c3$. As before, all the points along $c3c3$ are Pareto optimal, representing efficiency in exchange and thus fulfilling the first marginal condition. At point R3 on the transformation curve, the MRT$_X$ into Y is the same as the slope of the transformation curve (specifically, at R3, MRT$_X$ into Y = the slope of ww'). Given the selection of point R3, the third marginal condition will be satisfied at a point on the new $c3c3$ contract curve, R3* where the MRT$_X$ into Y will again equal the common MRS$_{of X for Y}$.

Moving from the interior commodity space to utility space we can now plot another point utility possibility frontier uniquely associated this time with point R3. Plotting $c3c3$ into utility space yields the point utility possibility frontier $c3c3$ with its unique point—R3* (see fig. A-13). Like R4*, R3* meets all three marginal conditions for the economy attaining a state of maximum social welfare. This process is repeated over and over by selecting each and every point on the transformation curve, generating a corresponding point utility possibility curve, and thereby yielding a collection of unique R*-ed

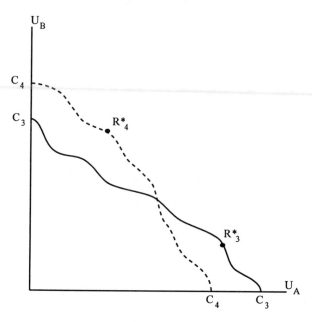

FIGURE A-13

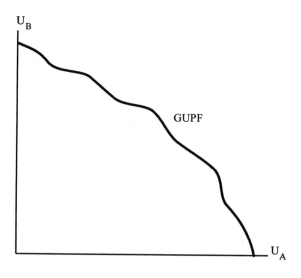

FIGURE A-14

points—each of which meets all three efficiency conditions. Connecting all the R*-ed points generates the *grand utility possibility frontier* (GUPF) in figure A-14, an infinite locus of all Pareto-optimal points, each one representing states of the economy that fulfill all three marginal conditions necessary for an economy to attain a state of maximum social welfare.

CLOSING OUT THE ANALYSIS: SOCIAL WELFARE FUNCTIONS

Given the infinite number of states of the economy that fulfill all three conditions for attaining maximum social welfare, in an attempt to close out the analysis, the existence of real-valued social welfare functions was postulated in order to give a basis upon which to choose among these optimal points.[4] Two types of social welfare functions were contemplated: social welfare contours in utility space and social indifference curves in commodity space. In either case, a social welfare function would have to be formulated, recognizing that political and/or ethical considerations must be made explicitly and imposed either through a collectivity or through a dictator. The social welfare function implies the existence of an ordinal ranking of alternative utility levels achieved by the various members of the community (in our case persons A and B). Thus the concept of a real-valued social welfare function is somewhat analogous to that of indifference curves: The idea of a family of indifference curves for an individual is conceptually aggregated into a family of social welfare contours for the society (SWC1, SWC2, SWC3, etc.) as depicted in figure A-15. Each social welfare contour defines a politically determined, subjective tradeoff between the utilities of persons A and B. As society moves to the northeast, each social welfare contour represents a higher level of societal welfare.

Of the infinite number of Pareto-optimal points comprising the grand utility possibility frontier (GUPF), Ω is the only point that has unequivocal prescriptive significance. It is not merely Pareto optimal; given the social welfare function and the political and/or ethical considerations subsumed in it, this point is also uniquely associated with maximum social welfare. In this regard, Pareto optimality (or efficiency) is said to be a *necessary* but not a *sufficient* condition for an economy's attainment of a position of maximum social welfare. The three marginal conditions yield only the Pareto-efficiency requirement; alone they do not guarantee a social welfare maximum. For the latter, an explicit social welfare function (derived solely from political/ethical considerations) is needed to attain, in the words of Kneese, the *optimum optimorum*.

Points to note:

- If the SWF is known, we could not maximize utility at Ω without simultaneously achieving efficiency in both exchange and production.

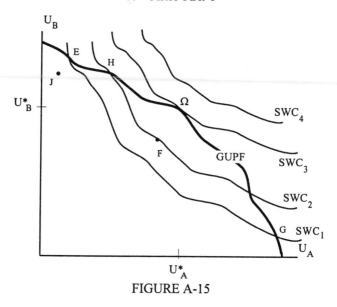

FIGURE A-15

- In accordance with the first optimality theorem, a perfectly competitive market may achieve efficiency which can lead the economy to attain a point on the GUPF, but not necessarily at Ω; perfectly competitive markets may instead have the economy come to rest at such points as H, G, or indeed anywhere along the GUPF.

- Certain moves can worsen social welfare but increase efficiency and vice versa. For example, a move from F to G in figure A-15 represents a gain in efficiency (a move from off to on the GUPF) but a loss in social welfare (from SWC2 to SWC1). Likewise, a movement from J to F (although neither Pareto superior nor Pareto efficient) does enhance social welfare as compared to the move from J to E, which is Pareto efficient but reflects a lower level of social welfare as compared to the inefficient F.

- Note that, given the existence of a social welfare function, the selection of Ω encompasses efficiency in exchange and production and yields:

1. a unique distribution of utility for persons A and B (U_A^*, U_B^*);

2. a particular X, Y aggregate output combination on the production possibility frontier;

3. a unique output allocation of commodities X and Y for person A and person B; and

4. a unique allocation of labor and capital for the respective production of each commodity, X and Y.

- Finally, it must be observed that without reference to a social welfare function, exclusive reliance on market solutions (under the conditions specified for perfect competition) will enable the economy to attain a some point on the GUPF, barring problems with information, externalities, and public goods. If society is not satisfied with that particular outcome, then the theory of welfare economics proffers the following:

> [The] observation . . . that the market mechanisms might produce a good (Pareto-optimal) result, but not the very best result, motivates the second basic theorem of welfare economics. Suppose someone . . . concludes that of all the Pareto-optimal distributions of goods possible in an economy, distribution X is the very best, the ideal of the optimal. The second basic theorem says that, with minor modifications involving transfers of cash among various people, the competitive market mechanism can be used to reach X. That is, X can be achieved via the interplay of profit-maximizing firms and/or utility-maximizing individuals. Consequently, it is unnecessary to have a huge bureaucracy to decide who gets what in the economy. (Feldman, 1980, pp. 3–4)

In summary, a Pareto optimum—being on the GUPF—can be interpreted as a state of the economy from which it is impossible to improve anyone's welfare, in the sense of moving a person to a position that (s)he prefers—either by "transforming" commodities through the realignment of resources in production, or by "trading" commodities in exchange—without impairing someone else's welfare. To the extent that a policy is set forth that conforms to the Pareto principle—that is, someone is being made better off and no one made worse off—it both provides the underlying rationale to go forward with a public policy or legal change, and is consistent with the thrust of Pareto, providing the recommendary force without the necessity of making interpersonal comparisons of utility and thereby avoiding the ambiguities involved in evaluating changes in welfare. Although the notion of a social welfare function was thought to serve to close out the analysis, it was largely put to rest by the work of Kenneth J. Arrow (1951) who demonstrated that there are no rules for collective choice—a social welfare function, even one with apparently reasonable and widely accepted conditions—that yields a complete and transitive, unambiguous ranking of social preferences. As an alternative to this search for global efficiency, the compensation principle offers a more piecemeal approach to evaluating legal change.

THE COMPENSATION PRINCIPLE: KALDOR-HICKS EFFICIENCY

The graphical analysis of the compensation principle is typically undertaken using point utility possibility curves,[5] and as such does not search for a globally efficient solution associated with the GUPF. Instead, it is more modest in that it is piecemeal and attempts to compare and evaluate (in as unambiguous a manner as possible) two different states of the economy brought on by the promulgation of a government policy or legal change.

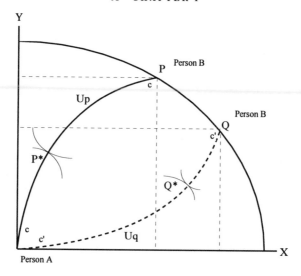

FIGURE A-16

For diagrammatic simplicity, it is assumed throughout that a government policy or legal change will take society (persons A and B) from a point such as P (the starting point) in figure A-16 to a point such as Q (the ending point) along society's transformation curve for commodities Y and X. The analytical concern is with the two associated point utility possibility frontiers, Up and Uq. Thus, in figure A-16, before the government promulgates its new policy or institutes the legal change, the economy is at point P with Up as the relevant contract curve *cc*.

Subsequently, once the government policy or legal change is in effect, the economy comes to rest at point Q with Uq as the relevant contract curve *c'c'*. It should be clear that the thrust of the compensation principle is the attempt to assess whether going forth with the legal change resulting in situation Q and contract curve *Uq*, together with a new distribution of welfare depicted as Q* (which is to the benefit of person A at the expense of person B), is or is not unambiguously preferable to maintaining the existing situation P and contract curve Up together with the P* distribution of welfare (this initial situation being to the benefit of person B vis-à-vis person A).

In assessing a movement from P to Q, and as we go from commodity space to utility space, there exist four possible cases to be analyzed, each depending upon the relative positioning of the point utility possibility curves before versus after the legal change.[6]

• Case 1: The two point utility possibility curves Uq and Up do not intersect, and Uq lies wholly outside of Up as in figure A-17. This case yields an unambiguous result. Clearly if the legal change results in a movement

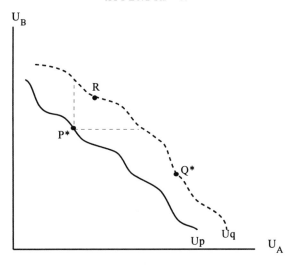

FIGURE A-17

from P* to Q*, total utility rises and person A's gain exceeds the loss of person B. Consequently, person A is in a position to compensate person B to agree to the change. The graphical test is whether there exists a Pareto-superior point (a point such as R to the northeast of P*) along Uq. In this case, with the legal change, in economic state Q, person A would be able to potentially compensate person B (along Uq) to a point such as R where both would be better off than under the economic state observed in state P along Up. The compensation principle would recommend going ahead with the government policy or legal change.

• Case 2: The two point utility possibility curves Uq and Up do not intersect, and Up lies wholly outside Uq as in figure A-18. This case also yields an unambiguous result. Clearly if the legal change results in a movement from P* to Q*, total utility falls and person A's gain does not exceed the loss of person B. Consequently, it is impossible for person A to compensate person B to agree to the change. Again, the graphical test is whether there exists a Pareto-superior point (a point to the northeast of P*) along Uq. As there is not, in this case, person A would not be able to potentially compensate person B (along Uq), and the legal change resulting in economic state Q should be foregone, since neither person could be made better off without the other being made worse off. The compensation principle would recommend maintaining the economic state associated with P.

• Case 3: The two point utility possibility curves Uq and Up intersect with P* and Q* as shown, respectively as in figure A-19. This case represents the Kaldor compensation principle as originally formulated, together with the in-

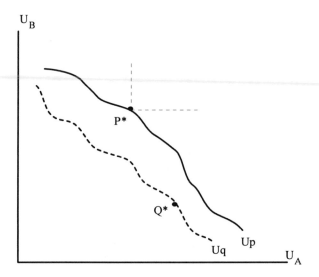

FIGURE A-18

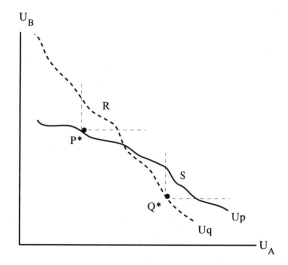

FIGURE A-19

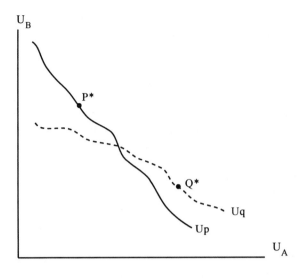

FIGURE A-20

herent paradox and ambiguity. The movement to Q can be shown to be preferable to the initial state of the economy P. For example, if the legal change
results in a movement from P* to Q*, and person A's gain exceeds the loss to
person B, person A is in a position to compensate person B to agree to the
change. Once again, the graphical test is whether there exists a Pareto-superior
point (a point to the northeast of P*) along Uq. Here, as in Case 1, there
is—point R. With the legal change to Q, person A would be able to potentially
compensate person B (along Uq) to a point such as R where both would be
better off then under the economic state observed in state P. The compensation
principle thus would recommend going ahead with the contemplated government policy or legal change.

   However, suppose that, once at Q*, we again employ the Kaldor criterion
using the graphical test to determine whether there exists a Pareto-superior
point, this time a point to the northeast of Q* along Up. It can be observed that,
indeed, such a point does exist, namely, point S. Thus, in going from Q back
to P, person B would be able to potentially compensate person A (along Up)
to a point such as S where both would be better off. Therein lies the paradox.
In this case, with the original legal change, from P to Q, the compensation
principle (as proffered by Kaldor) would recommend going ahead with the
change in government policy. However, once the change is instituted and the
economy is in state Q, the compensation principle would then recommend
reverting back to the initial policy associated with P. Under this welfare criterion, each state can be shown to be superior to the other.

- Case 4: The two point utility possibility curves Uq and Up intersect with P* and Q*, respectively, as shown in figure A-20. This case represents the Hick's formulation of the compensation principle which states that Q is superior to P if the loser cannot compensate the winner into forgoing the gains from the legal change. Note that, in figure A-20, person B's loss is not sufficient to compensate person A, the gainer, into forgoing the legal change. Thus, the *Hicks* compensation principle would recommend going ahead with the legal change. However, this raises another potential ambiguity. Notice that, in contemplating a policy change that would transform the economy from P* to Q*, person A cannot compensate person B to accept the change. That is, this policy change does not meet the *Kaldor* test (i.e., there are no points to the northeast of P* along Uq). Thus, the Hicks and Kaldor tests can give contradictory answers to the question of whether a given policy change will increase social well-being.

It is generally recognized, following the work of Scitovsky (1941–42), that it is only when both Kaldor's and Hick's conditions are satisfied that a legal change can unambiguously be judged an improvement. Thus, the modern-day formulation of the compensation principle is as follows: A change may be judged to improve society well-being if and only if both the gainers from the change could compensate the losers for their losses and remain better off themselves, *and* the losers could not have compensated the gainers to forgo their gains without being themselves worse off than in their original position.[7]

CHAPTER 2

Chicago Law and Economics

A second meaning of "justice," and the most common
I would argue, is simply "efficiency." When we
describe as "unjust" convicting a person without a
trial, taking property without just compensation, or
failing to require a negligent automobile driver to
answer in damages to the victim of his carelessness,
we can be interpreted as meaning simply that the
conduct or practice in question wastes resources.
(Posner, 1975, p. 777)

INTRODUCTION

While the roots of law and economics go back at least to Adam Smith and
Jeremy Bentham, it came of age as an intellectual discipline within economics
and law in the 1960s and 1970s through the work of such notables as Ronald
Coase, Guido Calabresi, Henry Manne, Gary Becker, and Richard Posner.[1]
The work of these scholars, of whom Posner—as professor, scholar, and
judge—is perhaps the foremost exponent, form the core of the Chicago approach to law and economics, an approach that has attracted a large following
and has come to dominate scholarship within the economic analysis of law.
For the purposes of this discussion, the Chicago school is deemed to encompass not just the work of Posner et al., but most of what falls under the um-
brella of "mainstream" law and economics, as reflected in, for example, the
Journal of Law and Economics, the *Journal of Legal Studies*, *Research in Law
and Economics*, and many of the major law reviews.[2]

This having been said, the history of law and economics at the University of
Chicago begins well before the birth in the 1960s of the "new" law and economics that is now synonymous with the Chicago school. The distinction between the "old" and "new" Chicago law and economics continues within the
Chicago oral tradition, though it is more folklore than fact.[3] To appreciate this
distinction, it is useful to mention a few of the highlights of this earlier era of
economics and law. As will become evident, although part of the early history
and subsequent success of Chicago law and economics is attributable to scholars in the Department of Economics at Chicago, much of the credit owes to the
intellectual edifice provided by the faculty of the law school.[4]

As noted in chapter 1, the Realist-Institutionalist interaction of the 1920s and 1930s did a great deal to bring law and economics together. A similar interaction commenced at nearly the same time at Chicago but with a distinctly different flavor. Within the law school, the early origins of Chicago law and economics can be traced back to the latter part of the 1930s, when the faculty, under the deanship of Wilber Katz, instituted a four-year interdisciplinary legal studies curriculum that included courses in economics and accounting (Katz, 1937). Not long thereafter, in 1939, the law school appointed its first economist, Henry Simons, to the faculty. Simons had been a lecturer in the Department of Economics and was a former student of Professor Frank Knight, who was in many respects the father of the modern neoclassical price-theoretic tradition of Chicago economics (Kitch, 1983a, p. 167).[5] Simons's appointment to the law school was the culmination of many episodes of political infighting between Frank Knight and Paul Douglas within the Department of Economics. Douglas—a strong proponent of Keynesian thinking and advocate of economic intervention—and others within the economics department fought both Simons's promotion and tenure. As a result, Simons was ultimately appointed to the law faculty to teach a course entitled "Economic Analysis of Public Policy," and, in 1945, he became the first economist granted tenure by the law school. By the mid-1940s, Simons had established himself as a contributing, but by no means seminal, figure at the headwaters of the Chicago law and economics movement,[6] and his anti-interventionist stance reflected the perspective that has come to be associated with Chicago law and economics. His tenure at the law school helped to lay a solid foundation and a receptive environment for the then-emerging field of law and economics.

Simons helped to ensure the continuity and growth of Chicago law and economics through his role (together with Friedrich A. Hayek and financial backing from the Volker Fund) in bringing to the law school the individual most responsible for firmly establishing the Chicago law and economics tradition, Aaron Director. Director had been a member of the economics faculty in the early 1930s; he had authored articles that had a distinct Chicago price-theoretic flavor[7] and was also a student of Frank Knight. In 1946, Director assumed the directorship of a university center (affiliated with the law school) dedicated to undertaking "a study of a suitable legal and institutional framework of an effective competitive system" (Coase, 1993, p. 246). Upon Simons's death, Director took over responsibility for teaching Simons's course on "Economic Analysis of Public Policy."

Subsequent to his law school appointment, Director was invited by Edward Levi to collaborate in the teaching of the antitrust course (an area of law particularly open to the influence of economic ideas) and, through his teachings, Director had a formidible influence on Chicago law students, including several individuals—among them, Robert Bork, John McGee, Ward S. Bowman Jr., and Richard Posner—who went on to be prominent scholars. During his tenure at the law school, Director formally established the nation's first law and economics program (derivative of the school's antitrust project), which maintained visiting fellowships for law and economics scholars, set in place the workshop in the law school (an arena of vigorous debate over issues of current research, already an established tradition within the economics department), and, in 1958, founded the *Journal of Law and Economics*. Throughout his tenure at Chicago he imparted a persuasive message to the students—that regulation was the proper function of markets, not government. This message was one that often resulted in legal reasoning losing out to economic analysis and was, to the students of law, "a message which was at once both unfamiliar and yet quite understandable" (Duxbury, 1995, p. 344).

Nowhere did early Chicago law and economics make a greater and more enduring impact than on the field of antitrust law, the goal of which, within the Chicago tradition, is said to be the promotion of efficiency. Over the past several decades, the existing legal-economic scholarship demonstrates that, as Herbert Hovenkamp (1986, p. 1020) has pointed out, "the Chicago School has done more for antitrust policy than any other coherent economic theory since the New Deal. No one . . . can escape [its] influence on antitrust analysis." Reflecting the emphasis within the Chicago tradition on the efficacy of the competitive system (see below), monopoly was viewed as occasional, unstable, and transitory—a potential outcome of the competitive process, but one that would soon be removed (in effect if not in existence) by competitive pressures. Given this, rigorous antitrust enforcement was thought to be unnecessary, and, even when monopolies were shown to generate long-term inefficiencies, the governmental cure was thought to be often worse than the disease, owing to the inefficiencies of government. This emphasis on efficiency has been challenged by scores of critics who contend that the goal of antitrust law is distribution- rather than efficiency-oriented, and who argue for strong limits on monopoly power through rigorous antitrust enforcement. Nonetheless, the Chicago view has become firmly established within this area, and, in this sense, the Chicagoans can claim a partial victory in the "battle for the soul of antitrust" (Fox, 1987)—that the intent of antitrust legislation is to promote allocative efficiency and thereby the economic interests of producers and consumers.

Perhaps Edmund Kitch, a Chicago-trained lawyer (1961–64) and later the director of the Law and Economics Program at the University of Chicago Law School, best described the thrust of law and economics at the Chicago law school during this earlier era when he said that

> [t]he interest . . . in economics did not come out of any anti-interventionist thinking. It essentially came out of the idea that the legal system is going to be doing this [i.e., intervening in the economic system] now and that means we need to

learn how to do it right and maybe economists know something about how to do it right. . . . There is a great legitimacy given to the idea that government is going to be doing these things and we in the law schools should try to help the government do it right. (Kitch, 1983a, pp. 175–76)

Although the events in the law school laid the foundation for the development of law and economics at Chicago, a full understanding of its development necessiates an appreciation of the scholarship generated by the faculty of the Department of Economics, both before World War II and thereafter. Especially with respect to methodology, there were really two Chicago schools of thought, roughly divided in time by the war (Duxbury, 1995, p. 367; Reder, 1982).[8] The perspective of the prewar Chicago school was largely derived from the works of Frank Knight, Jacob Viner, Paul Douglas, and Henry Schultz, who were themselves by no means of a homogeneous perspective. From this group, it was was Knight who had the most impact on what has come to be known as Chicago law and economics. In simple terms, proponents of the early Chicago approach generally accepted the propositions that had been at the heart of economics since the writing of Adam Smith (1776): Within a liberal democracy, the rational pursuit of economic self-interest by economic actors was taken as given, competition was seen as inherent within and intrinsic to economic life, and market-generated outcomes were said to be superior to those resulting from government interference with the market mechanism. Although, during the 1930s, these propositions (the latter two in particular) were being increasingly called into question within the profession at large, their continuity within the Chicago school served (and continues to serve) to set the Chicago perspective apart from much of the rest of the economics profession.

It was Knight who, among this earlier generation of Chicago economists, had the greatest influence on subsequent Chicago thinking, and, concomitantly, on Chicago law and economics. Although his writings are not unimportant within this, of greater import is the perspective that he imparted to his students—most importantly, for present purposes, Milton Friedman, George Stigler, and Aaron Director. Knight's interest and strength did not lie in the use of formal mathematical and quantitative tools, but rather in the economic way of thinking and in applying this way of thinking to the development of economic ideas and to the tearing down of what he saw as false theories that were becoming increasingly fashionable within economics (Reder, 1982, pp. 4, 6).

As Duxbury (1995, p. 368) has pointed out, whereas the earlier generation of Chicago economists "had grasped and applied certain of the basic insights of Adam Smith . . . [p]ost-war Chicagoans were more intent on elaborating and extending these insights." In line with this, the new generation undertook to demonstrate, in formal terms, the detailed nexus between competitive markets and efficient outcomes. The nature of these price-theoretic undertakings was necessarily abstract and typically ahistorical, largely relying on positive, empirical research and mathematical analysis (toward which methods Knight had been rather hostile), approaches very much in keeping with broader movements within neoclassical economics at the time.[9] In this sense, then, as Reder (1982, p. 6) has noted, "Knight contributed to the formation of their minds but did not influence the direction of their research." Following the lead of Milton Friedman and George Stigler, postwar Chicago economists, buttressed by their empirical research, emphasized the efficacy of the competitive market system, arguing for less government intervention, fewer wealth redistribution policies, reliance on voluntary exchange with a concommitant reliance on the common law for mediating conflicts, and an across-the-board promotion of more private enterprise—which, based on the evidence provided by their empirical research, would facilitate a more efficient allocation of resources.

In addition to Friedman and Stigler, another important contributor to the Chicago school during this era was Gary Becker. Seizing upon the idea that economics is the science of choice, Becker employed the Chicago price-theoretic framework to explain choices across a broad range of nonmarket behavior, including race discrimination in labor markets (Becker, 1957); crime (Becker, 1968); the organization of the family, including marriage and divorce, the decision to have children, and the division of labor within the household (Becker, 1976); altruism (Becker and Barro, 1988; Becker and Murphy, 1988a); and addictive behavior, including drug-taking (Becker and Murphy, 1988b; Becker, Grossman, and Murphy, 1991). All this illustrates Becker's distinct approach to the economic analysis of law and typifies, perhaps better than any other scholarship, what has come to be known as the "imperialism of economics."[10]

The final contribution from Chicago economists to be described here is embodied in the work of Armen A. Alchian and Harold Demsetz on the economics of property rights.[11] The property rights approach emerged as economists began to appreciate that legal-institutional arrangements that constrain the behavior of individuals and firms might have a crucial effect on the allocation of society's scarce resources. The main postulate of the economics of property rights is that the nature and form of property rights have a fundamental effect on the allocation of resources and the distribution of income in the economy (Veljanovski, 1982, pp. 68–70). Consequently, the proponents of the study of alternative property right regimes believed that such studies could uncover insights into the performance of the economy.[12] Their argument consisted of two parts. First, they argued that the value of resources is tied directly to the bundles of rights running with the resources; that is, the more complete and definite the specification of property rights (the less attenuated is the rights structure), the more uncertainty is diminished, which, in turn, tends to promote a more efficient allocation of resources. Second, proponents of the property rights approach inquired whether the standard theory of production and exchange was capable of explaining the emergence of the institution of property rights over scarce resources. Their empirical research[13] suggested an affirmative answer to this question—that an economic explanation of the development of property rights can be deduced—arguing that the emergence and development of new property rights can be explained as a consequence of value-seeking behavior brought on by new technologies and market opportunities.

The property rights approach, although owing its origins to the work of many Chicago-oriented economists, now serves as a fundamental intellectual underpinning for Neoinstitutional law and economics (described below in chapter 5) and has moved well beyond orthodox Chicago thinking. Nonetheless, core elements of the property rights approach remain at the heart of Chicago law and economics.

In summary, the intellectual direction and concerns of both the law school and the economics department, the various manifestations of the institutionalization of Chicago law and economics, the growing imperialism of the science of economics, and the emerging concern with the economic consequences of alternative rights structures partly describe the intellectual environment that Ronald Coase entered upon moving to the University of Chicago Law School in 1964. One of his major reasons for going to the law school was to assume the editorship (with Aaron Director) of the *Journal of Law and Economics*. He describes his motivation in going to Chicago as follows: "I don't think that I would ever have come to the University of Chicago had it not been for the existence of the *Journal of Law and Economics*. That's what I wanted to do. I wanted to get what Aaron had started going for the whole profession—and when I say the profession, I mean the economics profession; I have no interest in lawyers or legal education" (Coase, quoted in Kitch, 1983a, p. 192).

Of course, Coase could not have anticipated that the force of this movement would be at least as great within law as within economics. But Coase's "The Problem of Social Cost" (1960) and Guido Calabresi's "Some Thoughts on Risk Distribution and the Law of Torts" (1961) raised many issues for both economists and lawyers, including revealing the economic nature of many of the questions of legal analysis—that legal rules and decisions across many traditional fields of law beget both benefits and costs, and thus are amenable to analysis in efficiency terms—and the potential for the application of economic analysis to the law. This idea began to stimulate economic analyses of legal questions in the areas of property, contract, and tort law. Then, in 1968, came Gary Becker's pathbreaking economic analysis of criminal behavior and criminal law. By the early 1970s the economic analysis of law had emerged as a recognized field of inquiry.

FUNDAMENTAL BUILDING BLOCKS OF
THE CHICAGO APPROACH

The defining characteristic of the Chicago approach is the straightforward application of microeconomic (or price-theoretic) analysis to the law. As such, this approach embodies the following premises: (1) individuals are rational maximizers of their satisfactions in their nonmarket as well as their market behavior; (2) individuals respond to price incentives in nonmarket as well as market behavior; and (3) legal rules and legal outcomes can be assessed on the basis of their efficiency properties, along with which comes the normative prescription that legal decision making should promote efficiency. Each of these premises will be discussed in turn.

The Rational Maximization of Satisfaction

The assumption that economic agents are rational maximizers—that is, they make purposeful choices so as to pursue consistent ends using efficient means[14]—stands as a cornerstone of modern economic theory. Under this view, individuals are assumed to have a set of preferences which are complete, reflexive, transitive, and continuous. Given these conditions, it can be shown that consumer preferences can be represented by a utility function,[15] based on which, assuming that individuals are able to perfectly process all relevant information about the alternatives available to them, individuals can rank all possible outcomes according to their relative desirability and will choose to consume the bundle of goods/activities that maximizes utility. Similarly, firms are viewed as profit maximizers, with the result that the level of output produced, the price charged, the composition of inputs and of payments thereto, the contracting practices of the firm, and so on are those which will maximize the firm's profits.

The assumption of rational maximization leads to a straightforward result as to the process of decision making: Individuals will engage in additional units of an activity (be it the consumption of goods, production, the supply of labor, and so on) as long as the additional benefit derived from another unit of that activity is greater than or equal to the additional cost, that is, as long as marginal benefit is greater than or equal to marginal cost. Thus, for example, the decision as to how many apples to consume comes down to an evaluation of whether the additional benefit from each additional apple consumed is greater than or equal to the cost of consuming that apple. In the present context, undertaking actions with respect to the prevailing law (e.g., to breach a contract, to take precaution against breach, to engage in potentially tortious conduct, or to hold up a liquor store) becomes a matter of comparing marginal benefits with marginal costs. From this perspective, those who break the law are not essentially different from the rest of the population; they simply have different preferences/opportunity costs/constraints and engage in "illegal" activities because these are the activities that maximize their net benefit. Some commentators have challenged this idea on the grounds that individuals do not have full and complete information. The response is that information is a good, additional units of which are consumed only as long as marginal benefit is greater than or equal to marginal cost. Thus, it may be rational to be ignorant, and as the price of information rises, so does the level of ignorance. This, in fact, is the economic rationale for the failure to fully specify all contingencies in a contract.

The "rational" individual of economics contrasts, of course, with the "reasonable" individual of traditional legal theory—an individual who is socialized into the norms and conventions of a community, and whose behavior corresponds to these norms. The law is said to reflect these norms and conventions, and thus is obeyed by reasonable individuals. Those who engage in "illegal" activities are seen as unreasonable in that they have violated these norms and conventions. In contrast, the economic approach says that behavior can be (and usually is) rational even when it conflicts with these social norms (Cooter and Ulen, 1988, pp. 11–12).

Legal Rules as Prices

The idea that individuals are rational maximizers implies that they respond to price incentives—that consumers will consume less of a good if its price rises and that producers will produce more of a good as its price rises (all this, *ceteris paribus*).[16] Within the legal arena, legal rules establish prices, such as fines, community service, and incarceration, for engaging in various types of illegal behavior. The rational maximizer, then, will compare the benefits of each additional unit of illegal activity with the costs, where the costs are weighted by the probability of detection and conviction.

The adjustment—through public/legal policy—of the level of illegal activity, be it tortious acts, breach of contract, or criminal behavior, thus becomes a matter of adjusting the prices reflected in the legal rules. To reduce the amount of such activities, one simply raises their price through the imposition of higher fines or greater jail time by an amount sufficient to induce the desired degree of behavioral change. As Posner (1983, p. 75) has said, "The basic function of law in an economic or wealth maximizing perspective is to alter incentives." An increase in the price of engaging in an illegal activity will induce certain individuals to reduce or eliminate their involvement in such activities, whereas those who continue on are those whose benefits continue to exceed the higher cost.

Thus, the imposition of a liability rule on a polluting firm will raise the price of pollution and induce the firm to reduce the level of pollution as long as the marginal benefits (e.g., foregone damage payments) exceed the marginal cost (e.g., of pollution abatement). Similarly, the institution of higher damage payments for negligence in tort (e.g., punitive damages, pain and suffering, etc.) will induce potential tortfeasors to take additional precaution to prevent the occurrence of a tort. And, perhaps most controversially, higher fines and longer jail terms will reduce the amount of crime.

Efficiency

The third defining characteristic of the Chicago approach to law and economics is that legal decision making and the evaluation of legal rules should be analyzed from the perspective of economic efficiency. One criterion employed is Pareto efficiency—that a situation is efficiency-enhancing if at least one person can be made better off without making anyone else worse off. The Pareto criterion is generally recognized to be quite limited as a guide to legal decision making on the grounds that the ubiquity of losses due to legal change, and the impossibility and/or prohibitive cost of compensating all losses, would forever perpetuate the status quo. The standard definition of efficiency within the Chicago approach is Kaldor-Hicks efficiency, or wealth maximization: A legal change is efficiency-enhancing if the gains to the winners exceed the losses to the losers[17] or, alternatively stated, if the wealth of society (as measured by willingness to pay) is increased. "The economic task from the perspective of wealth maximization," says Posner (1990, p. 382), "is to influence [individuals] so as to maximize [their] output."

An example will easily demonstrate this efficiency concept in action. Suppose that a firm dumps chemicals into a stream, the effect of which is to reduce the property values of downstream landowners by a total of $1 million. Suppose further that the downstream landowners file suit seeking a permanent injunction against this dumping. If the downstream landowners have no way of preventing the damage, but the firm could eliminate the damage by installing a filtering device at a cost of $600,000, efficiency would dictate that the firm install the filter, since the cost of abatement is less than the damage from the chemical discharge. Thus, the injunction should be granted, which in turn would induce the firm to install the filter, increasing societal wealth by $400,000. But suppose that, due to the nature of the damage and the technology available, the downstream landowners could, in fact, eliminate the damage themselves for a cost of $300,000. In this case, efficiency would dictate a denial of the injunction, as the landowners could eliminate the harm at a lower cost than could the firm, and would in fact do so if the injunction were denied, since the gain from doing so ($1 million) exceeds the cost ($300,000).

The concept of efficiency as justice is what many of the critics of the Chicago approach to law and economics find so troubling.[18] Posner (1992, p. 27), however, avers that efficiency is "perhaps the most common" meaning of justice and says that "a moral system founded on economic principles is congruent with, and can give structure to, our everyday moral intuitions" (Posner, 1983, p. 84).[19] Posner (1983, p. 89) attempts to ground the ethical basis for a rule of wealth maximization in the principle of consent, which, as he describes it, is "an ethical criterion congenial to the Kantian emphasis on treating people as ends rather than as means, in a word, on autonomy." The notion of consent employed by Posner is based on *ex ante* compensation. The connection between consent and *ex ante* compensation lies in the idea that individuals would consent to wealth maximization as a criterion for establishing common law rules of adjudication as long as there is a sufficient probability that they will benefit (i.e., be net winners) from the application of such rules in the long run, even though they may be losers from the application of a particular rule. It is not necessary to compensate those who lose from the application of a particular wealth-maximizing decision rule because these individuals have garnered *ex ante* compensation in the form of the greater wealth (lower costs) that accompany the adoption of these wealth-maximizing rules.[20]

Posner also suggests that wealth maximization, which he sees as blending certain elements of the utilitarian and Kantian traditions (with its emphasis on human respect and autonomy), is superior as an ethical concept to both utilitarianism and Kantianism. First, he says, "the pursuit of wealth, based as it is on the model of the voluntary market transaction, involves greater respect for individual choice than in classical utilitarianism" (Posner, 1983, p. 66). Second, "Economic liberty . . . can be grounded more firmly in wealth maximization than in utilitarianism" (Posner, 1983, p. 67). Third, "the wealth-maximization principle encourages and rewards the traditional 'Calvinist' or 'Protestant' virtues and capacities associated with economic progress" (Posner, 1983, p. 68). Finally, "Wealth maximization is a more defensible moral principle also in that it provides a firmer foundation for a theory of distributive and corrective justice," along with a firmer commitment to the principle of rights than is evident in utilitarian and Kantian thinking (Posner, 1983, p. 69). But the strongest argument for wealth maximization, says Posner, is pragmatic: "We look around the world and see that in general people who live in societies in which markets are allowed to function more or less freely not only are wealthier than people in other societies but have more political rights, more liberty and dignity, are more content . . . so that wealth maximization may be the most direct route to a variety of moral ends" (Posner, 1990, p. 382).

CHICAGO LAW AND ECONOMICS AT WORK

We have seen that the Chicago approach to law and economics has as a primary goal the adoption of efficient legal rules. But how does this analysis proceed? First, the Chicago approach has been concerned with assessing the degree to which prevailing common law doctrines comport with the dictates of economic efficiency—what is generally described as the efficiency analysis of the common law, or *positive* law and economics. Second, where the common law is seen to depart from the dictates of efficiency, or where new common law issues present themselves, these scholars are concerned with determining efficient legal rules to guide judicial decision making—what is generally known as *normative* law and economics. The goal of this section is to present the basic framework of these two branches of analysis.

The Efficiency of the Common Law

Whereas many observers of the legal process may believe that the common law is a grouping of largely separate fields of analysis (e.g., property, contract, tort, etc.), each with its own set of judge-made legal rules and doctrines, the Chicago approach to law and economics suggests that the common law as a whole has an underlying economic logic. This point, first raised within the Chicago tradition by Coase (1960, p. 19) in "The Problem of Social Cost," has been probed in numerous studies by Posner and others that purport to describe the common law's economic logic.[21] Proponents of this line of research refer to it as the *positive* branch of the economic analysis of law. As Posner (1987b, p. 5) defines it, the economic theory of the common law (broadly conceived to include all judge-made law) "is that the common law is best understood not merely as a pricing mechanism but as a pricing mechanism designed to bring about an efficient allocation of resources, in the Kaldor-Hicks sense." Simply stated, the hypothesis is that the development of the common law can be explained *as if* its goal was to maximize allocative efficiency. That is, the basic thesis is that the common law (especially the law of torts) is best explained *as if* the judges who created the law through decisions operating as precedents were trying to promote efficient resource allocation.

Two aspects of this trend toward efficiency can be identified in the literature: First, that the institutions of the common law have been designed to promote efficiency by fostering market transactions through contract; second, that common law decisions will result in outcomes that will bring about an allocation of resources that simulates that which the free market would have brought about had a market been feasible.

The first of these efficiency hypotheses uses the expected utility maximization model to provide insight into the issue of pretrial settlement versus formal adjudication and has been analyzed in the contexts of civil, criminal, labor, and antitrust cases. The issue facing each party is that of settlement versus adjudication, and the decision making by each party is assumed to turn on which course of action gives them the higher expected utility, given their resource constraints and the subjective probability of winning should the case go to trial.

A simple example will illustrate the working of this process in a civil case. Assume that both parties agree that the judgment, if the defendant is found liable, will be $100,000, and that the probability of the plaintiff prevailing is 0.40.[22] Suppose further that the plaintiff's trial costs are $20,000 and the defendant's trial costs are $10,000. The plaintiff's expected gain from going to trial is thus $20,000 ($100,000 × 0.40 − $20,000) and the defendant's expected loss is $50,000 ($100,000 × 0.40 + $10,000). Given that the plaintiff's expected gain from a trial is $20,000, she will be willing to settle out-of-court for any amount greater than this. Similarly, the defendant, with expected costs of $50,000 associated with going to a trial, will be willing to settle for any amount less than $50,000. There is thus a $30,000 range within which a settlement can occur, and if the transaction costs associated with the bargaining process are relatively low, it can be expected that the parties will reach a mutually agreeable settlement within this range.[23]

This same type of analysis can be extended to criminal law and issues surrounding criminal settlement. In a criminal case, the defendant weighs his expected sentence (including the probability of conviction) against the sentence offered in the plea bargain. The prosecutor, whose utility may be defined to include the number of convictions, weighted by the severity of the sentences, will consider the expected sentence (again, weighted by the probability of conviction) in determining what, if any, terms to offer in a plea bargain. If expected gains to both parties from a settlement exist, then there will be a range of sentences within which a settlement may be reached.[24]

Numerous factors affect the issue of settlement versus trial, and many of these have been introduced into the economic models of this process. These include differential bargaining costs across disputants, differences in their respective attitudes toward the risks associated with the adjudicatory outcome, and different estimates of the probability of prevailing at trial. Moreover, the various methods by which the legal costs of going to trial are allocated between the litigants (e.g., the standard U.S. method versus the English Rule) have been analyzed in an attempt to explain the trial settlement pattern under each method.[25]

The second aspect of the efficiency hypothesis, that common law judgments will tend to mimic the efficient result of a free market, is derivative of two underlying hypotheses. The first is that inefficient legal rules are likely to be more frequently and more intensively (an effort in the sense of time) challenged in court than are efficient ones. The reason for this is that inefficient rules generate higher expected judgments for the challenging parties, and thus individuals will be willing to spend more time, money, and effort in challenging inefficient rules than they will in challenging efficient rules. This is apparent when one recognizes that the overturning of inefficient rules generates both a greater quantity of total wealth and a redistribution of wealth, whereas the overturning of efficient rules *decreases* total wealth at the same time that it redistributes it (Cooter and Ulen, 1988, pp. 492–96; Posner, 1990, p. 360). Alternatively, parties may seek some form of alternative dispute resolution, such as arbitration, if judicial decisions continue to promote inefficient allocations (Posner, 1992, p. 535). As a result, we can expect to see inefficient rules overturned more frequently, thus increasing the stock of efficient rules over time.

When this idea is combined with the logic of the trial-settlement model we see what has come to be known as "the economic theory of the evolution of the common law," as evidenced, for example, in the work of George L. Priest (1977) and Paul H. Rubin (1977). Rubin describes this theory as follows:

> The presumed efficiency of the common law and the decision to use the courts to settle a dispute are related. In particular, this relationship will occur because re-sorting to court settlement is more likely in cases where the legal rules relevant to the dispute are inefficient, and less likely where rules are efficient. Thus, efficient rules may evolve from in-court settlement, thereby reducing the incentive for future litigation and increasing the probability that efficient rules will persist. In short, the efficient rule situation noted by Posner is due to an evolutionary mechanism whose direction proceeds from the utility maximizing decisions of disputants rather than from the wisdom of judges. (Rubin, 1977, p. 51)

Rubin continues:

> If rules are inefficient, parties will use the courts until the rules are changed; conversely, if rules are efficient, the courts will not be used and the efficient rule will remain in force. An outside observer coming upon this legal rule would observe that this rule is efficient; but this efficiency occurs because of an evolutionary process, not because of any particular wisdom on the part of judges. If judges decide independently of efficiency one would still find efficient rules. Intelligent judges may speed up the process of attaining efficiency; they do not drive the process. (Rubin, 1977, p. 55)

Thus, the driving force toward efficiency, according to Rubin and Priest, is that inefficient legal rules/decisions will be contested and litigated more frequently than efficient decisions.

John C. Goodman goes further than Rubin and Priest, attempting to set forth specific reasons why inefficient rules will be overturned. Goodman assumes

(1) that judges are amenable to persuasion by the litigants appearing before the court, (2) that judges are completely unbiased with respect to efficiency, and (3) that any increase in legal expenses by either party will increase that party's probability of securing a favorable judgment. Since the economic stakes are higher under inefficient rules, the party on whom liability initially rests has a greater incentive to spend a larger amount on litigation expense here than under efficient rules. The additional expenditures on litigating inefficient rules thus increase the likelihood that such rules will be replaced by efficient ones. Goodman describes this as follows:

> A model of an adversary proceeding is proposed in which the probability that a particular litigant will win a favorable decision depends upon the efforts of both litigants to influence the court and upon the weight of judicial bias. Since parties before the court have an obvious interest in the decision, they have incentives, not necessarily equal, to affect that decision through efforts that incur legal costs— expenses for legal research, factual investigation, forensic talent, and so forth. The fundamental assumption made throughout is that any increment in legal expenses . . . will induce an increment, however small, in the probability . . . of winning a favorable decision. . . . Even if the weight of past precedents favors inefficient solutions, the side with the greater economic stake in the issue will still have a higher probability of winning any succeeding case so long as the ratio of his economic stake to his opponent's exceeds . . . the ratio of legal expenses by the two litigants that must be maintained in order to insure that they both have the same probability of winning. (Goodman, 1978, pp. 394–95)

The second and more strongly held rationale for the efficiency of the common law lies in the view that judges—implicitly or explicitly—select legal rules that generate efficient outcomes. Broadly stated, "The hypothesis is not that judges can or do duplicate the results of competitive markets, but that within the limits set by the costs of administering the legal system (costs that must be taken into account in any effort to promote efficiency through legal rules), common law adjudication brings the economic system closer to the results that would be produced by effective competition—a free market operating without significant externality, monopoly, or information problems" (Posner, 1983, pp. 4–5).[26]

"It is," says Posner (1990, p. 356, emphasis in original), "as if the judges *wanted* to adopt the rules, procedures, and case outcomes that would maximize society's wealth."

Posner (1992, p. 252) suggests that economic logic pervades the common law and that, in general, when transaction costs are low the common law gives incentives for individuals to "channel their transactions through the market," whereas when transaction costs are high, making market allocation infeasible, "the common law prices behavior in such a way as to mimic the market." The instances where law and economics scholars have found common law rules comporting with the dictates of efficiency are far too numerous to detail here, and a few examples will suffice. The law of property structures property rights in such a way as to promote value-maximizing exchange. Tort law, through the application of the Learned Hand formula, promotes the taking of cost-justified precautions. The doctrine of impossibility in contract law places liability on the party who could most easily anticipate or insure against the unforeseen contingency. Other examples are found in admiralty, expectation damages, assumption of risk, and the application and nonapplication of punitive damages.[27]

Although Chicago law and economics does not have a clearly defined model of judicial behavior or motivation in decision making, there is a more-or-less general theme that judges have in mind the overall well-being of society—a concept incorporating numerous social values—in resolving cases. Utility maximization is sometimes rejected as a motivating force for judges on the grounds that judges almost never have any personal stake in the case at hand, and that the judicial system has been designed to insulate judges from significant economic incentives. Richard Posner (1993b) has recently questioned this view, arguing that judges, like everyone else, are rational utility maximizers, where the utility functions of judges are primarily a function of income, leisure, and judicial voting. In fleshing out the implications of this utility function in the context of the institutional structure within which judges make decisions, Posner is able to both explain certain aspects of judicial behavior and offer testable predictions that arise from the model.

Although the actual motivation underlying judicial decision making is still open to question, it remains the case that judges are, at times, called upon to "legislate" (Posner, 1993b, p. 40). Whereas societal well-being entails both efficiency and distributional considerations, Posner (1990, p. 359) suggests that "prosperity" (i.e., wealth maximization) is a goal "that judges are especially well equipped to promote," while judges can do little, if anything, to promote the redistribution of wealth.[28] Moreover, says Posner (1990, p. 359), judges wish to avoid controversy, and wealth maximization "is a relatively uncontroversial policy." Because the cases at hand are unrelated to judicial self-interest, and/or because it is difficult to rationalize the judge's personal considerations as to "deservingness" within the context of a judicial opinion, the judge is "[a]lmost by default . . . compelled to view the parties as representatives of activities," and "[i]n these circumstances it is natural that he should ask which of the competing activities is more valuable in an economic sense" (Posner, 1992, pp. 523–24).

Although critics have often maintained that the common law reflects no overt economic logic or phraseology, the proponents of the efficiency theory suggest that the underlying economic logic is clear, even if judges usually do not speak the language—that judges employ language other than efficiency to explain efficient arrangements (Cooter and Ulen, 1988, p. 497). Posner (1992, pp. 254–55) even goes so far as to suggest that these efficient doctrines simply reflect common sense, and that whereas the articulation of these doctrines in formal economic terminology lies beyond the capacity of most judges, the commonsensical intuition does not. Against those who suggest that efficiency is not a value that would enter into the judge's decision-making calculus, Posner (1992, p. 255) responds that justice is often "a version of efficiency" and maintains that efficiency "has always been an important social value," especially during the laissez-faire period of the nineteenth century when the common law received much of its modern shape.

It must be underscored that to the extent to which the proponents of this line of reasoning succeed in having it gain acceptance, it will serve as an ideological barrier to the general promotion of statutory law—more specifically, a barrier to the passing of statutes. The logic underlying the efficiency of the common law thesis generally follows the following contour: Whenever the market falls a bit short of providing an efficient allocation of resources due to externalities or some other source of market failure, one can rely on the common law and damage measures (a common law they purport to have demonstrated to be comprised of rules and doctrines that produce efficient results) to give the market a gentle nudge in the direction of maximum social welfare. Thus, given the existence of some form of market failure, society need not rely on the ever-ready legislative branch to adopt regulatory statutes or bureaucratic mechanisms to promote efficiency; all one needs to do is rely on the common law to generate the efficient outcome.

Normative Law and Economics: The Formulation of Efficient Legal Rules

The normative branch of Chicago law and economics is concerned with the determination of efficient legal rules to deal with situations where the common law departs from the dictates of economic efficiency. The starting point is the recognition by Coase (1960, p. 2) that situations of harm are reciprocal in nature. Examples are present throughout the fields of property, contract, and tort law so the concept applies generally. Suppose that A emits pollution, which causes harm to its neighbor, B. A legal rule calling for A to eliminate the pollution removes the harm from B, but, as Coase pointed out, it also imposes harm on A, through, say, the cost of pollution abatement. Thus, "We are dealing with a problem of a reciprocal nature. To avoid the harm to B would inflict harm on A. The real question that has to be decided is: should A be allowed to harm B or should B be allowed to harm A?" In line with the goal of efficiency, described above, Coase goes on to suggest that "[t]he problem is to avoid the more serious harm"—that is, to maximize society's wealth (Coase, 1960, p. 2).

Under the reciprocal view of harm, the problem of causation becomes much more open than under the traditional legal approach. Landes and Posner (1983, p. 110) provide a useful description of the economics of causation in tort:

> If the basic purpose of tort law is to promote economic efficiency, a defendant's conduct will be deemed the cause of an injury when making him liable for the consequences of the injury would promote an efficient allocation of safety and care; and when it would not promote efficiency for the defendant to have behaved differently, then the cause of the accident will be ascribed to "an act of God" or some other force on which liability cannot rest. In this view, the injurer "causes" the injury when he is the cheaper cost avoider; not otherwise.

The contrast between the economic approach and the traditional measures of "cause-in-fact" and "proximate cause" is apparent, but the most interesting characteristic of the economic approach here is that "causation becomes a result rather than a premise" of the economic analysis of torts (Landes and Posner, 1983, p. 110).

Perhaps the most intriguing, and certainly the most controversial, aspect of Coase's analysis lies in what has come to be known as the Coase theorem. Although this theorem has several variants, it says, in a nutshell, that if rights are fully specified and transaction costs are zero, parties to a dispute will bargain to the same efficient outcome regardless of the initial assignment of rights. The central idea underlying the Coase theorem can be illustrated in the context of the example of the polluted stream, discussed above. The pollution discharge causes $1 million in damage to downstream landowners. The polluter can prevent the damage by installing a filtering device at a cost of $600,000, whereas downstream landowners could eliminate the damage at a cost of $300,000. Efficiency clearly dictates that the pollution be eliminated, since the damage is greater than the cost of abatement, and that the optimal way of abating the pollution is for the downstream landowners to undertake the abatement. The Coase theorem holds that, no matter how rights are initially assigned, this is exactly the solution that will obtain.

Suppose that the court assigns downstream landowners the right to be free from pollution. The polluter can abate the pollution at a cost of $600,000. However, the polluter, recognizing that the downstream landowners can abate at a cost of $300,000, will be willing to offer them any amount up to $600,000 to undertake the abatement. The landowners, in turn, will be willing to accept any payment in excess of $300,000 to undertake this abatement. Thus, in the absence of transaction costs, a mutually beneficial bargain will be struck between these parties whereby the landowners agree to undertake the abatement. If, on the other hand, the polluter is given the right to pollute, the downstream landowners, faced with a choice between the $1 million in damage and the $300,000 cost of abating the pollution themselves, will choose to undertake the abatement.[29] Thus, regardless of the initial assignment of rights, the efficient result—abatement undertaken by the downstream landowners—will obtain. In either case, the actual distribution of the gains from this exchange will depend on the relative bargaining power of the two sides.[30]

Although the present example provides a useful context for understanding the legal-economic resolution of property and tort disputes, this approach is also applicable to contract law. Suppose that A signs a contract with B which stipulates that A will sell her house to B for $200,000. After this contract has been signed, C enters the picture, offering to pay A $210,000 if A will sell to him. A then breaches her contract with B and sells the house to C for $210,000. Here, it is clearly efficient for A to breach the contract with B and sell to C instead, since C values the house more highly than does B. Suppose next that B files suit against A for breach of contract, asking that the contract be enforced according to its terms. If the court rules against B, then C retains the house—the efficient result obtains. If instead the court finds in favor of B, the house is transferred from C to B, resulting in an inefficient solution. Just as in the above pollution example, however, this is not the end of the story. If C values the house at $210,000 and B only at $200,000, then C will be willing to offer B any amount up to $210,000 for the house. B, who values the house at $200,000, will be willing to accept any amount greater than that to give up the house. Thus, a mutually-beneficial bargain will be struck, and the efficient result—C owning the house—will obtain. In a world of zero transaction costs, we thus get the efficient result regardless of the initial assignment of rights—that is, whether or not the court rules on behalf of A or on behalf of B.

More generally, in a world of zero transaction costs, it does not matter, from an efficiency perspective, whether A or B is given the right. If A is given the right and B values that right more than does A, then there is room for a mutually beneficial bargain to be struck in which B purchases the right from A. Conversely, if A values the right more than B, then B will not be willing to offer A any price which A would be willing to accept to give up its right. A similar chain of reasoning holds if the right is initially assigned to B. Thus, in a zero transaction cost situation, the right will end up in its highest-valued use because all mutually beneficial bargains can and will be costlessly struck by rational maximizing individuals.[31] Given such a situation, the judge will not need to be concerned about efficient rights assignment, as the same efficient outcome will be reached regardless of the judge's decision.[32] Attempts by judges to engage in social engineering will inevitably be fruitless because rights, regardless of how they are initially assigned, will always end up in their highest-valued use.

The problem, of course, is that the real world is, at least for the most part, a world of positive transaction costs, where transaction costs include, at the most basic level, the costs of negotiating, monitoring, and enforcing contractual agreements.[33] If transaction costs are low, relative to the gains from bargaining, then it is expected that inefficient assignments of rights will be overcome through the bargaining process, along the lines implied by the Coase theorem. However, transaction costs may be sufficiently high that bargaining is precluded. If this is the case,[34] we have what may be called a legal flypaper effect—the right sticks where it hits—since transaction costs will preclude bargaining to a more advantageous state. Here, the court's decision on behalf of one party or the other will directly determine the final resting place of the right and thus will impact the efficiency of the end state. The goal of efficiency in Chicago law and economics manifests itself in the normative prescription that rights should be assigned in a way that maximizes the wealth of society.

To continue with the pollution example, above, since the least-cost method of reducing pollution is for the downstream landowners to abate that pollution, the efficiency criterion would dictate that the polluter be given the right to pollute. As we saw, this would induce the landowners to undertake abatement since the alternative is sustaining $1 million in damage. Of course the optimal amount of pollution may be some intermediate amount, as opposed to all or nothing. In this case, a property rule will not give the optimal result when transaction costs preclude bargaining. As Guido Calabresi and A. Douglas Melamed (1972) have pointed out, efficiency would dictate the use of a liability rule in such a situation, since the polluter would then pollute only as long as its benefits from additional pollution exceed its costs (as measured by compensatory damages), thereby engendering the optimal outcome. Similarly, referring back to the example from contract law, the court should, from an efficiency perspective, allow A to breach her contract with B and sell to C, since, in doing so, the house is placed in a higher-valued use.

This approach reflects what has been called "mimicking the market" and involves assuming a hypothetical zero transaction costs world, as in the Coase theorem. The question then becomes one of ascertaining where, in a zero transaction cost world, the ultimate resting place of the right will finally be. By engaging in this type of inferential analysis, courts can attempt to discern the efficient outcome that would have resulted from the market-like machinations of the Coase theorem. By assigning rights in such a way as to achieve this result, the courts can accomplish the goal of wealth maximization. Thus, in a dispute over terms or provisions that are missing from a contract because positive transaction costs in negotiating the contract made it uneconomical, *ex ante*, to fully specify the contract over all states of the world, the task of the judge is to attempt to infer which party would have accepted liability for the contingency at issue in a world of costless bargaining. Since it can be inferred that the party accepting liability would have been the one who could have done so at least cost, the efficient decision would be to place *ex post* liability on that party. Similarly, within the law of contracts, if the gains from a breach of contract exceed the costs of breach, then the court should allow the contract to be breached.

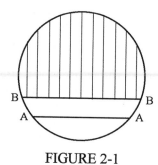

FIGURE 2-1

An Example from the Law of Torts

The unearthing of the efficiency of the common law is thought to be particularly evident in the field of tort law (though, as noted, much of the literature purports to offer evidence supporting the view that the common law doctrines of property, contract, etc., also promote efficiency). Here the subtle shift from the positive description to the normative prescription takes place. If society has an array of liability rules from which to pick (say, rules that may lead to the reduction of accidents or the abating of polluting activities), then the economic logic suggests choosing the least-cost alternative.

This line of reasoning was originally presented by Guido Calabresi (1961), coincidentally at about the same time Coase authored "The Problem of Social Cost." The logic inherent in the literature on efficient liability rules is based upon three suppositions: (1) that all loses can be expressed in monetary terms, (2) that the quantity of undesirable accidents or pollution can be reduced by devoting more of society's scarce resources to the accident prevention or pollution abatement, and (3) that those individuals who are potentially involved in accidents or polluting activities are sensitive to cost pressures (Burrows and Veljanovski, 1981, p. 11). The aim of efficiency-based tort law is to use *ex post* damage awards to replace what may be termed "*ex ante* unfeasible agreements" that would have occurred had a market been possible (that is, if transaction costs were sufficiently low).

The economic logic of this approach can be expressed with two simple examples. The first is to let figure 2-1 represent all the costs associated with, say, automobile accidents (including the actual damages suffered by victims, litigation expenses, legal administrative costs, enforcement costs, etc.) before the government acts in an attempt to reduce society's costs of accidents. Assume that the government first installs traffic signals and stop signs, with the net savings to society being the area beneath line AA. Now assume, additionally, that the government erects costly median barriers, again with some net savings, this time equal to the area ABBA. The area above line BB represents

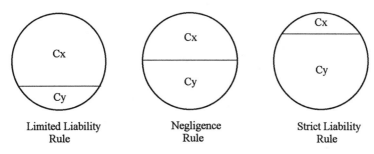

FIGURE 2-2

the residual costs of accidents, or, as they are commonly referred to, the *inter-action damage costs*. It is these costs that are the focus of the literature on economics of liability rules.

The economic approach to the analysis and selection of liability rules can be viewed as one method by which risks in society are determined to be either *background risks*, with the costs borne by the victim, or, alternatively, *compensated risks*, which arise from tortious acts and whose costs are borne by the injurer. The primary focus of the economic approach to liability rule formulation is to develop a standard of liability that minimizes the sum of interaction damage costs with full recognition that the selection of a specific liability rule will determine which actions will fall within the scope of background risks and which actions will be deemed compensated risks. Focusing only on the interaction damage costs (the area above the line BB in fig. 2-1, which is now equal to the three circles in fig. 2-2), we can easily describe the two facets of the problem.

First, in each panel of figure 2-2 let C_x represent all costs borne by victims because the liability rule chosen considers the risks associated with these interaction damage costs as background risks. In a like manner, in each panel of figure 2-2 let C_y represent all compensable costs borne by the injurers because the liability rule chosen considers the risks associated with these interaction damage costs as tortious and not part of society's background risks. As is evident, the liability rule which is chosen will determine the extent of non-compensable background risk vis-à-vis that of compensable risk. For example, with the limited liability rule, most risks are considered background risks, and most injurers are not liable for the damages caused (the victims bear most of the costs). At the other extreme, where injurers are held strictly liable, most risks are not considered background risks and thus the injurers are liable for most of the damages caused. Perhaps somewhere between the two lies a third liability rule, a negligence rule, that establishes a system under which injurers are liable for the damages only if they are negligent (i.e., at fault). The fundamental point illustrated here is that the legislative or judicial choice

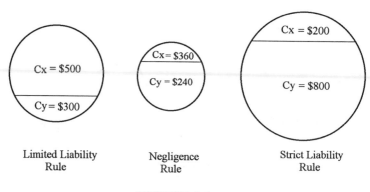

FIGURE 2-3

of one liability rule over another results in a different distribution of costs for society. It is only for expositional purposes that the three circles have the same area (i.e., represent the same interaction damage costs). Indeed, as stated above, the thrust of the economic approach to liability rule formulation is to develop a standard of liability that minimizes the sum total of interaction damage costs.

Figure 2-3 illustrates the economic approach that attempts to inform society of the efficiency consequences of the choice of one liability rule over another. The third circle, which illustrates a hypothetical strict liability rule, depicts both the distribution of costs (80 percent of which are borne by the injurers, with only 20 percent of the costs going uncompensated and thus being borne by the victims), and the total size of the interaction damage costs, here equal to $1,000. The second circle, by way of contrast, illustrates the situation for the rule of negligence, which yields (1) a different distribution of costs (50 percent being borne by the injurers and 50 percent of the costs going uncompensated and thus being borne by the victims), and (2) total interaction damage costs equal to $600. In comparing these two rules, the economic approach would suggest adopting the negligence liability rule on the grounds that it allocates risks, alters incentives, and thereby affects behavior so as to minimize the cost to society (as $600 is less than $1,000). Similarly, the negligence rule is preferred to the limited liability rule (the first circle) on efficiency grounds, since the limited liability rule results in total interaction damage costs of $800, as compared to $600 under the negligence rule. It should be noted that the explicit adoption of the least-cost solution carries with it the implicit adoption of the specific distribution of risk that goes along with the chosen rule. This is an important point of departure between the Chicago school and the traditional justice/fairness approach inherent in conventional law. Whereas the justice/fairness approach is concerned about the distribution of the costs associated with risk (i.e., in the circles, the question as to where one draws the line separating compensable risk from background risk), the Chicago approach to law and economics is concerned with minimizing the total costs associated with risk (that is, choosing the smallest circle), the distribution of the costs being irrelevant except as it affects the total cost.

The contrast between the Chicago and justice/fairness perspectives is seen in the following statements by Richard Posner and Richard Epstein. Speaking from the Chicago perspective, Posner (1973, p. 221) maintains that "[s]ince the efficient use of resources is an important although not always paramount social value, the burden, I suggest, is on the authors to present reasons why a standard that appears to impose avoidable cost on society should nonetheless be adopted. They have not carried this burden." Epstein (1973, p. 152), in contrast, argues that

> Once it is admitted that there are questions of fairness as between the parties that are not answerable in economic terms, the exact role of economic argument in the solution of legal questions becomes impossible to determine. It may well be that an acceptable theory of fairness can be reconciled with the dictates of economic theory in a manner that leaves ample room for the use of economic thought. But that judgment presupposes that some theory of fairness has been spelled out, which, once completed, may leave no room for economic considerations of any sort.

In essence, Posner is claiming that the goal of legal decision making should be efficiency, and that the burden rests with the advocates of the justice/fairness approach to demonstrate why fairness considerations should dominate efficiency. Epstein argues from the opposite pole, setting up fairness as the goal and stating, in a sense, that the burden rests with the advocates of the economic approach to show why efficiency considerations should dominate fairness.

An alternative way of illustrating the economic approach to liability formulation is as follows. Let us suppose that legal policymakers have come up with five different liability rules that can help diminish accidents. These liability rules, with their respective impacts, are shown in table 2-1. Each of the five liability rules generates a particular damage award to the victim (#1 lowest damage award → #5 the highest damage award). As a consequence, each liability rule induces a different level of precaution on the part of potential injurers (from #1 → #5).[35] Additionally, each subsequent liability rule (#1 → #5) reduces the probability of accidents and thus the expected accident losses.

It should be clear from this simple example that, either through statutory enactment or the wisdom of efficiency-oriented common law judges, the law of torts ought to include Rule #3, which is the most efficient (least-cost) rule— the rule that minimizes the total costs of accidents at $16. Each of the other liability rules, because of their respective impacts on precaution costs vis-à-vis expected accident losses, generates higher total costs to society than does Rule

TABLE 2-1

Liability Rules	Individual's Level of Precaution	Cost of Precaution	Accident Probability	Expected Accident Losses	Total Accident Losses
1	none	$0	15%	$20	$20
2	low	2	11	16	18
3	moderate	5	7	11	16
4	high	9	4	8	17
5	extreme	14	1	5	19

#3. For example, a move from Rule #3 to Rule #4 will induce potential injurers to spend an additional $4 on precaution while reducing the expected damages by only $3, which is not cost-justified. In addition, the adoption and application of Rule #3 in present cases serves as a signal to the rest of society that they will be held liable for failure to take the appropriate, cost-justified level of precaution. This signal provides the necessary incentives to induce efficient behavior and thereby comports with the efficiency dictates of the Chicago school of law and economics.

An Example from the Law of Contracts: Efficient Breach

The economics of contract law attempts to provide an alternative viewpoint and unique perspective on the rules, distinctions, categories, and boundaries of the evolving legal doctrine of traditional contract law.[36] Its major thrust is to help facilitate contracting parties to accomplish what they are trying to do—and to do so efficiently (Goldberg, 1989, x). Contract law concerns the structuring of contracts, the negotiation of settlements among the parties of interest in a dispute over their asserted legal rights, arbitration, and in a lawsuit, the defense of some breach of a contract. If the parties of interest had taken the time and incurred the costs to explicitly incorporate into the contract terms that deal with every type of nonperformance under every possible circumstance, then there would be no occasion for the courts to prescribe a remedy. However, disputes often arise because, for a variety of reasons, the contract terms fail to cover all foreseeable contingencies. Obviously, from an economic standpoint, contract rules are desirable and necessary because it is too costly to negotiate and draft contracts that provide for every conceivable contingency. In Coasean terms, the problem is one of transaction costs, and thus, as A. Mitchell Polinsky (1989, p. 27) describes it, "Contract law can be viewed as filling in these 'gaps' in the contract—attempting to reproduce what the parties would have agreed to if they could have costlessly planned for the event initially."

Obligations that arise consequent to a contract relate to two questions. The first has to do with the circumstances under which an otherwise binding promise would be excused, whereas the second concerns the issue of what legal consequences flow from breaching a contract. Thus, for our purposes here, legal rules of contract can be divided in to two distinct classes. In one class are the so-called *immutable rules*, rules that govern even if the parties try to contract around them. The other class consists of the so-called *default rules* that parties can contract around by prior agreement. These are the rules that fill the gaps in incomplete contracts (Craswell and Schwartz, 1994; Ayres and Gertner, 1989). A major line of literature of the economics of contract law concerns the default rules and the legal consequences that flow from breach. As observed by Robert Cooter and Thomas Ulen (1988, p. 290), "One of the most enlightening insights of law and economics is the recognition that there are circumstances where breach of contract is more efficient than performance." They go on to define efficient breach as follows: "the breach of a contract is more efficient than performance of the contract when the costs of performance exceed the benefits to all parties" (Cooter and Ulen, 1988, p. 290). The major thrust of the literature is to analyze under which rules we are more likely to encounter efficient defaults. As with much of Chicago law and economics, one must go back to Pareto efficiency and therefore to Coase. Markets and their attending contracts are not costless; thus, following Coase, if contracts are not costless, they should at least be structured to approximate the Coasean outcome by providing incentives for value-maximizing conduct.[37]

If a party breaches a contract, and the court determines that (1) the contract has been validly formed, and (2) performance will not be excused, then a remedy for the breach must be determined. For our purposes here we will consider only three options. The first two remedies to be considered are court-determined; these are *legal relief* and *equitable relief*. The third remedy—liquidated damages—is not court-determined, but structured by the contracting parties themselves, explicitly designating a remedy at the time the contract is formed in the event of subsequent nonperformance.

- *Legal relief*: This remedy consists of court-imposed money damages and is the remedy most often imposed by the court. Legal relief can take one of three forms (Polinsky, 1989, p. 28):

    Expectation damages: awards the victim of breach an amount of money that puts him in the same position he would have been in had the contract been completed.
    Reliance damages: awards the victim of breach an amount of money that places him in the position he would have been in had he never entered into the contract initially.
    Restitution damages: awards the victim of breach an amount of money corresponding to any benefits that he has conferred upon the breaching party.

- *Equitable relief (specific performance)*: Although not used often, equitable relief is the second court-determined remedy that can be imposed, and is termed *specific performance*. Specific performance protects the potential victim's right to performance by ordering the breaching party to perform the contractual promise. That is, the court essentially protects the victim's right with the equivalent of a property rule.
- *Liquidated damages*: Unlike the first two remedies—*legal relief* and *equitable relief*—that are imposed upon the parties by the court, the third remedy—*liquidated damages*—is imposed by the parties themselves. The liquidated damage remedy awards the breached-against party an amount of money agreed to by the parties in advance of the performance of the contract (Polinsky, 1989, pp. 64–65).

The economic analysis of breach of contract asks, at the most basic level, whether, and under what conditions, the expectation, reliance, restitution, specific performance, and liquidated damages remedies for breach of contract are efficient alternatives to a fully specified (ergo, Pareto efficient) contract. Putting it slightly differently, the goal, from an efficiency perspective, is to employ the legal remedy that at once prevents inefficient breach and at the same time induces breach when breach is efficient. Each of the above-mentioned remedies can be examined with this in mind, and we shall do so in the context of a simple example.

Suppose that Acme Autos has a car for sale at a price of $12,000. Fred is willing to pay up to $15,000 for the car, signs a contract with Acme to purchase the car at the $12,000 price, gives Acme a down payment of $5,000, and agrees to return in three days to make the remaining payment and take possession of the car. Fred then goes from Acme to an auto parts dealer, where he purchases new wheels and tires for this car during their going-out-of business sale, spending a nonrefundable $800 in the process. Shortly after Fred leaves Acme, Jim arrives and offers Acme $13,000 for the car—an amount equal to the value he places on owning it. Abstracting for the moment from the issue of damages, Acme will wish to breach its contract with Fred in order to sell the car to Jim, since it can realize an extra $1,000 from the transaction. However, since Fred values the car at $15,000, whereas Jim only values it at $13,000, such a breach would be inefficient, since it would place the vehicle in a lower-valued use. We can now examine the effect that the various remedies would have on the potential breach.

EXPECTATION DAMAGES

An expectation damages remedy makes the victim as well-off as if the contract had been performed. Thus, if Acme sold the vehicle to Jim, an expectation damages remedy would require Acme not only to refund Fred his $5,000 down payment, but also to pay Fred $3,000 (the surplus from the transaction that Fred lost due to the breach). Thus, Acme would decide not to breach the contract since the gain from selling to Jim ($1,000) is less than the damages that they would have to pay to Fred ($3,000) under the expectation damages remedy. If, on the other hand, Jim had offered Acme $20,000 for the car, a decision by Acme to breach would be efficient, since Jim would value the car more highly than Fred. And, in this situation, Acme would breach its contract and sell to Jim, since the gain from selling to Jim ($8,000) exceeds the damages that they would have to pay to Fred ($3,000). More generally, under the expectation damages remedy, Acme will refrain from breaching its contract with Fred for any amount less than $15,000 and will breach its contract for any amount greater than this.

From the vantage point of economics, the expectation damages remedy encourages efficient breach and discourages inefficient breach. The economic reasoning here is straightforward and can be generalized. The expectation remedy requires the breaching party to pay in damages the value of the good or resource to the breached-against party. If some other buyer enters the arena and values the good or resource more than the initial buyer, then it is efficient for that third party to have the good; that is, goods and resources should gravitate to their highest-valued uses. Consequently, with the anticipated court imposed expectation remedy, the seller will have an incentive to breach in order to obtain the higher offer, pay the breached-against party his expectation damages, keep the surplus, and thereby remain better off with no one made worse off. On the other hand, if some buyer had entered the arena who did not value the good as much as the initial buyer, the expectation remedy would appropriately and efficiently discourage the breaching of the contract.[38]

RELIANCE DAMAGES

Reliance damages place Fred in the same position as he was in prior to signing the contract, and as such compensate him for expenditures undertaken in reliance on the contract. In this case, Fred had made a nonrefundable $800 expenditure on wheels and tires, and thus, under a reliance damages remedy, Acme would be forced to compensate Fred in the amount of $800, plus refund his down payment.

It should be apparent that the reliance damages remedy provides an incentive for inefficient breach. With Jim's offer of $13,000, Acme can gain an additional $1,000 by selling the car to Jim, and, since Acme must only compensate Fred in the amount of $800, this provides Acme with an incentive to breach the contract. But, since Fred places a higher value on the car ($15,000) than does Jim ($13,000), this breach is inefficient—resources would not be gravitating to their highest-valued use. More generally stated, reliance damages do not internalize to the potential breacher the full cost of the breach to the victim (i.e., the "price" of breaching is inefficiently low) and, as a result, can lead to breaches where the social costs are in excess of the social benefits.

RESTITUTION

Under the restitution damages remedy, the breacher need only return to the victim any monies received from the victim—here, Fred's $5,000 down-payment. Given this, Acme will breach its contract with Fred and sell to Jim, and, indeed, would do so at any price in excess of $12,000. As with reliance damages, restitution damages do not internalize all costs of breach to the potential breacher, and, as a result, give rise to the potential for inefficient breach.

Thus, among the monetary remedies, only expectation damages, by internalizing the full cost of his actions to the potential breacher, act simultaneously to discourage inefficient breach and to promote efficient breach.[39]

SPECIFIC PERFORMANCE

Specific performance involves an order by the court that the contract be completed according to its terms. Thus, in the context of our example, Acme would be required to sell the car to Fred for $12,000. As such, specific performance eliminates the possibility of inefficient breach. It might be argued, however, that specific performance will have the effect of preventing efficient breaches. For example, if Jim had offered $20,000 for the car, the court's requirement of specific performance, awarding the car to Fred, would generate an inefficient outcome. Yet, in such a situation there exists a subsequent exchange that would exhaust gains from trade. Jim would presumably also be willing to pay Fred $20,000 for the car, and Fred, valuing the car at $15,000, would be willing to part with it at the $20,000 price. Thus, unless transaction costs are prohibitive, we would expect that specific performance subsequently would result in the efficient outcome, and the difference between specific performance and expectation damages (previously shown to be efficient) will be purely distributional; that is, under specific performance, Fred will capture the gains from Jim's greater willingness to pay, whereas, under expectation damages, Acme will capture those gains.

Based on this, it has been argued that courts should rely more heavily on specific performance as a remedy for breach.[40] This is particularly true if the good is one for which the value of performance to the victim is difficult for the court to discern with certainty. If, for example, the victim places a very high subjective value on the good in question (a value much higher than others would place on it), the court, in questioning whether the victim is accurately revealing his preferences, may well award insufficient damages. Under a specific performance remedy, however, the breacher will have every opportunity to negotiate with the victim and pay him his full value if he is to consent to the breach. More generally, since valuations are more likely to be accurately reflected through the bargaining process than through court-stipulated damages, specific performance offers a greater potential for an efficient resolution of the dispute than do monetary damages as long as transaction costs are low; conversely, monetary damages are to be preferred when transaction costs are high.[41]

LIQUIDATED DAMAGES

Liquidated damages clauses are inserted into the contract by the parties themselves during the contract-formation process and specify the damages that one party must pay to the other in the event that the contract is breached. Nonetheless, courts have traditionally been unwilling to enforce such clauses when the specified damages appear to be overly burdensome or punitive (that is, appear to exceed compensation for the harm caused to the victim). However, the economic approach places these damages in a somewhat different relief. Since rational maximizing agents will only agree to a contract that both believe to be in their interests, these clauses would seem to be efficient; otherwise, the parties would not have agreed to their inclusion in the first place. There are two important reasons why maximizing agents might agree to such terms. First, the potential victim might place a very high subjective value on performance of the contract—much, much higher than the average person. The high level of liquidated damages specified in the contract may thus reflect the high subjective value placed on performance by the victim, and, in a sense, insurance against nonperformance. Alternatively, the potential breacher may be willing to insert such a clause as a quality signal to attract customers. In either case, the clause is mutually beneficial *ex ante* and thus, from an efficiency perspective, should be enforced.[42]

AN ASIDE: THE NEW HAVEN SCHOOL OF LAW AND ECONOMICS[43]

Proponents of the New Haven school take as their field of study the entire modern regulatory welfare state and base their approach on the twin intellectual foundations of public policy analysis and social choice theory.[44] As a consequence, their view of the task of law and economics is (1) "to define the economic justification for public action," (2) "to analyze political and bureaucratic institutions realistically," and (3) "to define useful roles for the courts within this modern policymaking system" (Rose-Ackerman, 1992, p. 3). Proponents of this view suggest that their approach to law and economics is made necessary and essential by the increasingly prominent role played by the regulatory process and administrative law within the modern welfare state. As they underscore, this legal transformation has "forced both judges and legal scholars to reexamine the roles of Congress, the agencies, and the courts" (Rose-

Ackerman, 1992, p. 8). They adhere to the proposition that once one truly understands the *functional* role of government, the modern regulatory system is seen as superior not only to more highly collectivist alternatives, but also to its common law predecessor. In fact, it is argued that in many contexts "the problem is one of too little rather than too much regulation" (Sunstein, 1990, pp. 227–33). The goal, for the New Haven school, "is a reformed administrative law that will incorporate a richer range of both empirical and theoretical concerns and will respond more effectively to the needs of public officials, politicians, and private citizens" (Rose-Ackerman, 1992, p. 8).

Although recognizing the existence of the problem of scarcity and the virtues of the market for allocating resources, the New Haven school emphasizes the presence of multiple sources of market failure that necessitates some form of government intervention. In maintaining that government intervention should be justified based on existing market failures, they argue that legal-economic policy should be limited to correcting these failures with a recognized concern for *both allocative and distributional impacts* (Rose-Ackerman, 1992, pp. 6–7, 9), as well as a continuing concern for *justice and fairness*. Moreover, the market-failure-correcting policies should be set in place based on cost-benefit analysis whenever possible, and this process should include the evaluation of *all* benefits and costs (e.g., lives saved, acres of wilderness preserved, and so on), not just those benefits and costs that can be measured in explicit dollar terms (Rose-Ackerman, 1992, pp. 16–17).

The origins of the New Haven school can be traced back to the seminal contributions of Guido Calabresi. Two of his early articles—"Some Thoughts on Risk Distribution and the Law of Torts" (1961) and, with A. Douglas Melamed, "Property Rules, Liability Rules, and Inalienability: One View of the Cathedral" (1972)—are classics in the economic analysis of law. The former article attempts to provide a detailed economic analysis of tort law, focusing on the relationship between rules of liability and the spreading of loss. The latter article takes off from Coase's analysis in "The Problem of Social Cost" (1960) to analyze the choice of remedies for resolving disputes over incompatible property uses. In a situation where one party has illegitimately interfered with another party's property (i.e., given the existence of an externality) and the assignment of rights (or, in their words, entitlements) has been determined, the court may choose to protect this entitlement in one of two ways: through an injunction or through mandating the payment of compensatory damages. Calabresi and Melamed argue that, in making the choice between these alternative remedies, the court should base its decision on the ability of the parties to cooperate to resolve the dispute. If there are significant obstacles to bargaining, compensatory damages should be mandated. Alternatively, if transaction costs are perceived to be low and thus there are few obstacles to cooperation, the injunctive remedy is preferable because the parties themselves can then bargain to the efficient result.[45]

In 1970 Calabresi published his now classic book *The Cost of Accidents: A Legal and Economic Analysis*, which provided an economic analysis of the goals and functions of liability rules and laid the foundation for further explorations into the economics of tort law.[46] In this book Calabresi argues that the principal aim of rules of liablity for accidents is the reduction in accident costs. Specifically, he contends that the goal of accident-cost reduction includes (1) the reduction in the number and severity of accidents (which he terms primary accident-cost reduction), (2) reduction in the social costs of accidents (secondary accident-cost reduction), and (3) reduction in the administrative costs associated with accidents (the tertiary or efficiency accident-cost reduction) (Calabresi, 1970, pp. 24–31). Both here and in a later extension of his argument (Calabresi and Hirschoff, 1972, p. 19), Calabresi argues that liability should be placed on the least-cost avoider—that is, on the person who is in the best position to make cost-benefit analysis between accident costs and accident-avoidance costs and to act on the decision once it has been made. Both in *The Cost of Accidents* and in a more recent article analyzing four alternative rules of liability (Calabresi and Klevorick, 1985), Calabresi concludes that specific remedies can only be proffered after extensive empirical research. The problem, he says, is that the data necessary to make these empirical judgments is very difficult to obtain (Calabresi, 1970, p. 14).[47] It is in this context that one must understand, for example, the assessment of Izhak England (1993, p. 32), who concludes that "Calabresi's economic analysis, for all its sophistication and subtlety, can do no more than demonstrate the relevant considerations . . . concrete solutions still require policy decisions."

Directly related to this policy-decision-making process and of major import as regards the New Haven school, one must recognize that Calabresi's writings have not focused exclusively on the efficiency of tort law, but, rather, have had a continuing concern for justice and fairness—one of the hallmarks of the New Haven approach. As Calabresi (1970, p. 24) has emphasized, any system of accident law has two principal goals: "First, it must be just or fair; and second, it must reduce the costs of accidents." Calabresi then went on to state that "[n]o system of accident law can operate unless it takes into account which acts are deemed good, which deemed evil, and which deemed neutral. Any system of accident law that encourages evil acts will seem unjust to critic and community even if economically it is very efficient indeed" (Calabresi, 1970, p. 294).

As England has observed, "Calabresi denies that economic efficiency is the exclusive value in allocating accident losses. He insists on the distinctness of wealth efficiency and its distribution from the notion of justice" (England, 1993, p. 33; see also Calabresi, 1980).[48] Indeed, Calabresi himself has argued forcefully that "lawyer-economists can have a great deal to say, as scholars, about what is distributively desirable. . . . We can develop scholarly definitions of just distributions, both theoretical definitions, and definitions based on empirical studies" (Calabresi, 1991, p. 1228). Thus, the New Haven school's continuing concern for efficiency and distribution, as well as justice and fairness, has its origins in the seminal works of Guido Calabresi.

The school's focus on efficiency and justice is worked out within the context of a system that establishes a presumption in favor of individual choice and the use of mechanisms such as the market and the democratic political process which promote such choices. Given this, they prefer policy mechanisms that create incentives to influence individual choice, such as taxes and subsidies. Consequently, they place less emphasis on the use of the common law remedies relied upon so heavily within the Chicago approach to law and economics. Within the New Haven school, there is a much wider role for the use of statutes and regulations, and a greater reliance on well-structured government institutions to help remedy pockets of market failure in society. Because of this, they emphasize the importance of studying the operations of governmental institutions and the use of the tools of public policy analysis and social choice analysis (always with an eye on both allocative and distributional impacts) in the search for solutions to legal-economic problems (Rose-Ackerman, 1992, p. 6).

The New Haven school's emphasis on the study of all aspects of the governmental policy process necessitates a model of governmental behavior, and the model used here is that of the rational actor. As will become evident, this rational actor model has certain commonalities with the various other schools of thought explored in this book. What is absent from the New Haven approach is the normative presumption favoring the status quo distribution of wealth and property and the conservative ideological element often attributed to the Public Choice and Chicago approaches to Law and Economics. Rather, the proponents of the New Haven approach "recognize that the existing distribution of property rights [and hence wealth] is highly contingent and lacks strong normative justification" (Rose-Ackerman, 1992, p. 6). They argue that policy analysts should endeavor to determine the various available policy options in dealing with situations of market failure, and that they should do so without privileging the status quo, as in the case of Public Choice, and without a presumption in favor of common law resolutions, as in the case of the Chicago school (Rose-Ackerman, 1992, pp. 3, 16).[49]

The dichotomy between the Chicago emphasis on the efficacy of the common law and the New Haven emphasis on a more broadly based policymaking approach to law and economics is well illustrated in the area of torts. Whereas the Chicago school promotes the design of least-cost-avoider rules to promote efficient common law remedies for dealing with situations of harmful effects, the New Haven approach emphasizes a much greater reliance on statutes to address these situations. Under the New Haven approach, the role of the common law should be narrowly defined and channeled to "augment regulatory enforcement" and to deal with "situations that would be poorly resolved by broad-based regulations" (Rose-Ackerman, 1992, p. 131).

As evidence for this point, Steven Shavell (1987, pp. 277–90) suggests several advantages that pertain to a statute-based system: (1) statutes are preferable when harms are diffused through the population, creating reduced incentives for individuals to sue and high costs of organizing for group lawsuits; (2) statutes can provide deterrence in situations where those causing the harm lack sufficient resources to pay for the harm caused and who will thus not be strongly deterred by *ex post* common law compensation systems; (3) *ex ante* statutes get around the problem of demonstrating causation that often affects tort cases; (4) when various injury situations have similar benefit-cost effects, statutes can impose uniform rules on similarly situated injurers, thereby avoiding the need to adjudicate many individual cases; (5) there are many situations where the costs of administering a statutory system are lower than the costs of administering a tort system.[50] Expanding on this theme, Susan Rose-Ackerman (1992, p. 121) suggests that toxic torts, products liability, and medical malpractice are especially suited for statutory control. It is argued that such statutes should take the form of *ex ante* incentive schemes, whereby firms respond to the cost of damages set forth in the statute. In such situations, the law of tort should submit to the greater authority of the statute and courts should be content with (1) adjudicating disputes over gaps in statutes and (2) resolving situations where statutes have not yet been enacted or are not feasible given the idiosyncratic nature of tortious acts (Rose-Ackerman, 1992, pp. 128–31).

CHAPTER 3

Public Choice Theory

> That which emerges from the trading or exchange
> process, conceived in its narrowest or its broadest
> terms, is not the solution to a maximizing problem,
> despite the presence of scarce resources and the
> conflict among ends. That which emerges is
> that which emerges and that is that.
> *(Buchanan, 1975, p. 226)*

INTRODUCTION

Public choice theory is defined as the economic analysis of nonmarket decision making—a body of theory that treats individual decision makers as participants in a complex interaction that generates political outcomes. Alternatively, it is also defined as the application of economic analysis to political
decision making, including theories of the state, voting rules and voter behavior, apathy, party politics, logrolling, bureaucratic choice, policy analysis, and
regulation.[1] As such, it constitutes an approach to Law and Economics that
focuses predominately on the creation and implementation of law through the
political process, as opposed to the common-law-oriented nature of Chicago
law and economics.

The modern scholarly interest in public choice theory stems from the work
of the public finance scholars of the mid-1950s as they branched out beyond
government tax and expenditure policies in an effort to explore voting theory.
Two notable pioneers in this tradition are Duncan Black and Anthony Downs.
Works that predate the formal inception of public choice include a series of
articles by Duncan Black in the late 1940s, culminating with his pathbreaking
book *The Theory of Committees and Elections* (1958). Anthony Downs's early
contribution is the well-known *Economic Theory of Democracy* (1957). The
formal inception of public choice theory can be marked with the establishment
of the Thomas Jefferson Center for Studies in Political Economy at the University of Virginia by James M. Buchanan and Warren Nutter in 1957. In 1963 the
Public Choice Society was founded (initially under the title "Committee on
Non-Market Decision-Making"), and in 1966 an economic journal was established entitled *Papers on Non-Market Decision Making*. Two years later, its
name was changed to *Public Choice*. In 1969 the Center for Study of Public

Choice was established at Virginia Polytechnic Institute; not long thereafter, the Japanese and the European Public Choice Societies were separately formed. Most recently, in 1982, the Center shifted its entire operations to George Mason University where it continues today. Public choice theory has developed to the point where it is now made up of what may be termed (1) axiomatic social choice theory, (2) conventional public choice theories of bureaucracies, legislatures, and the state, and (3) catallaxy, the contractarian public choice theory.[2]

The branch of conventional public choice theory that concerns itself with the analysis of bureaucracies, legislatures, and the state is largely organized around the concept of *homo economicus*—the conventional basic maximizing paradigm of microeconomics[3] where individuals (in both political and economic arenas) are modeled as behaving as if they were maximizing utility (with appropriate arguments specified in their utility functions). The predominant areas of application within this branch of public choice include regulation,[4] legislatures[5] and political parties,[6] and theories of bureaucracy.[7] The catallaxy theory of public choice directs attention to the *processes* of exchange, trade, agreement, and contract, that is, to all processes of voluntary agreements among persons in political as well as economic arenas.[8] Within catallaxy, understanding of collective action is garnered through models that have individual decision makers as the basic unit of analysis and then examine politics and the political process in terms of a complex exchange paradigm.

In each of these areas, public choice theory has both a positive and a normative component.[9] With respect to the positive branch, on the basis of the efficiency criterion, public choice investigates (1) the political process underlying the legislative sector and the emergent statutes, (2) the rules underlying bureaucratic decision making and the decisions of the bureaucracy, (3) the regulatory process together with the promulgated rules and regulations, and (4) the constitutional process with an emphasis on the rules for making rules at the constitutional stage of choice. With respect to the normative branch, each of these same areas is analyzed with the prescription being to adopt that legislative statute, bureaucratic rule, regulatory reform/regulation, and/or that constitutional provision that is efficiency enhancing. From the perspective of Law and Economics, it should be clear that the emphasis of public choice theory is on the nonjudicial facets of lawmaking, leaving the efficiency analysis of judge-made law (though not entirely[10]) to the Chicago school of law and economics.

It must be noted from the outset that, if there is one defining characteristic of public choice theory, it is that its proponents refuse to accept two basic tenets of conventional political science. First, they reject the political science organic conception of the state; second, they reject the view that government officials (legislators, regulators, bureaucrats, etc.) seek to act for the common good or in the public interest (Gwartney and Wagner, 1988, p. 7). It might further be noted that the two branches outlined above generally follow (though, of course, not for all contributors) the delineation between the Chicago-based public choice scholars and the Virginia-based theoreticians. Generally those who contribute to Chicago-based public choice literature engage in empirical work and rely on the "maximization-scarcity-allocation-efficiency" paradigm. Alternatively, those who advance the Virginia tradition of public choice, although acknowledging the work of the Chicago-based empiricists, emphasize theoretical work related to the constitutional stage of choice within the context of the theory of catallaxy. The tension that persists between these two branches of Law and Economics is perhaps most clearly delineated by Buchanan (1986, p. 20), who argues that we should "exorcise the maximizing paradigm from its dominant place within our tool kit, . . . quit defining our discipline . . . in terms of the scarcity constraint, . . . [and] stop worrying so much about the allocation of resources and the efficiency thereof." As described above, both the *homo economicus* and catallaxy branches of public choice theory have positive and normative components. For our purposes here, however, the positive work is largely explained in the context of "the *homo economicus*–legislature and bureaucracy–the Chicago school" and the normative contributions are explained in the context of "the catallaxy–constitution–the Virginia school."

METHODOLOGICAL "CLOSURE"

Public choice theory (both branches) is concerned with political processes and, as such, can be viewed as an "opening up" of the conventional neoclassical economic paradigm (where political processes are typically taken as given). As with market exchange, the motive for agreement in political exchange is mutual advantage and the gains from trade that are garnered from participation. At the same time, public choice theory can be understood as a movement toward "closure" with respect to the nature of the analysis. Each view deserves some elaboration.

On the one hand, public choice theory represents an "opening up" in the sense that contributors to the literature perceive their approach as extending beyond the narrowly conceived limits of neoclassical economic theory and into an examination of the political, legal, and social constraints which are typically taken as given in neoclassical economics. The formal application of economic analysis to such subject matters as the theory of the state, voting rules and voter behavior, party politics, logrolling, bureaucratic choice, and regulation distinguishes conventional public choice from mainstream neoclassical economics.

From the methodological perspective, public choice represents a movement toward the analysis of closed systems (Buchanan, 1972). In neoclassical economics, political institutions, political decision makers, and thus political decisions are perceived as *exogenous* to economic activity, whereas in public choice theory the institutions and decisions are *endogenous*. That is, rational, utility-maximizing individuals do not act solely in the marketplace where goods, services, and factors of production are exchanged, and through the exchange process exhaust the gains from trade; these same individuals also participate in the political decision-making processes to enhance their utility. Consequently, society's scarce resources are allocated by both the marketplace and the political process—by the same individuals acting in several separate capacities. James M. Buchanan has described this methodological movement toward closure as follows:

> The critically important bridge between the behavior of persons who act in the marketplace and the behavior of persons who act in political process must be analyzed. The 'theory of public choice' can be interpreted as the construction of such a bridge. The approach requires only the simple assumption that the same individuals act in both relationships. Political decisions are not handed down from on high by omniscient beings who cannot err. Individuals behave in market interactions, in political-government interactions, in cooperative-nongovernmental interactions, and in other arrangements. *Closure of the behavioral system*, as I am using the term, means only that analysis must be extended to the actions of persons in their several separate capacities. (Buchanan, 1972, p. 12, emphasis added)[11]

PUBLIC CHOICE THEORY—*HOMO ECONOMICUS*

The *homo economicus* branch of public choice theory attempts to develop a logical, positive, consistent theory linking individual behavior to collective action. It seeks to explain how political processes—political structures, bureaucratic working rules, and constitutional provisions—actually work. That is, this work represents an attempt to understand and explain the legislative and bureaucratic outcomes that can be expected to follow from the rational behavior of those engaged in legislative and bureaucratic choice under prevailing or alternative political rules. As aptly described by James Gwartney and Richard Wagner (1988, p. 7), "Public choice analysis is to governments what economic analysis is to the markets. In both cases, the outcomes will reflect the choices of individuals and the incentive structure which influences those choices. In the political arena, the major players are the voters, politicians, and the bureaucrats." The theory focuses its analysis on the political rules of collective order (hereafter 'political rules')—both those rules prevailing at a given point in time and the formulation of new rules. These political rules are the rules under which legislators and bureaucrats make political decisions. The rules provide both discretion for and constraints upon their capacity or latitude to make choices.

Within positive public choice theory, the goal is to describe and explain political results in terms of rational, utility-maximizing behavior of individuals and groups of individuals as they participate in the political process. Propositions derived from these models will find empirical support or refutation in the observable behavior of individuals in their capacity as participants in collective decision-making processes. The theory examines the outcomes and issues of voting rules under direct democracy, as well as the workings of the legislatures and bureaucracies in representative democracy, with an emphasis on the analysis of the political rules that serve to structure incentives and therefore influence the behavior of the political decision makers in making their choices.[12] Given that the prevailing political rules in a representative democracy provide both a range of discretion and various degrees of constraints upon the legislators and bureaucrats, the latitude of choice associated with a particular political rule can often be ambiguous in its scope due to this combined discretion/constraint phenomena.

Much of the work in this area (the *homo economicus* branch) of public choice theory is undertaken either in the context of direct democracy or representative democracy. From the perspective of Law and Economics the issue is typically framed along the following lines: Which voting rules or procedures (under either direct democracy or representative democracy) will provide voters with an incentive to vote (or become informed on the relevant public issues) so as to enhance the prospect of realizing a political outcome that serves to provide for an efficient allocation of society's scarce resources? The concern is with such questions as which voting rules or procedures will structure incentives for voters (be they individuals or representatives) to vote for, against, or abstain on such issues as which public goods to provide, how much of the public good in question should be provided, and the amount to authorize for expenditure.

Direct Democracy—Rules and Issues

The literature dealing with public choice issues within the context of direct democracy focuses on the analysis of the voting mechanisms and criteria that should be used to pass laws or structure policy.[13] At the constitutional stage of choice, where the basic "rules of the game" are being framed, one is faced with the issue of determining the baseline voting rule for society. One alternative is the rule of unanimous consent. The attractiveness of the unanimity rule is that it is the only rule that ensures that legal changes constitute movements to a Pareto-better state; if someone will be made worse off by the proposed law or regulation under consideration, that person can vote against it and thus prevent its passage. The origin of this idea dates back to the work of Knut Wicksell with his proffering the unanimity rule for the provision of public goods. The rule requires that each decision authorizing a government

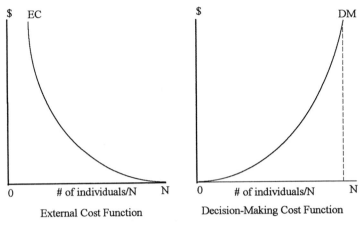

External Cost Function   Decision-Making Cost Function

N = total number of eligible voters

FIGURE 3-1

expenditure be accompanied by a related tax bill to finance that expenditure, and further, that the joint expenditure-tax package be passed with unanimous consent.[14] Subsequent work by Eric Lindahl (1919) and others has revealed that by the proper apportioning of benefits and burdens, unanimous consent can be obtained.[15]

In spite of its seemingly attractive efficiency properties, the unanimity rule has two important difficulties associated with it. First, it is very costly, in terms of time and other resources, to design a proposal which will command unanimous consent. Second, the unanimity rule gives individuals an incentive to engage in strategic behavior—to hold out, threatening to veto the proposed law or rule unless additional benefits or lower burdens are apportioned to them. Given this incentive, it is unlikely that many new laws or rules will be passed (Johnson, 1991, p. 161; Mueller, 1989, pp. 50–52).

Given the difficulties associated with the unanimity rule, some form of majority rule is often seen as the optimal voting criterion. The problem here is that the majority rule fails to guarantee that only proposed laws or rules that are Pareto superior (i.e., make no one worse off and at least one person better off) will be passed into law. The starting point for determining the efficient voting rule is the recognition that all voting rules are costly, these costs being the sum of (1) the *external costs of decision making* (EC)—the costs borne by those who disapprove of a decision, and (2) *the decision-making costs* (DM)—the bargaining costs associated with making a decision (see fig. 3-1).

EC decreases as the number of voters required to pass a proposal (N) increases, since fewer and fewer costs can be imposed on external parties as we consider adopting decision rules which come closer and closer to the unani-

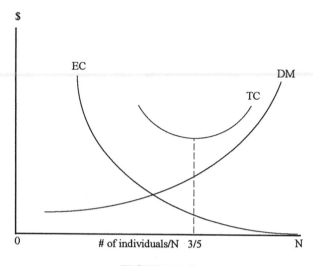

FIGURE 3-2

mous consent requirement. DM is an increasing function of N, since it is more and more costly to bring more and more individuals into the decision-making process as we consider adopting decision rules which come closer and closer to the unanimous consent requirement. The sum of these external and decision-making costs (TC in fig. 3-2) shows the total cost of imposing any particular consent requirement. The goal, at the constitutional stage of choice, is to determine, for each specific category of public policy, the decision rule (i.e., the share of the votes required for a proposal to be adopted) that will minimize the sum of these two costs (the minimum point on the U-shaped cost curve TC). In departing from the unanimous consent requirement and selecting the "least-cost optimal majority" rule, society in effect selects the most efficient rule (Buchanan and Tullock, 1962, pp. 43–84).

It is in this sense that we can observe that a "rationally" (or perhaps more accurately, "economically") constructed constitution will allow for specific collective decisions to be made that do not meet the strict Pareto criterion. Viewed in isolation, a collective decision with respect to a particular category of public policy can be made that does not meet the strict unanimous consent requirement. However, when viewed from a broader perspective, at the constitutional stage of choice, a collective choice as to which decision rule to employ does attain a legitimated status. It does so because, although the decision may not be Pareto efficient (here requiring only, say, a three-fifths vote instead of unanimous consent), the decision will have been made based on a rule that has the virtue of being cost minimizing; that is, it is a rule that a priori minimizes the sum of the external costs and the decision-making costs to society. As such, it attains a legitimated status.

The size of the majority necessary for the passage of a proposed law (e.g., simple majority—50 percent-plus-one, or a supramajority of, say, two-thirds) is of significance in Law and Economics, as it influences not only the likelihood of a law's passage, but the specific form that the law will take in the first place. Under a simple majority rule, the median voter theorem suggest that the outcome of a given vote will reflect the preferences of the median voter if voters do not have multipeaked preferences (in simple terms, do not prefer both extremes to the middle ground).[16] Given this, one can expect that laws or regulations will be written (and perhaps amended) so as to satisfy the preferences of the median voter. In the case of a supramajority voting rule, a greater proportion of the electorate must have their interests served to secure a law's passage, and thus it may be necessary to structure the law or regulation differently (e.g., with a different level and/or allocation of benefits and burdens) than one would under a simple majority scheme. In addition, there is an understanding that the order in which proposals are voted upon may be important in determining which proposals pass. This is the issue of agenda control—organizing the order of the votes to ensure a favorable outcome. Thus, both the voting rule adopted and the voting agenda play an important role in determining the form that legal-economic policy actually takes.

It should be clear that a majority rule does not guarantee that proposals that secure passage will be efficient in the Pareto sense. In addition, it does not guarantee Kaldor-Hicks efficient changes (that the gains to the winners will exceed the losses to the losers). The problem is that a simple one-person, one-vote system does not allow individuals to register the intensity of their preferences for or against a proposal. For example, although a proposal may pass with 70 percent of the vote, that 70 percent of the electorate may gain less than the 30 percent who voted against the proposal lose. One way to get around this would be to allow the selling of votes. However, this is illegal. One mechanism that is employed to get around this is logrolling, or vote-trading. Voters in the minority on an issue about which they feel strongly may be willing to trade their votes on other issues about which they feel less strongly in exchange for the votes of others. From an efficiency perspective, logrolling is a two-edged sword: It allows efficient proposals that would not otherwise command a majority to in fact do so; however, it also allows for the passage of inefficient proposals that would not otherwise be adopted.[17]

Representative Democracy—Rules and Issues

In the context of representative democracy, public choice scholars turn their attention to the voting patterns of campaigning or elected politicians. Assuming all voters can rank their positions on a scale (perhaps over a range from extreme liberal to extreme conservative) the vote-maximizing campaigning legislator or the elected legislator will adopt the preferred program of the median voter so as not to be "outflanked" by an opponent or member of the partisan opposition. Both the politician and the bureaucrat are placed under close scrutiny with particular attention paid to the incentives surrounding the voting and working rules of the decision-making arena.

POLITICIANS

In the *homo economicus* branch of public choice theory, various models are set forth that postulate that legislators or politicians make decisions that maximize their own self-interest based on such factors as votes, power, and political income: for example, some models within this branch of public choice theory focus on the behavior of legislators and political parties both during a political campaign and while in office.

With respect to the political processes, the primary insights of public choice theory reflect the analysis of how and why the outcomes of the political process are often inefficient. The dissatisfaction with the prevailing political processes is typically expressed in the following manner: "If the behavior of politicians in seeking and securing 'political income' while holding elective office does nothing but create some slack between the working of practical government and an idealized drawing-board model, there would be no cause for concern here. But if this behavior of politicians biases results consistently in the direction of larger governments, it becomes relevant for our purpose. The presence of such bias seems clearly established" (Buchanan, 1977, p. 13).

At center stage are the concepts of the rational ignorance of the voter and the self-interested legislator looking to maximize the likelihood of (re)election. As to the latter, in public choice theory legislators are motivated not by a desire to enhance the public interest, but by endorsing programs and/or voting for laws that maximize their appeal to their constituents or by voting for those programs or laws that are most responsive to active special interest groups (e.g., major financial supporters, those energizing effective publicity, or those providing politically meaningful endorsements) thereby enhancing their prospects for (re)election (Shepsle, 1985).

As to the former, given majority rule, voters will have little reason to invest the time, money, or energy that would be required to cast a well-informed vote because they know that there is only the slightest of chances that their vote will be decisive. Given the high probability that the outcome of an election will be unaffected by whether a voter makes an informed choice or simply chooses on the basis of existing knowledge, it is sensible (rational) for voters to remain uninformed on many issues; that is, it is rational to be ignorant. Given the weak incentives for voters to acquire all relevant information, and the ever-present incentives for politicians to look to short-term strategies or policies to enhance their reelection possibilities, political outcomes—outcomes that comprise a facet of the Law in Law and Economics—are typically inefficient. These short-term, inefficient policies and strategies are pursued due to their political attractiveness and are characterized as being detrimental to the aggregate economy in the long run. It is in this sense that public choice theory sees itself as focusing on the continuing conflict between the so-called *good politics* and *sound economics* (Gwartney and Wagner, 1988, pp. 7–14).

THE BUREAUCRACY

The *homo economicus* branch is also concerned with examining the economic consequences of bureaucratic decision making. The role of the bureaucrat takes on importance because of the gaps that often exist in legislation—legislation that specifies certain goals but may not be fully specific with respect to implementation.[18] The greater is the scope for bureaucratic discretion in implementation, the greater is the potential for divergence between the legislative intent reflected in the political choice process and the final impact of that legislation. It thus becomes necessary to analyze and understand the role of, the incentives placed upon, and the resulting actions of the bureaucrat to gain a full understanding of the implementation of legislation. In addition, public choice theory also looks at the interrelationships among (1) the bureaus of the government, (2) the bureaucracy and the surrounding special interest groups, and (3) the bureaucracy and the legislature. In all this there is a focus on the problems relating to information with respect to costs and evaluation of bureaucratic output.

With respect to the bureaucracy, the primary insights of public choice theory reflect the analysis of how and why the outcomes of bureaucratic choice are wasteful and inefficient. The dissatisfaction with the prevailing bureaucratic process is typically expressed in the following manner:

> As the public sector has grown during the last decades, charges of bureaucratic inefficiency and unresponsiveness have become increasingly widespread. In the past, criticism of bureaucratic decision-making arose primarily from sources seeking to reduce the size of government. However, in recent years, advocates of public sector action have often been at the forefront of those charging that the bureaucracy has failed to carry out legislative intent and has been insensitive to the needs of the average citizen. (Gwartney and Stroup, 1980, p. 451)

The central issue here is that the bureaucrat's utility-maximization process is not coterminous with the maximization of social welfare. Various models of the bureaucracy postulate that power, prestige, the size of the bureau's budget, job security, perquisites, future salary, and working conditions enter the utility function of bureaucrats. To the extent that the pursuit of these goals conflicts with social welfare, social welfare is correspondingly reduced. Furthermore, legislators lack the incentive to curb the inefficient and wasteful performance of government bureaus. Several reasons for this are typically identified in the public choice literature: (1) bureaus do not have an easily identifiable index of performance (i.e., no bottom line or quantifiable unit of output), (2) biased information regarding performance (i.e., information on a bureau's performance is typically acquired from the bureau), (3) the fact that, for political reasons, inefficient performance rarely terminates the operation of a bureau, and (4) the bureaucrats and their clients can form powerful coalitions, thereby forming an interest group capable of effectuating political decisions. As described by Gwartney and Wagner (1988, p. 16), "[Public choice theory] indicates that bureaucrats confront a perverse incentive structure that will lead to both high per unit costs and a rate of output for which the marginal value of the bureau's output is less than its cost."

It is important to note that this branch of public choice is not concerned only with analyzing the prevailing political rules. It is generally recognized that the rules of collective order are not given once and for all time, but are subject to revision. Such revisions are accomplished through a complex process in which various parties may work to alter political rules in an attempt to foster their own interests. For example, legislative or bureaucratic rules may be altered as a result of the direct political activities of the community at large. These political activities are often directed at the legislature as opposed to bureaucracies. Bureaucratic rules are often altered through political activities of specific interest groups (e.g., farm, labor, or education lobbies) as well as the bureaucrats themselves. In an attempt to maximize their utility, the parties of interest alter the political rules, which results in a broadening or narrowing of the range of discretion and the degree of constraint on the legislature and bureaucracy.

In normative public choice theory, the goal is to prescribe what political reforms should be adopted (often with an emphasis on the efficiency of decision-making processes). Based on their empirical findings, normative public choice scholars have proffered a variety of recommendations that they believe will improve the performance of existing political institutions.

CONTRACTARIAN PUBLIC CHOICE THEORY—CATALLAXY

Within the catallaxy approach, the concepts of spontaneous coordination and spontaneous order take center stage over the principle of maximization. In this the emphasis shifts from simple to complex exchanges, that is, to all processes of voluntary agreements among persons in political as well as economic arenas. The central thrust of catallaxy is to take individual decision makers as the basic unit of analysis and to view both politics and the political processes in terms of the exchange paradigm (Buchanan, 1986, pp. 20–21).[19] The positive branch of catallaxy applies the public choice paradigm at the level of simple exchange within well-defined rules. At the most basic level, this approach is concerned with the constitutional stage of choice where the basic rules of collective order are resolved, whereas at a more intermediate level the discussion concerns the determination of the structure of government institutions (Buchanan, 1975, p. 228). Hence, catallaxy represents the extension of the economic perspective to institutional settings in which persons interact collectively.

Catallaxy is distinguished from conventional political science by its focus on the science of complex exchanges. Whereas catallaxy views politics and the political process in terms of the voluntary exchange paradigm, the focus of political science is on the nonvoluntary relationships among individuals involving power and/or coercion.[20] The thrust of the positive work within catallaxy is to describe how differences among people are reconciled under the prevailing political institutions. More specifically, this branch of public choice theory, in attempting to describe what is transpiring, hopes to enhance our ability to differentiate between those institutional arrangements that bring individual self-interest and the general welfare into harmony and those institutional arrangements that leave them in conflict (Gwartney and Wagner, 1988, p. 8).

However, there is an immediate shift to normative catallaxy which asks: How *should* differences in various arenas be reconciled? That is, as one accepts that which is inherent in the catallaxy approach—a view of the world as an arena for complex exchanges—normative implications arise which drive the public choice approach to institutional reform. In describing this normative element and the proclivity of public choice economists to favor market-like arrangements whenever and wherever they seem feasible, Buchanan (1986, p. 22) has stated that "[t]o the extent that voluntary exchange among persons is valued positively while coercion is valued negatively, there emerges the implication that substitution of the former for the latter is desired, on the presumption, of course, that such substitution is technologically feasible and is not prohibitively costly in resources."

The manner by which this is accomplished is closely associated with what the proponents of catallaxy believe should be the role of economists in public policy. Simply put, within the context of politics and political decision making, the role of the economist is to search out, invent, and broker social (re)arrangements which will embody Pareto-superior moves (Buchanan, 1975, p. 227). Toward this end, public choice theory focuses on the potential for complex exchange in the political arena under the rules of unanimous consent (to ensure Pareto-superior results), and the compensation requirement.[21] That is, the normative thrust of public choice theory is to structure a political process where values are revealed through the political actions of individuals, and consensus among the individuals of the choosing group becomes the sole affirmation of social value. Like the market, political institutions are to be structured around the common unifying principle of gains-from-trade with a prescriptive focus on cost-minimizing rights structures together with conflict resolution by contracted agreements, vote trading, vote selling, package deals, compensation, and compromise (Reisman, 1990, p. 176).

The catallactic approach to public choice envisions the economist as proffering a social policy solution (or solutions) as "presumptively efficient" (that is, as a tentative hypothesis that a proposed solution is efficient) and then observing whether the solution finds support through the consensus of the individuals in the society. To the extent that a presumptively efficient policy (structured around inclusive, complex trading and exchange agreements) can garner unanimous agreement, the proponents of the catallactic approach can unambiguously recommend that particular policy.

It is here that we see a departure from the *homo economicus* branch of public choice theory. Inherent within much of the literature of the Chicago school branch is the maximization-scarcity-allocation-efficiency paradigm with its emphasis on the efficient outcome—"a presumably objectifiable allocative norm that remains conceptually independent of individual choices" (Buchanan, 1986, p. 25). The essential points made by the Virginia proponents of catallaxy are, first, that there is no external standard or scale (e.g., efficiency) through which end states can be valued, and, second, that the appropriateness or correctness of a public policy (or legal change) is *not* the improvement in an independent, observable assessment of allocative efficiency, but is instead agreement—consensus among the group. In a sense, a policy is fair because the individuals in the society unanimously adopted it; they did not adopt it because it was a priori "fair."[22]

Notwithstanding this subtle difference in approach between the *homo economicus* branch and the catallaxy branch, both comprise what has been termed the inclusive theory of public choice: "In the 1960s, 1970s, and early in the 1980s varying contributions have represented differing weighted combinations of the two central elements in the inclusive public choice perspective. Works on the theory of bureaucracy and bureaucratic behavior and on the theory of regulation have been weighted toward the *homo economicus* element, whereas works on constitutional analysis have been more derivative from the politics-as-exchange paradigm" (Buchanan, 1986, p. 26).

RENT-SEEKING BEHAVIOR

One of the major concerns of public choice is the practice of political rent seeking. The term rent seeking is used to describe "the resource-wasting activities of individuals in seeking transfers of wealth through the aegis of the state" (Buchanan, Tollison, and Tullock, 1980, ix).[23] In the public choice analysis of rent-seeking behavior the focus is not so much on the special privileges or resulting monopoly positions (and the associated resource misallocations) granted to certain individuals through government action, but on the so-called wasteful use of resources expended to acquire and/or maintain these privileged positions—costly lobbyists, lawyers, accountants, press agents, and economists—resources that could have instead been used in economically productive activities.[24] As succinctly described by David B. Johnson (1991, pp. 329–30), "The nation's resources are withdrawn from productive activity and put to rent-seeking activity by the monopolist because he is willing to pay a higher price. The monopolist gains a monopoly right, but citizens lose because the resources which could have been producing real goods and services, are used to chase rents."

Prescriptively, the public choice literature recognizes that the wastes associated with rent seeking may be the product of political investments that are consistent with the rational behavior of all participants (Buchanan, 1980, p. 9). Rational behavior notwithstanding, this waste must be minimized, and the remedies prescribed by the public choice approach to avoid waste include (1) attenuating the role of government regulation, (2) avoiding the establishment of rent-creating government institutions, and (3) adopting constitutional reforms that require supramajorities (two-thirds or three-fourths majorities) to pass rent-seeking-type legislation (Johnson, 1991, pp. 330–32, 334–35). The key is to design institutions that facilitate competition for those rents that accompany newly created surpluses or new wealth creation and that discourage the wasteful competition for existing rents (Mueller, 1989, pp. 244–46).

AN ASIDE: THE MODERN REPUBLICAN CIVIC TRADITION AND PUBLIC CHOICES

Many public choice scholars contend that their purpose, far from being cynical, is merely to describe dispassionately the operation of the political process—to provide an economic analysis of the mechanisms of government for combining private preferences into social decisions.[25] In this regard, public choice is a model of political life that rests on the modern political notion of interest group pluralism. Within interest group pluralism, individuals—cognizant of their original endowments, the costs of transacting, and both the costs of political defeat and the benefits of political victory—are seen to bring their own set of arbitrary, external, and (relatively) unalterable preferences to the political marketplace and to engage in those "deals" that leave them better off than before the political undertaking. As described by Farber and Frickey (and outlined above), the core of the economic models of public choice maintain a rather jaundiced view of the motivation of legislators and bureaucrats (Farber and Frickey, 1991, pp. 2, 22). The antithesis of the public choice portrayal of government is provided by what has come to be known as "the modern republican civic tradition."[26] As recounted by Kathryn Abrams (1988, p. 1591), civic republicanism—a collectivist strain of American politics—was a major focus of concern for historians in the 1960s, and later, in the 1980s, became an alternative to Rawlsian liberalism. In the mid-1980s, legal scholars appropriated the core ideas culminating in what today is termed "the modern republican civic tradition." In some respects, the proponents of civic republicanism are more closely aligned with the work of the New Haven school of law and economics and, accordingly, are at odds with many of the core ideas of the Virginia and Chicago strands of public choice theory.

In the simplest of terms, modern civic republicanism contains disparate elements, some of which help to provide an alternative normative scheme to modern liberalism. Civic republicanism is a scheme that is relevant to both the judiciary and the legislature.[27] It represents an alternative vision of public decision making—a version of democratic self-governance, combined with an aspiration for collective decision making that goes beyond the mere aggregation of individuals' preferences into some vector of public decision making (Mashaw, 1988, p. 1685). The underpinnings of civic republicanism lie in the corpus of ideas proffered by James Madison in his revision of classical republican thought.[28] Experience had shown that the classical republican belief in small-scale democracy—a system of direct, active citizen participation—was unworkable and unrealistic, due primarily to the rise of factional warfare over a variety of public policies. As a consequence, Madison's version of republicanism included the idea of a large republic with comparatively well-insulated representatives. With a large enough republic, political factions would be so numerous that they would tend to hold each other in check. Consequently, representatives would be able to escape the pressures of powerful political factions and, instead, concentrate on the deliberative tasks of politics and thereby promote the common good.

From these underpinnings, modern civic republicanism places much faith in both the need to appeal to norms broader than individual private interests and the existence of shared values together with the possibility of identifying a common good. As such, it envisions a public arena in which decisions are made in the courts and in the legislature through principled deliberation and reasoned dialogue by individuals who think rationally and who are capable of abstracting from their private position and experiences.[29]

In Cass R. Sunstein's formulation, the republican civic tradition is characterized by commitments to four central principles:[30]

> **1.** *Deliberation* in politics is made possible by civic virtue; private interests, although relevant inputs into politics, are neither prepolitical nor exogenous to the decision-making process: they are the object of critical scrutiny. Republicanism maintains the aspiration that the preferences of political actors, with a measure of distance from prevailing issues/practices, are revisable in light of the collective discussion and debate. The requirement of deliberation is designed to ensure that political outcomes will be supported by reference to consensus among political equals. In the context of Law and Economics, emergent laws must be supported

by argument and reason, rather than being the exclusive outcome of self-interested deals (Sunstein, 1988, p. 1544).

2. Civic republicanism includes an *equality* among political actors together with a commitment to eliminate both disparities in political participation and asymmetrical influence among individuals or social groups.

3. Civic republicanism also includes *universalism*, which includes the belief in the possibility of mediating different approaches to politics or different conceptions of the public good through deliberation, dialogue and discussion. As such, universalism is a regulative ideal, a process of mediation based on practical reasoning that yields outcomes that are substantively correct and reflect the common good.

4. Finally, civic republicanism includes *citizenship*, as manifested in the broad guarantee of rights of participation, a participation that is both functional (e.g., monitors the behavior of representatives and their decisions) and instrumental (e.g., a vehicle for inculcating empathy, virtue, and other feelings of community and citizenship). It seeks to have citizen control over national institutions and promotes local control through decentralization and self-determination.

Thus, in modern civic republicanism, political participants are seen to subordinate their private interests to the public and common good in *and* through the ongoing process of collective self-determination. Republicanism views politics as a distinct sphere—in many respects a superior sphere—from the private sector ordering of life.[31] For republicans, political life goes well beyond the use of government to further the ends of private life (an underlying tenet of liberalism); a citizen's participation in political life enables him to work to further a common enterprise and thereby rise above the mere private concerns of the private sector.

In the modern civic republican tradition, the role of government is, in part, to serve as a creative force; it is both a moral teacher and a reflection of public opinion. Government is the arena in which individual preferences (those held so sacrosanct in public choice theory) are formed and reformed in the ongoing public-spirited debate and dialogue as to what public policies fall within the domain of the common good. Existing desires are revisable in light of collective discussion and debate over relevant information and alternative perspectives. Republicanism does not require a romantic dissolution of political differences and disagreements. Indeed, political differences and disagreements form the very basis of the political dialogue, and hence constitute a creative and educational force. Frank I. Michelman (1979, p. 509) has commented regarding this that "[p]olitics must be a joint and mutual search for good or right answers to the question of directions for our evolving selves." As the informed debate moves forward, preferences take shape, and individuals, now armed with an understanding of the greater good that is being sought, subordinate their own private interests and accordingly discipline their own private pursuits so as to realize the greater common good.

Cass Sunstein's application of civic republican thinking to the *Lochner*[32] era serves as a useful illustration of this approach. The *Lochner* era was a period in time (from 1905 through the early 1930s) when the judiciary relied heavily upon the due process clause of the Constitution to invalidate what were held to be unduly restrictive (and hence arbitrary and capricious) economic regulations. In *Lochner v. New York*, the U.S. Supreme Court struck down a New York State statute that set a maximum number of working hours for confectionery and bakery workers at ten hours per day or sixty hours per week. The Supreme Court held that the statute violated the due process clause of the Fourteenth Amendment and stated: "The [legislative] act must have a . . . direct relation, as a means to an end, and the end itself must be appropriate and legitimate, before an act can be held to be valid which interferes with the general right of an individual to be free in his person and in his power to contract in relation to his own labor" (*Lochner v. New York*, pp. 57–58).

In reviewing the *Lochner* era from the vantage point of modern civic republicanism, Sunstein argues that the court's positing of the existence of a natural and prepolitical private sphere served as a brake on economic legislation.[33] Civic republicanism is skeptical of judicial approaches to law and politics that rely on rights that are said to antedate legal and political deliberation. Thus, the underlying problem with the decision by the *Lochner* court was that it relied on self-described, status quo, common law baselines. As Sunstein argues, the values supporting such classifications are the product of social power; they must be subject to political and legal scrutiny and review. Accordingly, the Court in adopting its position in *Lochner* ignores the constitutive functions of law and therefore the ways in which existing practices are dependent on past and present choices of the legal system.

In Law and Economics, both the development of law and the underlying principles from which that law emerges remain at issue. The deliberative nature of modern civic republicanism remains an alternative to the interest group pluralism inherent in the Chicago and Virginia variants of public choice theory. As is evident, republicanism and public choice theory are in direct conflict with one another. This conflict is well illustrated in the following characterization by Farber and Frickey:

> [W]here public choice theory risks cynicism, republicanism can verge dangerously close on romanticism. . . . Where public choice theorists find voter turnout inexplicable, republicans find it a paradigm case of civic virtue. Where public choice theorists see self-interest behind every statute, republicans hope to find a quest for the public good. And where public choice theorists see haphazard cycling and strategic behavior, republicans discern the possibility of genuine political dialogue. (Farber and Frickey, 1991, p. 45)

CHAPTER 4

Institutional Law and Economics

We are interested here in what governs institutional
and systemic performance and how we may,
objectively and nonpresumptively, analyze
and understand the variables governing performance.
The underlying motivation is twofold: First, to enable
us to better know what is going on in the economy
and the polity; and second, to enable us to better
choose and effectuate meaningful and consequential
institutional changes. The focus is on human
interdependence and how alternative property
rights affect its outcome.
(Schmid, 1987, xi)

INTRODUCTION

The institutional approach to law and economics has its roots in the work
of economists such as Henry Carter Adams (1954) on economics and jurisprudence, Richard T. Ely (1914) on the relation of property and contract to
the distribution of wealth, John R. Commons (1924, 1925) on the legal foundations of the economic system, and Wesley C. Mitchell (1927) on the role
of the price system and its place in the modern economy. Important elements
of the institutional approach can also be found in the work of one of the
founding fathers of institutional economics, Thorstein Veblen (1889, 1904),
of lawyer-economists such as Robert Lee Hale[1] and Walton H. Hamilton
(1932), and of legal scholars such as Karl Llewellyn (1925), Jerome Frank
(1930), and Roscoe Pound (1911a,b, 1912). Institutional economics (a label
said to have been coined by Walton H. Hamilton in 1919) is essentially
an American contribution to economic thought that, like Legal Realism, is
said to have "had its heyday in the 1920s and early 1930s" (Bell, 1967).
Nonetheless, it continues to have a relatively strong presence today in the
United States and, to a lesser extent, in Europe. So that the reader can better
understand the foundations upon which present-day institutional law and
economics rests, we will begin our discussion with a brief overview of institutional economics.[2]

Institutional Economics

Institutional economics developed as a rather heterodox approach to the study of economic society. As its name implies, institutional economics places at the center of analysis the study of the institutions of the economic system. Institutions are variously and broadly defined within institutional economics. John R. Commons (1934) defined an institution as "collective action in control of individual action" and as "collective action in restraint, liberation, and expansion of individual action," thereby emphasizing the social bases of the individual which orthodox economists took as given and self-subsistent. Thorstein Veblen (1899) defined institutions as "widely followed habits of thought and the practices which prevail in any given period," thereby emphasizing their problematic and belief-oriented nature. Herbert J. Davenport essentially combined the two definitions in his description of an institution as "a working consensus of human thought or habits—a generally-established attitude of mind and a generally-adopted custom of action as for example, private property, inheritance, government, taxation, competition, and credit" (cited in Srivastava, 1965, p. 470).

Institutional economics has often been described as part of "a revolt against formalism" (Spiegel, 1971, p. 629), a revolt that took place in law, in history, and in economics at about the same time. Institutional economics, as part of that revolt, was led by a group of young American scholars who, after World War I, engaged in a critique of the predominate, formalistic economic doctrines of the day. In economics, formalism was taken to be the abstract *deductive* reasoning of orthodox economic analysis that enthroned universally valid reason, assumed passive, rational utility maximizing behavior, and demonstrated an inordinate concern over the equilibria of comparative statics (in particular, utility analysis of consumer behavior and the marginal productivity theory of distribution).

Instead, institutionalists engaged in *inductive* analyses of specific institutional aspects of the American economy. While their principal emphasis was on using the inductive method to describe the constituent elements of the economy, the institutionalists never employed the inductive method to extremes and thereby were still able to make substantive theoretical generalizations. As noted by Walter S. Buckingham (1958, pp. 107–8), "the development of generalizations gave institutional economics more of a theoretical content than the largely descriptive [German] historical school was ever able to attain. Institutional theory is by no means as refined and exact as orthodox theory, but is not so abstract and lacking in empirical content either."

Charles J. Whalen (1996) describes three distinct influences that contributed to the emergence of the institutionalist school of thought. One was the German historical school, which influenced such early institutionalist thinkers as

Richard T. Ely. The German historical school, founded by Wilhelm Roscher (1817–94) and later dominated by Gustav von Schmoller (1838–1917), emerged at least in part as a reaction against classical economic thinking in the mid–nineteenth century. The Historical school emphasized the dynamics of economic development, the need to use empirical data (rather than abstract ideas) to ground economic theories, and the necessity of paying particular attention to human institutions. This emphasis on gathering facts and studying them in relation to their historical significance rather than as isolated, objective data in static, timeless models had a direct bearing on the methodology of emerging institutionalist economics.

The second influence was from American pragmatic philosophy as set forth by, among others, Charles Peirce, William James, and John Dewey. Proponents of American pragmatic philosophy recognized an uncertainty inherent in understanding and looked for philosophical methods for establishing the meaning of concepts and beliefs. The analysis of social phenomena had to be conducted within systems of relationships among individuals in their empirical settings. They largely replaced a priori abstract reasoning with empirical studies. Contrary to the narrow, uniform "rational behavior" assumption in orthodox microeconomics, choices were pragmatically perceived—to be made in a world of ever-changing empirical objects and emerging economic, political, and social institutions. "True" ideas are those to which responsible investigators would assent after thorough examination, that is, after considering what conceivable effects of a practical kind a theory or object holds. Thus, only those hypotheses that contributed to organizing data garnered through sense perceptions related to the real world (i.e., held practical significence), and did so in a progressive and unifying manner, were taken to be legitimate. In short, an idea was right if it had "fruitful" consequences. The pragmatist emphasis on the uncertainty inherent in understanding served to provide an epistemological foundation and a social philosophy upon which to erect the basic tenets of institutional economic thought.

The third influence came through Thornstein Veblen's turn-of-the century writings focusing on the evolutionary facet of economic development, within which one can trace many of the origins of and early insights into institutional economic thought. Veblen studied political economy and philosophy, spoke some twenty-six languages, and is considered by most the founder of Institutionalism. In his studies he was most influenced by John Bates Clark, professor of political economy at Carleton College, and he subsequently received his doctorate from Yale. In 1892 he was brought to the newly founded University of Chicago by J. Laurence Laughlin, the then head of the Department of Economics, and during his tenure there, he edited the *Journal of Political Economy* for over a decade. Thereafter he moved around through several different academic positions.

A strong critic of orthodox economic thinking, Veblen rejected the mechanistic view of economic society reflected in static equilibrium analysis and instead focused on what he termed an evolutionary method of economic analysis. He believed that the material environment, technology, and propensities of human nature condition the emergence and growth of institutions, and he insisted on a critical examination of capitalistic institutions—especially what he termed industry and business, along with the economic power they were able to exercise—to understand economic society. Toward that end, he emphasized that it was necessary to understand both group habits and institutions, and not merely how these institutions worked, but how they evolved. In his most renowned book, *The Theory of the Leisure Class* (1899), Veblen provided a critique of the pecuniary behavior of people in the context of their cultural background and inherited traits, and argued that the orthodox hedonistic conception of man as a lightning calculator of pleasure and pain was overly narrow and outmoded. In his book he described the idea of a two-class society—the productive class (those who produced socially) and the leisure class (those who depended upon the wasteful effort of acquisition), and from this developed a theory of consumption based on broad cultural factors that influence human personality, avoiding what he considered to be the narrow, individualistic thrust of orthodox economics. Veblen's (e.g., 1904, 1923) analysis of industrial capitalism was couched in terms of a dichotomy between business and industrial interests, the former negative and the latter positive. Business, he said, is about the making of money and the acquisition of economic power. Industry, in contrast, is the amalgam of tools and skills in the production of goods and services. There is, according to Veblen, a conflict between these interests, in that the tendency of industry is toward greater productivity, which would result in lower profits, a factor which worked against business interests. This, he argued, leads businessmen to attempt to retard industrial progress that would benefit consumers. In doing so, Veblen attempted to demonstrate what he considered to be the managerial and administered character of the modern capitalist economic system, as against the individualist and competitive nature attributed to it in public discourse and within economic theory.[3]

Certain of Veblen's ideas were given further development by Clarence E. Ayres, who received his doctorate from Chicago in 1917 and became interested in institutional thought during the course of his studies of philosophy (under Dewey) and economics (under Veblen). Upon taking up a position at Amherst, he came under the influence of Walton Hamilton, a severe critic of orthodox economic thinking. It was during his tenure at Amherst that Ayres came to reject marginal analysis—the keystone of neoclassical economic thought; he was to spend the remainder of his career in search of a new economic framework that could better explain the economic forces shaping modern economies. Indeed, it was Ayres who became the chief exemplar of Institutionalist economic thought in the post–World War II period, when from his base at the University of Texas–Austin he and his students developed the Veblenian-Ayresian perspective within Institutionalism (Breit, 1973, pp. 244–45).

Ayres's perspective is perhaps best reflected in his treatise *The Theory of Economic Progress* (1944), in which he undertook to both explain and apply institutional economic thought with respect to the field of economic development. In short, as described by Breit (1973), it is a theoretical work that attempts to explain the forces that have shaped the economy, isolating on those factors that accelerated the development as well as those that have impeded it. Ayres saw human activity as reflective of two basic and ever-present forces: "technological" behavior, a productive and progressive force, and "ceremonial" behavior (as manifested in, for example, hierarchies, mores, culture, and ideology), which is counterproductive and inhibits change, acting as a curb on technological progress. The central theme of this work is that exponentially expanding and advancing "technology" (defined broadly as all human activities involving the use of tools, and thus including both human and physical capital) is responsible for the enormous changes in the welfare of society. The focus is not so much on the individuals, but on the technological progress as related to the advancement of the tools (i.e., the objective instruments capable of being variously combined) and the role of this in enhancing economic progress. Since the ceremonial institutions resist change, he argued, progress is a function of the relative strength of these progressive and inhibiting forces, the variance of which relative strength helps to explain the differential rates of development across societies and cultures. Thus, for Ayres, the challenge confronting economics is to "devise new organizational forms, to pragmatically develop organizational arts to match, rather than contradict, our science and technology" (Breit, 1973, pp. 255–56).

Robert Lee Hale received his L.L.B. from Harvard University in 1909 and his Ph.D. in economics from Columbia University in 1918. He subsequently held a joint appointment in the economics department and the law school at Columbia and moved to the law school on a full-time basis in 1928.[4] His emphasis on the integration of economics and law was reflected both in his teaching—particularly his course on "Legal Factors in Economic Society"— and in his writing, much of which dealt with the regulation of railroads and public utilities—fields in which an understanding of the interface between economics and law has always been fundamental.[5] Hale wrote extensively on the legal and economic theory of rate-base valuation, as well as on the regulation of rate structure and level, and his writings were instrumental in the adoption by the courts of the "prudent investment" doctrine of valuation for public utilities (Dorfman, 1959, p. 161).

Hale can perhaps best be described as a Legal Realist who drew upon the emerging tradition of Institutionalism (Duxbury, 1995, pp. 107–8). Consistent with the Realists of the day, Hale's work was very much a challenge to and critique of the dominant tradition of laissez-faire capitalism. Like John R. Commons (whose contributions will be reviewed below), Hale was influenced by Wesley H. Hohfeld's articulation of "fundamental legal conceptions," which, in Hohfeld's mind, were the "lowest common denominators of law" (Cotterrell, 1989, p. 88). As described by Samuels, Hale's paradigm was comprised of the concepts of voluntary freedom, volitional freedom, coercion, power, and government. Legal and economic processes were viewed as inseparable. Hale described the economy as a structure of coercive power arrangements and relationships which necessitated an understanding of the formation and structure of the underlying distribution of economic power. As such, the economy was seen as a system of power operating through a system of coercion, and thus the economic freedom expressed by the courts of the day was merely freedom to engage in economic coercion. The evolution of Hale's brand of legal economics—as reflected in both his writing and his teaching—gradually evolved into a "theory of the economy as a system of mutual coercion and the legal basis thereof" (Samuels, 1973, p. 25); his perspective was most fully spelled out in his classic book entitled *Freedom through Law* (1952).

Hale did not view this coercion as something to be condemned, but, rather, as a basic fact of economic life. As such, he argued, if, for example, income is in fact the fruit of coercion, abetted actively or passively by government, then it cannot be said that overt coercive redistributions of income by government are themselves wrong (Dorfman, 1959, pp. 162–63). Hale's Hohfeldian perspective on rights led him to view nearly every statute with economic implications as impacting negatively upon someone's liberty or property. Given this, he believed that it was essential for the courts to undertake an intelligent balancing of the gains and losses brought about by the particular statutes brought before them—a process which, he said, requires "a realistic understanding of the economic effect of the legislation" (quoted in Dorfman, 1959, p. 163). Although Hale believed that ethical judgements must ultimately be the basis upon which the court's decisions are made, he felt that the judicial application of economic principles was necessary in order to ascertain the economic consequences—allocative and distributive—of the legislation whose constitutionality the court was asked to evaluate (Hale, 1924, 1927).[6]

Finally, of particular and importance to institutional law and economics, is the work of John R. Commons. Like Veblen, Commons was a student of Ely, who instilled in his students the inductive method of study and emphasized both the historical facets of and legal issues within the study of economics. Early on, Ely interested Commons in the field of labor and later was instrumental in helping to place Commons at the University of Wisconsin, where he spent most of his academic life. Commons's intellectual interests ranged across industrial relations, labor reform legislation, public utility regulation, and price stabilization. Besides teaching and writing at the University of Wisconsin, he was also very involved in public life and served on an array of state and federal commissions. It was while at Wisconsin in 1934 that Commons published *Institutional Economics: Its Place in Political Economy*. For Commons, institutional economics was an economics of rights, duties, liberties, and exposures. Commons rejected the exclusive emphasis on methodological individualism reflected in orthodox theory; instead he gave collective and corporate action its due place in economic analysis. Likewise, he rejected the economics of a harmony of interests and instead centered his analysis on the conflict of interest inherent in a modern economy. Commons optimistically believed that the primary economic institutions could be formed and reshaped (as needed) to conform to the social changes inherent within a society, a belief that led him to probe extensively the impact of institutions, such as the law, on economic structure and performance, and to become actively involved in various reform activities.

Based on the writings of these early contributors and the many who followed in their footsteps, what emerged as Institutionalist economics is a rather heterodox approach to analyzing economic society. In its more modern form, as a school of thought, institutional economics suggests a series of propositions, which, when taken together, provide an alternative approach within economic analysis. As will become evident, these propositions, together with the focus contributed by Commons, provide the foundation upon which institutional law and economics rests:[7]

- Economic behavior is strongly conditioned by the institutional environment within which economic activity takes place, and, simultaneously, economic behavior affects the structure of the institutional environment.

- The mutual interaction between the institutions and the behavior of economic actors is an evolutionary process, hence the need for an "evolutionary approach" to economics.[8]

- In analyzing the evolutionary processes contained therein, emphasis is directed to the role played by the conditions imposed by modern technology and the monetary institutions of modern, mixed-market capitalism.

- Emphasis is centered upon conflict within the economic sphere of society as opposed to harmonious order inherent within the cooperative, spontaneous, and unconscious free play of economic actors within the market.

- There is a clear and present need to channel the conflict inherent in economic relationships by structuring institutions to establish a system of social control over economic activity.

- Institutionalism requires an interdisciplinary approach calling on psychology, sociology, anthropology, and law to help understand the behavior of economic actors and thereby generate more accurate assumptions in describing their behavior.

It should be clear that these propositions offer a partial rejection of the positivist, price-theoretic approach proffered by the more orthodox neoclassical microeconomics, and are a manifestation of the Institutionalist position that the framework of orthodox economic analysis does not allow it to get at certain fundamentally important features of economic activity. On the other hand, institutional economics—an evolutionary theory—is proffered as being based on more "realistic" behavioral assumptions derived from a broad array of social science knowledge and a full appreciation for and understanding of the institutions driving a mixed-market economy.[9] Both Veblen and Commons incorporated the research findings of the behavioral sciences into economics. Following that tradition, contemporary Institutionalists reject the assumption of fixed preferences and, consistent with Herbert Simon's concept of procedural rationality, explore the hypothesis that law systematically influences the learning of preferences (Schmid, 1987, ch. 10).

Commons and the Development of Institutional Law and Economics

Although each of the above-mentioned scholars played an important role in the development of the institutional approach to economics, and therefore ultimately to institutional law and economics, it is Commons who, through the Wisconsin tradition, stands as the central figure within the development of this approach. Commons's central concern was with uncovering the development, evolution, and workings of the institutions that ultimately impact the performance of the economic system. A major part of this work involved an examination of the legal foundations of the capitalist economic system, particularly in his classic treatise *Legal Foundations of Capitalism* (1924). *Legal Foundations of Capitalism* was a theoretical work unlike anything that had come before and benefited from Commons's close contact with law through his involvement with the courts, his serving on government commissions, and his drafting of legislation. The emphasis of the book is on describing the role of law and the courts and how they determine the elements of an economic system. Like his predecessors, Commons believed all economic institutions were subject to evolution. Whether describing the institution of capitalism, private property, or the state itself, each was shown to receive its sanction from the authorities—the church, the state, the courts—through an evolutionary process. Commons undertook an analysis of a wide variety of cases, working rules, and statutes to probe their impacts on the development of modern capitalism, and thereby to illuminate the interrelations between legal and economic processes. Through this analysis, Commons showed how, on the one hand, economy influences law as the economic system brings to bear pressures on political and legal systems for legal change that facilitates a particular direction of evolution, and, on the other hand, how law influences economy—that is, how legal change facilitates the development of economic activity in a particular direction.

Commons's primary interest in *Legal Foundations* was to uncover the values underlying the working rules that govern social-economic relations, and he found this in the courts' use of the term "reasonable value." He found that legal history showed certain well-defined tendencies on the part of the courts to eliminate the destructive practices of capitalistic institutions, while at the same time ascertaining the "reasonable" policies that should be followed in a competitive system. Thus, "reasonable values" could be used to ground policies that would bring about compromises in arenas of economic conflict, namely, labor disputes, public utility rate making, tax policy, pricing, and so on (Bell, 1967, pp. 556–57). Specifically, as the definition of what types of activities were considered reasonable evolved over time, so too did the legal rules governing social-economic relations. Thus in the West was engendered a movement from a feudal and agrarian society to a capitalist system, with economic change driving legal change, which in turn facilitated the economic transformations.

Much of Commons's analysis consisted of tracing this unfolding legal-economic evolution to illustrate the pervasiveness of this legal-economic nexus, for example, the effects of the transformation of the legal definition of property and its impact on business, and the effects of law on the employment relation within the firm, on the market mechanism, and on the wage bargain. But Commons also lays out, in great detail, the mechanisms through which law and economy influence one another. Of particular import here is his analysis of the role played by rights and working rules within the economic system, where he lays out, in a systematic way, why rights matter (and thus law matters) within the economic system, and why the development of economic theory should proceed with attention to the role of law and legal change in structuring economic activity and performance. Moreover, through his work on proportional representation, Commons (1907) explored the manner in which rules influence whose preferences will count within the political process, and through this he laid the foundation for an Institutionalist approach to the study of constitutional choices.

Whereas many of the roots of institutional law and economics emanate from economists trained at the University of Wisconsin, today the major contributions come from Michigan State University through the work of Warren J. Samuels and A. Allan Schmid. Others at Michigan State University who continue to contribute to this tradition are Harry Trebing,[10] who has made substantial and influential contributions to the analysis of regulation and public utilities, and Robert A. Solo,[11] much of whose work focuses on monpoly regulation and institutional change. The focus of the institutional approach is on the relations between legal (or governmental) and economic processes, rather than the application of microeconomic theory to the law. Although most economists identify the beginning of law and economics with the Chicago school, the roots of law and economics, as pointed out in chapter 1, actually lie in part within the Institutionalist tradition several decades earlier (Samuels, 1993). Whereas the Institutionalist law and economics literature has been quite critical of the Chicago approach, Samuels (1981, pp. 148–49), for one, has praised Posner for the usefulness of his analysis in once again bringing to the attention of economists and legal scholars alike how economic conditions affect the law, and conversely.

In contrast to the other approaches examined in this book, the institutional approach draws no distinction between jurisprudential, legislative, bureaucratic, or regulatory treatments, seeing them all as particular manifestations of the interrelation of government and the economy, or legal and economic processes. Underlying the major thrust of the institutional approach to law and economics are two complementary modes of analysis. From the perspective of the *Logic of Law and Economics*, described above, we have seen that

$\triangle$ law or legal structure $\rightarrow$ $\triangle$ behavior or conduct in the mixed-market economy $\rightarrow$ $\triangle$ economic performance.

However, for institutional law and economics, the emphasis is on the interrelations and *mutual* interaction between government and the economy, with the effect that its perspective is described by the relation

$\triangle$ law or legal structure $\leftrightarrow$ $\triangle$ behavior or conduct in the mixed-market economy $\leftrightarrow$ $\triangle$ economic performance.

Much, though not all, of the work of Schmid has tended to concentrate on the "structure $\leftrightarrow$ performance" linkage, with an emphasis on empirical work that explores the economic impact of alternative legal structures.[12] Schmid brings to the forefront the many varieties of human interdependence, focusing on both (1) the various types of transactions—bargained, administrative, and status and grant transactions, and (2) the varied interdependencies that emerge—technological, pecuniary, and political externalities arising from incompatible use, exclusion costs, information costs, and economies of scale. As posed by Schmid, the institutional approach to law and economics must ask, "How do the rules of property structure human relationships and affect participation in decisions when interests conflict or when shared objectives are to be implemented? How do the results affect performance of the economy?" (Schmid, 1987, p. 188).

The work of Samuels, in contrast, has tended to concentrate on describing the conduct or behavior of individuals and groups in the legal-economic arena—on the "conduct $\leftrightarrow$ performance" linkage. For Samuels, the organizing concept is that of the *legal-economic nexus*, wherein, as Samuels (1989a, p. 1567) describes it, "the law is a function of the economy, and the economy (especially its structure) is a function of law. . . . [Law and economy] are jointly produced, *not* independently given and *not* merely interacting." Through the legal-economic nexus is worked out the structure of the law and the economic system, where each serves as both dependent and independent variable in the construction of legal-economic reality. Legal rules govern "the terms of access to and participation in the economy by potential economic actors," and "property and other rights . . . govern whose preferences will be given effect through the market" (Samuels, 1975, p. 66). The focus of the institutional approach is thus on delving into the workings of the legal-economic nexus to understand its processes and thereby conduct an in-depth analysis of the consequences of choice. Resource allocation and the distribution of income and wealth are explained "in terms of a complex causal chain involving both allocation and distribution as functions of market forces that depend in turn on power, rights, and the use of government" (Samuels and Schmid, 1981, p. 4).

Both branches of the institutional approach are avowedly positive. As Samuels and Schmid (1981, p. 1) describe it in the introduction to their book on institutional law and economics, "Our principal goal is quite simply to understand what is going on—to identify the instrumental variables and fundamental issues and processes—in the operation of legal institutions of economic significance," and to promote "the development of skills with which to analyze and predict the performance consequences of alternative institutional designs."[13] The institutional approach to law and economics is best understood as two complementary branches that differ only with respect to the relative emphasis given to "structure" and "conduct," as outlined above. In total, the institutional approach emphasizes the need to explain and analyze the available alternatives and the consequences of choice at three distinct stages: (1) the constitutional stage of choice—the social contract that binds people together; (2) the institutional stage of choice—the structuring and restructuring of political-legal-economic institutions, and (3) the economic impact stage of choice—describing the economic impacts of existing or potentially revised legal-economic relations, be they in the form of private property rights, status rights, or communal property (Mercuro, 1989, pp. 3–6).

For purposes of exposition, the remaining sections lay out the central themes of the institutional approach to law and economics as they relate to the understanding of legal-economic processes and do not further explore the nuances of the two complementary branches. The final two sections deal with the formulation and application of a comparative institutional approach to doing law and economics. The comparative institutional approach is presented by the Institutionalists as an integrated response to the alternative paradigms to better understand the interrelations between legal and economic processes and thereby help fill the void left by the Legal Realists.

CENTRAL THEMES: EVOLUTION, INTERDEPENDENCE, AND ORDER

Several central themes emerge in the institutional law and economics literature, and these themes are clearly related to fundamental elements of institutional economics in general. Institutional economics represents a system of thought that originated in America in the first quarter of the century, and its central premise is that economic institutions motivate all economic activities. Within Institutionalism, habits, customs, social patterns, and legal and economic arrangements are seen to be the primary factors and forces governing economic life. Economic institutions are considered to be the combined product of evolution, power, and technology. Thus, much of the work of the Institutionalist economists has concentrated on describing and analyzing economic life in the context of the full array of surrounding social institutions.

The Evolution of Law and Economy

One of the factors emphasized by Commons in his discussion of the legal foundations of the capitalist economic system is the evolutionary nature of the economic system, and, most importantly for the present discussion, the role of the evolution of law in structuring the evolution of the economic system. One prominent example of this is his discussion of the evolution of the law of property.

Prior to the late nineteenth century, the U.S. courts held to a physical conception of property, a view that defined property as value in use rather than value in exchange (Commons, 1924, p. 12). One of the implications of this definition of property was that governmental deprivations of exchange value did not require compensation under the Fifth and Fourteenth amendments. As Commons points out, it was only in the 1870s that the idea of property as value in exchange first began to creep into dissenting opinions of the U.S. Supreme Court, and it was not until the 1890s that the Court finally made the transition from a definition of property as a thing having only use value to a definition that conceived of property as the exchange value of anything (Commons, 1924, pp. 12–14). In making this transition, the Court was saying not only that physical things are property, but that "the *expected earning power* of those things is property," and thus "[t]o deprive the owners of the *exchange value* of their property is equivalent to depriving them of their property" (Commons, 1924, p. 16, emphasis in original). Thus, no longer were physical seizures of property the only "takings" requiring compensation; it now became the case that activities (including government regulations) that reduced the exchange value of things could give rise to claims for compensation. In the Allegeyer Case of 1897 this was further expanded to include liberty of access to markets, an important component in the determination of exchange values (Commons, 1924, p. 17). The definition of property as corporeal property had been expanded to include both incorporeal property (e.g., debt instruments or promises to pay) and intangible property ("anything that enables one to obtain from others an income in the process of buying and selling, borrowing and lending, hiring and hiring out, renting and leasing, in any of the transactions of the modern business") (Commons, 1924, p. 19). The import of this for the development of the capitalist system is set forth by Commons in the context of farming:

> The isolated, colonial or frontier farmer might produce and consume things, attentive only to their use value, but the modern farmer lives by producing "social-use-values" and buying other social-use-values produced and sold by other business men. In this way he also "produces" exchange-value, that is, assets. He farms for sale, not for use, and while he has the doubtful alternative of falling back on his own natural resources if he cannot sell his products yet his farm and crops are valuable because they are business assets, that is, exchange-values, while his liabilities are his debts and his taxes, all of them measured by his expectations and realizations on the commodity markets and money markets, in terms of exchange-value or price. (Commons, 1924, p. 21)

That is, what distinguishes capitalism from the colonial and feudal systems it replaced is the transition from production for one's own use to "production for the use of others and acquisition for the use of self" (Commons, 1924, p. 21), and it was in part the adoption of this more expansive definition of property that helped to facilitate this economic transition.

Following on the work of Institutionalists such as Commons, the institutional approach to law and economics is evolutionary, emphasizing the importance of the historical process and the evolutionary change of law through time. As described by Samuels (1989a, p. 1578), the legal-economic nexus "is a continuing, explorative, and emergent process through which are worked out ongoing solutions to legal problems." The structure of legal-economic institutions—the state (whether in the context of the legislature, the bureaucracy, or the judiciary), the firm-corporation, or the market—channels legal-economic decision making, and this structure is seen as the outcome of an evolutionary process of legal-economic change rather than as movement to a steady-state equilibrium (Schmid, 1989, p. 66). Legal change, although gradual, has been continuous and "has led to major transformations of the legal system and of the pattern of rights and, thereby, of the system of economic organization and control" (Samuels and Mercuro, 1979, p. 167). The pervasiveness of legal change and the ongoing process of legal-economic reconstruction through the nexus process thus makes necessary an evolutionary-historical approach that accounts for the array of factors and forces promoting both continuity and change over time.[14]

Continuity versus Change

Another of the fundamental ideas explored within the Institutionalist approach to law and economics is the ever-present tension between continuity and change. The evolutionary path of the legal-economic system is derivative of the legal-economic policy choices that are made over time. Within this policymaking process (be it legislative, bureaucratic, or judicial) arise forces that, through acts of commission or omission, serve to maintain the status quo structure of legal-economic institutions and relations—that is, continuity— while other forces promote an alteration in these institutions and relations— that is, change. The ongoing choice process within the legal-economic arena will thus determine both the institutional structures that obtain at any given point in time and whether the status quo institutional structures, or some other, will prevail in the future—whether there will be change, and if so how much. It must be recognized, say the Institutionalists, that the formation of legal-economic policy takes place in an arena within which there is the ever-present tension of both continuity and change. Each is the outcome of the policymaking process, and, more specifically, of the interaction between the groups supporting the respective forces of continuity and change and the power that each can bring to bear on this process (Samuels, 1966, pp. 267–73).

Mutual Interdependence, Conflict, and the Problem of Order

The Institutionalists view the legal-economic system as a system of mutual interdependence rather than atomistic independence. The economy, says Schmid (1989, p. 59), is "a universe of human relations," not merely "a universe of commodities," and within this world each individual has scarcity relationships with others. Although it may be that part of life deals with movements from positions off of contract curves to positions on contract curves in the process of exhausting gains from trade, the Institutionalist approach places strong emphasis on (1) who gets to play, (2) where one starts in the game, and (3) the strategic behavior (i.e., the conscious, calculated choices) of participants that frame the position, role, and status of each individual.

Given the importance of human interdependence and the emphasis on who plays and what are the starting points within the Institutionalist approach, the emphasis of this approach is on conflict rather than harmony, where "The role of the legal system, including both common and constitutional law, is to provide a framework or a process for conflict resolution and the development of legal rights" (Samuels and Mercuro, 1979, p. 166). The fundamental problem here is that of order, which Samuels (1972a, p. 584) defines as "the reconciling of freedom and control, or autonomy and coordination including hierarchy and equality, with continuity and change." "The ultimate meaning of the legal and economic processes," says Samuels (1971, p. 449), "is in terms of their functioning toward resolving the problem(s) of order." The existence of conflicting interests necessitates both a process (or processes) for deciding between these competing interests and a method (or methods) for determining how these conflicts are to be resolved.

Thus, society is recognized, at least in part, as a cooperative venture for mutual advantage where there is both an identity and a conflict of interests in ongoing human relations. Within this system of mutual interdependence, societal institutions, including the legal system, both enhance the scope of cooperative endeavors and channel political-legal-economic conflict toward resolution (Mercuro, 1989, p. 2). The resolution of these conflicts, of whose interests government will give effect through law and otherwise, is the resolution of the problem of order in society—a working out of a societal structure that promotes coherence, security, and orderliness in human relations. Indeed, the manner by which a society comes to channel conflict says much about its ultimate character.[15]

RIGHTS, POWER, AND GOVERNMENT

From the institutional perspective, law is fundamentally a matter of rights creation and re-creation. Consistent with the positive, descriptive nature of this approach, Institutionalists are concerned with the rights (re)creation process and the impact of this process on legal-economic decision making and activity. To understand the importance of rights from the institutional perspective, it is first necessary to understand the Institutionalist conception of the determination of the individual choice process and the activities open to individuals.

Individual decision making is a function of one's opportunity set, which "consists of the available alternatives for action or choice, each with a relative opportunity cost, which are open to the individual" (Samuels, 1974, p. 120). However, these opportunity sets are not without limit in their scope; rather, reflecting human interdependence and scarcity, each individual's opportunity set is constrained, and indeed shaped, by the opportunity sets of others in society. Each individual desires to make choices from a set that is as unconstrained as possible, which, in turn, means that individuals will wish to control the choices, and hence opportunity sets, of others who may constrain their choice. The extent of each individual's ability to determine his or her own choices and to influence the opportunity sets, and hence choices, of others is the outcome of a process of *mutual coercion*, where the ability to coerce is simply the ability of A to impact B's opportunity set without B's consent. An individual's capacity to exercise coercion is, in turn, a function of that individual's *power*, defined as "the means or capacity with which to exercise choice" (Samuels, 1972b, p. 65), and this power is relative to the power of others. Thus, "The opportunity set of the individual, within which he attempts a constrained maximizing equilibrium, is a function of the total structure of mutual coercion, grounded upon relative power" (Samuels, 1972b, p. 65). Moreover, power is also a dependent variable in this process, being a function of the choices made from opportunity sets that exist and evolve through time (Samuels, 1972b, p. 66).

The ongoing delineation and redefinition of opportunity sets, through the machinations of power and mutual coercion in the face of conflicts, gives rise to disputes which necessitate resolution. For example, the upstream polluting factory's choice of production technology impacts and conflicts with the choice of activities of the downstream water user, and conversely. The upstream user cannot exercise choice without impacting the choice of downstream users, and conversely. The resolution of such conflicts comes through the creation and assignment (or reassignment) of legal rights, which define the scope of choices open to each individual and the degree to which each is exposed to the choices of others. Thus, power, and hence coercion, and the resulting opportunity sets and choices, are a function of rights.

The origin of rights in the resolution of conflicts of interest brings to the fore the point that rights have a dual nature—"the opportunity set enhancement of those who have rights and the opportunity set restriction of those who are exposed to them" (Samuels, 1974, p. 122). Virtually every legal change imposes both benefits and costs, the enhancement of some opportunity sets and the simultaneous restriction of others. Externalities are thus ubiquitous and reciprocal—any (re)definition, (re)allocation, or change in the degree of enforcement of rights benefits some interests and harms others; the externality remains; it is merely shifted. In institutional law and economics, systems of property, tort, and contract law, then, do not provide *solutions* to situations of externality, but rather only *resolutions*, as externalities, and hence benefit and harm, are channeled in a particular direction through the legal delimitation of rights.

Government is seen to play a central and inevitable role within this process, for rights are not rights because they are preexisting, but rather are rights because they are protected by government.[16] Rights are thus relative to and contingent upon "the legal limitations inherent in their identification and interpretation, the exercise by others of their rights, and legal and nonlegal change"

(Samuels, 1974, p. 118). Each of these factors is a function of the rights-creation (and re-creation) process, and hence of the ability of individuals to secure rights (or a change therein) through the use and control of government. Government thus becomes an object of control for those seeking private legal-economic gain or advantage, "a mode through which relative rights and there-fore relative market (income securing) status is given effect" (Samuels, 1971, pp. 441–42). The question is not, then, one of more versus less government, but rather of whose interests government gives effect through law—that is, through the process of rights creation and re-creation. The Institutionalists thus see terms such as regulation, deregulation, and government intervention as misleading, in that government is omnipresent (Lang, 1980; Breimyer, 1991). For example, although it is often said that the adoption of workplace safety regulations constitutes an intervention of government into the market, the In-stitutionalists claim that such activity represents merely a change in rights (or the interests to which government gives effect)—a movement which expands the rights/opportunity sets of workers and reduces the rights/opportunity sets of employers. The issue as to who will have rights thus turns on whose inter-ests government allows to be realized and who is able to use government for what ends. The critical matter, says Samuels, is who is able to control and use the legal-economic nexus to control legal-economic continuity or change (Samuels, 1971, p. 440).[17]

The reciprocal nature of externalities has the effect that the decision as to whose interests are protected as rights is necessarily a function of a choice process—choice as to who will have rights and who will be exposed to the exercise of those rights, of who will be able to inflict gains and losses on others, and to what extent (Samuels and Mercuro, 1979, pp. 172–74). This inevitable necessity of choice reveals that law is not something that is given or to be discovered, but is instead a human artifact marked by deliberative and nondeliberative human choice (Samuels, 1981, p. 168). This human choice process necessitates the introduction of value judgments in choosing between competing interests, and legal-economic outcomes are thus "an ex-pression of the values of those who have participated and prevailed at each stage of choice in the political-legal-economic arena"—that is, those who are able to most effectively use government to further their own ends (Mercuro, 1989, p. 10).

Recognition of the necessity of choice reveals the tentative, selective, and partial nature of the application of specific legal rules, which are themselves both subject and outcome of the choice process. The use of tests, rules, and the like "is essentially selective and arbitrary. Their use in any particular case is a matter of decision, of ultimate pure choice. . . . There is no automatic litmus test by which the tests themselves can be selected for applicability. They are categories (empty boxes) with variable selective contents whose adoption is almost if not wholly subjective" (Samuels and Mercuro, 1979, p. 177). The rights generated through the use of tests, rules, and so on reflect selective perception both with respect to the test or rule actually applied and with respect to facts, gains, and losses as applied. Justice, then, reflects not some given set of high foundational principles, but rather a normative valuational process that determines the laws, norms, and values that are to govern living (Samuels, 1971, p. 444).[18] The legal-economic nexus is that sphere of decision making that reflects the working out of whose interests are to count as rights, whose values are to dominate, and who is to make these decisions. The resolution of these issues determines not just rights, but the allocation and distribution of resources in society, and hence power, income, and wealth.

THE PROBLEMATIC NATURE OF EFFICIENCY

One of the hallmarks of the institutional approach is the rejection of the Chicago emphasis on the determination of *the* efficient resolution of legal disputes. The Institutionalists do not reject efficiency as an important variable in legal-economic analysis, but rather maintain that efficiency is not unique and therefore cannot determine the assignment of rights (Samuels, 1989a, p. 1563). It is not merely a question of adding something to the concept of efficiency, but, rather, of what is subsumed or included within the concept.

The starting point here is the recognition that economic activity—prices, costs, outputs, risk, income, wealth, and so on—is not some sort of natural phenomenon, but rather is determined by the structure of rights that exists in society, with the levels of and changes in each of these variables being in part a function of rights, and hence of the legal structure and legal change over time.[19] Each particular rights structure will give rise to a particular set of prices, costs, outputs, and the like, and thus to a particular efficient allocation of resources. Hence, there is no unique efficient result. For the Institutionalists, the purportedly positivist Chicago school rhetoric of "atomistic industries" or "contestable markets" and the associated concept of "price-taking behavior" is exposed as nothing more than deeply normative "rights-taking behavior" (Samuels and Mercuro, 1984). The Institutionalists maintain that inasmuch as rights underlie product prices and thus costs, to talk of "price-takers" bypasses virtually all that is important in Law and Economics.

Because efficiency is a function of rights, and not the other way around, it is circular to maintain that efficiency alone can determine rights. Since costs, prices, outputs, wealth, and so on are derivative of a particular rights structure, so too are cost minimization, value-of-output maximization, and wealth maximization. Different specifications of rights will lead to different (and economically noncomparable) minimizing or maximizing valuations. The result is that an outcome that is claimed to be efficient is efficient only with regard to the assumed initial structure of rights (Schmid, 1989, pp. 68–69). Thus, as

Samuels (1981, p. 154) asserts, "To argue that wealth maximization [or any other efficiency criterion] can determine rights serves only to mask a choice of which interests to protect as rights. Legal decisions or changes can be said to be efficient only from the point of view of the party whose interests are given effect through the identification and assignment of rights."

Moreover, the definition of "output"—of what it is that one is to be efficient about—requires an antecedent normative specification as to the appropriate performance goal for society. Social output (the aggregate well-being of society), consumptive output (the value of goods from the consumer point of view), and productive output (the value of goods from the producer point of view, i.e., profits) are three examples of the alternatives that are available. The value-laden choice of a particular definition of output as the maximand, which in effect is the choice of a particular social welfare function where many are possible, will drive the decision as to what constitutes the efficient allocation (Samuels, 1978, pp. 102–4).

The recognition of the multiplicity of efficient solutions and the contingency of any given efficient solution on the presumed structure of rights and the definition of output reveals the inherent normative element that is present in efficiency-based decision making. Each possible legal solution points to a different efficient outcome, and "There is no independent test by which the law's solutions can be said to be *the* efficient solution" (Samuels, 1981, p. 155). The determination of a particular efficient solution involves a normative and selective choice as to whose interests will be accommodated, who will realize gains, and who will realize losses.

Because of the nonuniqueness of efficiency (the Chicago school's claim to the contrary notwithstanding), efficiency is inevitably bound up with distribution; as Samuels and Schmid (1981, p. 2) describe it, "the concept of efficiency as separate from distribution is false." Rights determination is a normative activity with both efficiency and distributional consequences, determining which efficient allocation and which distribution of benefits and costs will carry the day. Rights determine the distribution of income and wealth, which in turn determines the efficient solution that is reached. But at the same time, the specification of rights, and the resulting efficient outcome, structure the future distribution of income and wealth in society. The choice of rights, then, is ultimately a distributional issue: "With no unique optimal use of resources and opportunities independent of rights identification and assignment, the legal system must select the [distributional] result to be pursued: *the definition of the efficient solution is both the object and the subject of the legal system*" (Samuels, 1978, p. 106, emphasis in original). Thus, as described by Schmid (1989, p. 69), "the whole point is that global welfare maximization is meaningless," and "To recommend one right over another, analysts must take their stand as naked normativists without the comfort of the Pareto-better cloak or any other formalism." In part because of this, then, the Institutionalists maintain that "[t]he distribution problem, viz., of power, income, wealth, opportunity, exposure, and sacrifice, is critical to legal-economic research and policy" (Samuels, 1975, p. 70).

This line of reasoning also leads Institutionalists to reject the efficiency theory of the common law. Any given rights structure will produce an efficient or wealth-maximizing outcome, and thus "The so-called efficiency of the common law is an 'empirical regularity' only in the sense that every common law specification of rights can produce an unique, wealth-maximizing outcome" (Samuels, 1981, p. 162). If different interests had been protected as rights, different efficient outcomes would have occurred. The choice of certain rights structures reflects a normative choice for a particular efficient pattern of law and economic development over time, where different decisions would have led to different patterns of efficient development. Thus, says Samuels (1981, p. 162), the literature purporting to explain the efficient development of the common law "'explains' everything and nothing." "Wealth maximization," he says, "cannot . . . explain the evolution of the common law: any developmental logic concerning rights in a market economy would have led the common law to some wealth-maximizing result" (Samuels, 1981, p. 154).

Consistent with their rejection of the efficiency theory of common law, proponents of Institutionalist law and economics also reject the theory of rent seeking (as described earlier in the chapter on Public Choice), which defines rent-seeking activities as "resource-wasting activities of individuals in seeking transfers of wealth through the aegis of the state" (Buchanan et al., 1980, ix). In this view, if scarce resources are expended by agents in an attempt to garner a privileged position (e.g., an exclusive monopoly franchise) from the state, or, if the state is used (e.g., through legislative activities or lobbying) to alter product and/or factor prices to enhance profits without a concomitant increase in output, such activities are termed rent seeking and deemed wasteful. The normative thrust of this theory thus becomes one of promoting policies designed to avoid wasteful, rent-seeking activities, which often involves a greater, more exclusive reliance on markets and a scaling back of government.

The intellectual construct employed by proponents of the rent-seeking literature is that of the competitive market economy and the legitimized product and factor prices and thus profits that obtain therefrom. Prices and profits that occur consequent to standard marketplace phenomena—such as the entering and exiting of firms into and from industries, adopting new technologies, altering the scale of plant, and so on—are all legitimate. However, when prices and profits are altered by and/or through the aegis of the state, this is said to result in waste.

From the standpoint of Institutional law and economics, this characterization of rent seeking is an exercise in selective perception and market legitimation (Samuels and Mercuro, 1984, pp. 55–70). As the Institutionalists have pointed out, to use today's market prices and profits as a basis to determine rents and wastes is to give propriety to extant laws governing the production of goods while at the same time selectively culling out one subset of rights to make claims of rent-seeking, wasteful activity. It is the proponents' reliance on the model of competition that gives effect to this selective perception. As is made clear in Institutionalist law and economics, models of the economy predicated on price-taking behavior are in reality models of rights-taking behavior. Market prices are not absolute, predetermined, and independent of law, but, rather, are a partial function of rights—the latter related directly to the government's ubiquitous role in creating, defining, assigning, enforcing, and altering rights. Moreover, it is emphasized that today's prevailing market prices of products and factors of production are all predicated upon the past use of the state and past rent-seeking activities. Market-generated product and factor prices that make up a firm's revenue-cost calculation are property-rights specific; as a consequence, so too is its net revenue calculation a function of rights. The government's role in the economy remains ubiquitous, and, accordingly, a theory that purports to identify rent-seeking behavior and the economic wastes therefrom begs the question. There are no *correct* rights, prices, profits, or correct structure of rents. Thus, rent-seeking theory is characterized as an artificial, misguided normative theory that will "mislead positive analysis and generate artificial distinctions and thereby provide no real basis for distinguishing between permissible and impermissible activities" (Samuels and Mercuro, 1984, p. 67).[20]

COMPARATIVE INSTITUTIONAL ANALYSIS

The foundation for an Institutionalist law and economics is thus a coming to grips with the interrelations between legal (broadly conceived) and economic processes. Samuels (1975, p. 72) identifies three efforts that are central to this process: (1) "models of legal-political and economic interaction" must be developed; (2) "objective, positive, empirical studies of government as both a dependent and independent variable, and of economic activity as both an input and an output of political-legal processes" must be undertaken; and (3) efforts must be made "to wed both theoretical and empirical analyses toward a self-consciously objective, positive comprehension of law and economics." According to Samuels (1975, p. 72), such analysis will serve the twin purposes of deepening the understanding of legal and economic processes and their interrelations, and provide "a more realistic and knowledgeable basis on which to predict the probable performance consequences of both political and economic change or reform."

The import of this becomes clear in the Institutionalist assertion that the essential normative element in political-legal-economic decision making means that a choice must be made between alternative efficiency-distributional results and hence between alternative political-legal-economic institutional structures. This, in turn, necessitates a comparative institutional approach to legal-economic analysis.[21] The institutional structure cannot, in this view, merely be assumed away or taken as given. Rather, it must be the subject of study and, more specifically, the legal-economic decision-making process must involve a comparison of the effects of institutional alternatives on social well-being.

The comparative institutional approach is general rather than partial (Samuels, 1972a, pp. 582, 585), and its scope consists in describing and analyzing "the systematic relationship between 1) the structure of political-legal-economic institutions, focusing on the rights and rules by which they operate; 2) the conduct or observed behavior in light of the incentives (penalties and rewards) created by the structure of institutions; 3) the consequent economic performance, i.e., the allocation *and* distribution of resources that determine the character of economic life under these institutions" (Mercuro, 1989, p. 11, emphasis in original).

The object, then, is to explain and compare the outcomes that will occur under real, discrete, alternative institutional structures, and to do so not just in terms of efficiency, but in terms of the distribution of income and wealth, employment rates, and any other factors that may affect the quality of life or the productive capacity of firms. Regarding this point, Samuels suggests that "[f]or law to be preoccupied solely with economic maximization would rob law of life and of much of what makes for human meaning and significance" (Samuels, 1981, p. 165). The goal here is not normative judgment, but description: "A viable approach to the study of the interrelations between law and economics should be content with describing the full array of economic impacts (including both the allocation and distribution of resources) of alternative institutions and legal arrangements together with an articulation of whose interests will be served and at whose expense" (Mercuro, 1989, p. 12). Such analysis will not privilege one set of interests over others, but it will enable those who study and participate in the processes of the legal-economic nexus to better understand these processes and their resulting effects on law and economy (Samuels, 1989a, p. 1578).[22]

But of course normative judgments must be made in the process of reaching legal decisions. Recognizing this, the institutional approach emphasizes the need for openness and values clarification in the political-legal-economic decision-making process, a legacy of the Legal Realist movement within the law (Samuels, 1989a, p. 1573). Economists, legal scholars, policymakers, and judges should strive to make the value premises underlying their conclusions as explicit as possible, so that the choice process can be effectuated "carefully and overtly" rather than "carelessly and covertly" (Samuels, 1978, p. 113).[23] This call for openness is clearly tied to the comparative institutional method:

Not only should normative premises be made explicit, but an array of studies should be conducted on the basis of *alternative* normative (and factual) assumptions. To do only one study is to give effect to only one perception and specification of outputs, costs, benefits, and rights. Alternative studies call attention to the subtle intrusion of ideology and partisanship, emphasize the necessary and inevitable critical choice of underlying values, highlight the fundamental distributional consequences that depend on the political determination of output definitions, and so forth. (Samuels, 1978, p. 112, emphasis in original)

The obfuscation of values and underlying normative premises within so much of the Chicago and Public Choice approaches to law and economics is the bane of the comparative institutional approach. Relying solely on the Pareto-efficiency criterion serves to obfuscate and impede the normative choice process that is necessarily at work in the legal-economic nexus.[24]

APPLICATIONS OF THE INSTITUTIONAL APPROACH

Application #1: Schmid—Structure and Performance

The Institutionalists' above-mentioned qualms about the overuse of efficiency analysis translate into an approach that is concerned not with making assessments based on abstract ideals, such as attaching labels of "efficient" or "inefficient" to particular legal rules or institutional structures, but with describing and making comparisons among the real alternatives that are open to society. As evidenced, for example, in Schmid (1987), such analysis takes place under a situation-specific structure-conduct-performance paradigm, in which alternative institutional structures (e.g., different definitions and assignments of property rights) and inherent sources of interdependency are identified. These, in turn, are linked to the (dis)incentives created and the consequences for individual, firm, and government behavior, and, in general, for economic performance and quality of life. As such, it reflects a "total" approach to policy analysis (Schmid, 1987, pp. 257–58), one that emphasizes the link between structure and performance.

To see how the institutional approach to these issues works, and how it contrasts with the mainstream economic approach, let us consider Schmid's example of water pollution and the choice between regulatory standards and charges (or user fees).[25] The conventional economic approach to this issue is to recommend charges (pollution taxes) over standards on the grounds that they are more efficient—they accomplish the same reduction in pollution at a lower cost.[26] The reasoning behind this is as follows. Regulatory standards mandate that, to accomplish an x percent reduction in pollution, each producer must reduce its discharge by this same x percent. However, this across-the-board approach does not take into account the fact that the costli-

ness of pollution abatement may vary widely across firms. Efficiency considerations would suggest that those who can reduce pollution at lower cost be
forced to bear a larger share of this burden, to accomplish this aggregate reduction in pollution at the minimum cost to society. The charges approach, in
contrast, sets a fee to be charged for each unit of pollution emitted. Under
such a scheme, each polluter will compare the cost of abating an additional
unit of pollution with the cost of the charge. Those firms that can abate pollution more cheaply will find it profitable to undertake relatively more abatement
(and thus less polluting) as compared to those firms with higher costs of abatement. Thus, a tax which is set at a level sufficient to achieve an x percent
reduction in aggregate pollution will have the effect of pushing a larger
share of the burden of this pollution reduction onto the firms with lower costs
of abatement and will, in the process, achieve the x percent reduction in pollution at a lower total cost than would obtain under the use of a regulatory
standard; that is, a system of charges is more efficient than the employment of
a regulatory standard.

Schmid (1987, pp. 264–65) maintains that such analysis is incomplete, in
that it focuses exclusively on costs, ignoring their distribution and thus the
differential effects of these policies across firms (see also Samuels and
Schmid, 1976). The comparative institutional approach toward law and economics that he advocates entails not only an examination of these differential
costs, but also of looking beyond them to the underlying property rights and
opportunity sets and their distributional implications. Schmid maintains that a
regulatory standard implies that each firm has a right to discharge a certain
quantity of waste,[27] whereas "third-party environmentalists" are given a de
facto ownership claim over the remaining share of the water. The use of regulatory standards, which require each firm to reduce its discharge by the same
percentage, holds the relative property rights of each firm constant at their
preregulatory levels.[28]

A charge on emissions alters the property rights and opportunity sets relationship, in that it implies that rights over the resource are owned by the government and that firms can, in a sense, purchase a portion of these rights by
paying the specified charge. Under this system, the firms with higher abatement costs are allowed to substitute the lower tax cum discharge costs for the
higher-cost abatement and thus receive a greater right to the use of the stream
than would obtain under the system of regulatory standards. As compared to
the standards scheme, we see, in effect, a transfer of rights to the use of the
stream from low-cost to high-cost abaters. And because the payments for these
rights to use the stream go to the government, rather than to the low-cost
abaters whose rights to the stream have been reduced, we also see a redistribution of income between the firms. Thus, the decision as to which abatement-
inducing scheme to adopt impacts the relative well-being of the firms in-

volved. One might expect, given the above, that low-cost abaters will prefer a regulatory scheme, whereas high-cost abaters will prefer a system of charges. This, and the size of each group, in turn will affect the relative pressures brought to bear upon government for one system versus the other.

As Schmid (1987, pp. 265–66) points out, the comparative institutional approach reveals that "[w]hen the rights of third-party environmentalists are expanded, a conflict arises between . . . industrial firms in the sharing of the costs of redistribution. Thus, there is a conflict between achieving equal treatment between two firms and achieving the lowest cost of attaining a given stream quality." The decision, then, is not simply about costs, but about the distribution of these costs between affected parties. Of course, the same analysis applies to the decision one step previous to that considered here—the distribution of rights between firms and third-party environmentalists; that is, the decision to adopt a policy to reduce pollution or to maintain the status quo. This decision influences the distribution of rights, and thus costs and incomes, between firms and third-party environmentalists. Decision making at either of these levels does not, under the comparative institutional approach, admit to an easy answer. The goal is an evaluation of the substantive effects of alternative policy mechanisms (institutional structures) on affected parties. But beyond this, the decision as to which institutional structure to adopt becomes fundamentally a choice as to whose interests are to count.

Application #2: Samuels—The Legal-Economic Nexus

A useful application of the conduct-oriented approach advocated by Samuels is found in his discussion of *Miller et al. v. Schoene*. This case revolved around a 1914 statute passed by the Virginia State legislature which gave the state entomologist the power to investigate, condemn, and destroy, without compensation, red cedar trees within a two-mile radius of an apple orchard if it could be shown that the red cedar trees constituted a menace to the health of the apple orchards. Red cedar rust, a fungus harmless to red cedar trees, is harmful to the leaves and fruit of apple trees and is known to migrate from the former to the latter, causing an economic loss to apple orchard owners. The plaintiffs—red cedar owners—argued that this statute unconstitutionally deprived them of their property without just compensation. The case made its way to the U.S. Supreme Court, where the Court denied the challenge to the statute. Speaking for the Court, Mr. Justice Stone wrote:

> On the evidence we may accept the conclusion of the Supreme Court of Appeals that the state was under the necessity of making a choice between the preservation of one class of property and that of the other wherever both existed in dangerous

proximity. It would have been none the less a choice if, instead of enacting the present statute, the state, by doing nothing, had permitted serious injury to the apple orchards within its borders to go on unchecked. When forced to such a choice the state does not exceed its constitutional powers by deciding upon the destruction of one class of property in order to save another which, in the judgment of the legislature, is of greater value to the public. (*Miller et al. v. Schoene*, pp. 279–80, quoted in Samuels, 1971, pp. 437–38)

Commenting on this decision, Samuels (1971, pp. 438–39) points out the manner in which Justice Stone's opinion brings to the fore the inevitable necessity of choice in resolving questions of rights, and does so in a manner that is clearly tied to the themes of the institutional approach to law and economics, set forth above, while eschewing the search for any globally efficient solution:

The state had to make a choice as to which property owner was to be made not only formally secure but practically viable in his legal rights. The Court, as part of the state, had to make a judgment as to which owner would be visited with injury and which protected. The state, ultimately the Court, had to decide which party would have what capacity to coerce the other, meaning by coercion the impact of one party of [sic] the actions of the other. There was a direct conflict between two private interests (between two private rights claimants) which required choice, and choice on the basis of some (rational) criterion, in the instant case involving the criterion(ia) which the legislature and the courts embodied or read into the concept of public interest, public value, or the public welfare, ultimately through the vehicle of the police power. (Samuels, 1971, pp. 438–39)

Samuels argues that, in the absence of the cedar rust statute, the structure of rights puts the apple orchard owners at a disadvantage in that the law gives the cedar tree owners the freedom to visit injury upon them. They are also, moreover, at a coercive disadvantage in that the burden of coming to an agreement that mitigates the damage lies with them and the flow of attendant payments runs from them to the red cedar owners. Under the cedar rust statute, just the opposite conditions obtain. The orchard owners are protected from harm, injury is visited upon the red cedar owners, and the coercive advantage rests with the orchard owners (the burden of coming to an agreement that mitigates injury to the red cedar owners lies with the red cedar owners), meaning that the flow of payment for mitigation of injury runs from the red cedar owners to the orchard owners (Samuels, 1971, p. 439). Thus, as Samuels notes, "relative rights . . . , the pattern of mutual coercion . . . , the distribution of relative risk, business costs . . . , resource allocation, income distribution and the general level of income are a partial function of law" (Samuels, 1971, p. 440). In other words, more generally, economic activity, performance, and conditions are a partial function of law.

As Samuels (1971, pp. 441–42) goes on to point out, this case is also illustrative of the inevitability of governmental presence within the legal-economic process. In the absence of the cedar rust statute, the government is, through the status quo rights structure, giving effect to the interests of the red cedar owners, to whose advantage the status quo works. Under the statute, of course, the government is giving effect to the interests of the apple orchard owners. The point to be made, according to Samuels, is that the government is equally present in either case: "government had to choose between the effective promotion of one group or the other: government is in both cases a participant in the economic decision making process." When the cedar rust statute was enacted, it did not accomplish "an intrusion of government into a situation in which it had hitherto been absent, but rather a change of the interests to which effective legal support would be given" (Samuels, 1971, p. 441).

This case is also suggestive of the issue of individuals/organizations using government (in a nonpejorative sense) for their own ends and thus, more generally, of the idea of using government to direct the allocation and distribution of resources within the economic system and hence the idea that economic performance and conditions are a partial function of who is able to use government for what ends. In the present case, we see two groups competing to influence or use government: the owners of the red cedar trees, which, as Samuels (1971, p. 443) notes, "are of primarily ornamental use, with some use and value as timber," and apple orchard owners, who make up a major industry in Virginia. As Samuels points out, the apple orchard owners were a well-organized and influential group, whereas the red cedar owners were not, and the legislature was sensitive to the relative strength, economic and political, of these two concerns. Perhaps not surprisingly, then, it responded by protecting the interests of the more economically important and politically influential group. Again, the point being made here is not a negative one, but simply that competing interests will attempt to influence (or use) government to promote their own ends in a world of scarcity and choice. As such, an understanding of the legal-economic process, and of the determinants of the outcomes generated within the economic system, cannot be obtained apart from the recognition that government is a player in the resolution of scarcity-based conflicts and that such resolutions are a function of the relative pressures brought to bear upon government and of who is able to secure the promotion of their interests through government.[29]

A further issue raised by this case is that of compensation for harm and its relation to rights, allocation, and distribution. The cedar rust statute did not provide for compensation to owners for the value lost in the destruction of the red cedar trees. Samuels maintains that the larger question is not really compensation versus no compensation, since to compensate for all injuries visited by the law of property, or even changes therein, would impose a nearly impossible financial burden on society. Rather, the question really becomes "*when should compensation be paid?*" (Samuels, 1971, p. 446, emphasis in original).[30] The issue of compensation is part of the question of who visits injury upon whom, and thus of one pattern of cost and income distribution versus another. In this situation, one is speaking not so much of (to take the present example) red cedar owners versus apple orchard owners, but of one party (the party who, in the absence of compensation, would be injured) versus society as a whole, which is forced to bear the burden of the compensation payments. That is, the law of property determines not only the allocation and distribution of resources and income across claimants to a particular dispute, but, through the compensation principle, across society as a whole. Thus, the question of the extent of the ability of government to impact the use of private property without compensation (the use and extent of the police power) has implications beyond the parties to specific disputes.

Thus, this case, says Samuels, brings to the fore a number of important aspects of the interrelations between legal and economic processes:

> There is, first of all, an existential necessity of choice over relative rights, relative capacity to visit injury or costs, and mutual coercive power (or claims to income). The economy, in which the legal process is so obviously involved, is a system of relative rights, of exposure to costs shifted by others, and of the coercive impact of others. In choosing between conflicting rights' claimants, furthermore, the choice is between one interest or another. The choice is over capacities to participate in the economic decision-making process. . . . These choices are a function of rights which are a function of law; so that, *inter alia*, income distribution—through relative claims to income—is a partial function of law. It is ineluctable, then, that government is involved in the fundamental character, structure, and results of the private sector. Policy issues thus become which or whose rights will government operate to effectively secure, which rights will government no longer operate to effectively secure and which new rights, that is, the use of government to change the effective pattern of rights or realization of interests. (Samuels, 1971, p. 442)

The overtly positive and even agnostic approach of institutional law and economics is not comforting to those who would seek refuge in determinate solutions to the questions of legal-economic policy, and some may well be inclined to dismiss it on this ground. Against this, Schmid responds, "If [institutional law and economics] has no dispositive answer to resolve policy arguments, what is it good for? It can identify many less than obvious sources of power in an economy so that people can know where their welfare comes from. It can raise the level of normative debate so that issues can be joined and people can live with tragic choices rather than ignoring and dismissing them"

(Schmid, 1994, pp. 36–37). Whereas singular solutions to legal-economic issues reflect only one particular set of value premises and one particular conception of the facts, benefits, and costs at issue, the comparative institutional approach, by recognizing the multiplicity of potential solutions and underlying value premises, attempts to flesh out the alternative possibilities that are open to society in the ongoing social construction and reconstruction of legal-economic reality.

CHAPTER 5

Neoinstitutional Law and Economics

[T]he state is a two-edged sword: "The existence of
a state is essential for economic growth; the state,
however, is the source of man-made decline."
(Eggertsson, 1990, p. 317, quoting North, 1981, p. 20)

INTRODUCTION

Neoinstitutional economics (NIE), like Institutionalism, begins with the fundamental premise that institutions are important factors in the determination of economic structure, and hence performance. With this basic insight as a starting point, the NIE draws on early work by scholars such as Armen Alchian (1959, 1961), Steven Cheung (1969, 1970), Ronald Coase (1960), Harold Demsetz (1964), and Oliver Williamson (1963) on the role of property rights within the economic system;[1] by Coase (1937, 1960) and George Stigler (1961) on the effects of transaction and information costs on the exchange process; and by Buchanan and Tullock (1962) on the analysis of collective choice processes in an attempt to explicate the underlying relations between institutional structure, institutional change, and economic performance. Within the institutional structure lies the legal framework of a society—in modern terms, the body of constitutional, statute, and common law, and agency rules, that serve, in part, as the basis for economic relations.

Many of the contributions to this approach to law and economics are found in the *Journal of Law, Economics, and Organization* and the *Journal of Institutional and Theoretical Economics*. Although the NIE is rather heterogeneous within itself, two fundamental building blocks of analysis can be identified. The first is that individuals are assumed to rationally pursue their self-interest, subject to constraint. These constraints are more numerous and severe than those of neoclassical economic theory. These include the definition (as well as existence) of property rights and transaction costs, as well as a recognition of the limited computational capacity of the human mind (as reflected in Herbert Simon's (1961, xxiv) concept of "bounded rationality," wherein human behavior is said to be *"intendedly* rational, but only *limitedly* so"). The second building block of the NIE (at least within many quarters) is the idea of wealth maximization—the search for institutional structures that enhance society's wealth-producing capacity. The NIE also, from a more positive perspective, attempts to analyze the role of different institutional structures in giving rise to differential economic performance across time.

Douglass North (1990b, p. 3) defines institutions as "the rules of the game in a society or, more formally, . . . the humanly devised constraints that shape human interaction." As such, he says, these institutions "structure incentives in human exchange, whether political, social, or economic." These institutions include both formal rules, such as the law, and informal mechanisms, such as customs, conventions, and codes of conduct. Our discussion here will focus on formal legal mechanisms. The NIE analysis of institutions focuses on three central concepts: property rights, contracting, and transaction costs. *"Property rights,"* says Gary Libecap (1989a, p. 1, emphasis added), "are the social institutions that define or delimit the range of privileges granted to individuals to specific assets," and as such function in the determination of the value of an asset by setting the range of its productivity or exchangability. These rights may be endogenous or exogenous to individual actors. *Contracting* is the process through which property rights are established, assigned, or modified (Libecap, 1989a, p. 4; Eggertsson, 1990, p. 45). Thus, underlying the process of exchange—the physical transfer of assets—is the transacting, or contracting, process, wherein the legal rights to these assets are transferred.[2] In contrast, neoclassical economic theory focuses on exchange, which is sometimes simultaneous with and sometimes subsequent to the actual transaction. Moreover, the possibilities and limitations of exchange are a function of the transactional or contracting framework—the legal structure, the discussion of which is virtually absent from neoclassical theory. Within the NIE, contracting is seen to proceed both at a microlevel, wherein private individuals or groups bargain over rights, and at a macrolevel, wherein private individuals or groups, and/or politicians, and/or bureaucrats, and/or judges bargain over the basic legal framework which establishes social, legal, and economic structure (Libecap, 1989a, p. 4). *Transaction costs*, like contracting, proceed at multiple levels, but can be conceptualized, in a general sense, as the costs associated with the creation, maintenance, or modification of institutions, such as property rights.[3] Thus, at the microlevel, transaction costs consist of those costs associated with contracting between private parties, whereas, at the macrolevel, transaction costs may be said to consist of the costs involved in the bargaining process through which the institutional framework of society is established or modified (Furubotn and Richter, 1991, p. 8; Eggertsson, 1990, pp. 14–15).

As the above discussion suggests, the NIE analysis proceeds at two different levels, one more macro-oriented and the other more micro-oriented. These levels of analysis are perhaps best described by Davis and North (1971, pp. 6–7, quoted in Williamson, 1993a, p. 53), who draw a distinction between the institutional environment (macro) and institutional arrangements, or what Williamson (1993a, p. 53) calls the "institutions of governance" (micro):

The *institutional environment* is the set of fundamental political, social and legal ground rules that establishes the basis for production, exchange and distribution. Rules governing elections, property rights, and the right of contract are examples. . . .

An *institutional arrangement* is an arrangement between economic units that governs the ways in which these units can cooperate and/or compete. It . . . [can] provide a structure within which its members can cooperate . . . or [it can] provide a mechanism that can effect a change in laws or property rights. (emphasis in original)

In fact, however, the institutional environment and institutional arrangements are interactive, in that the institutional environment sets the general framework within which institutional arrangements take place, whereas institutional arrangements, their effects, or the difficulties in devising them may effect pressures for change in the institutional environment. As the legal-economic analysis of the NIE proceeds at these two levels, our discussion will treat each of these in turn.

THE LEGAL-ECONOMIC ANALYSIS OF
INSTITUTIONAL ENVIRONMENTS

As noted above, formal rules make up an important part of a society's institutional structure. North (1990b, p. 47) distinguishes between three types of formal rules that govern relations within a society.[4] First, the *political rules* of a society "broadly define the hierarchical structure of the polity, its basic decision structure, and the explicit characteristics of agenda control." Second, the *economic rules* "define property rights, that is, the bundle of rights over the use and income to be derived from property and the ability to alienate an asset or resource." Finally, *contracts* "contain the provisions specific to a particular agreement in exchange." Taken together, these rules, by defining opportunity sets, facilitate political and economic exchange—be it within the existing institutional structure or to change the institutional structure—that leads to gains from trade and thus increases in wealth. These rules are also interdependent, and the causation is multidirectional. That is, although a given set of political rules will give rise to a particular set of economic rules which in turn structures contracts, it is also the case that pressure for new forms of contractual structure can lead to changes in economic and political rules (North, 1989, p. 662). Much of the legal-economic analysis of institutional environments has been carried out within the so-called property rights approach to economic analysis, and is exemplified in the work of North (e.g., 1981, 1990b), Yoram Barzel (1989), Libecap (1989a,b), and Steven Cheung (1969, 1970).[5]

Common Pools, Property Rights, and Transaction Costs

The importance of property rights in economic analysis and performance rests on two facets of their operation.[6] First, property rights determine ownership as well as benefits and costs of resource use and the allocation thereof across individuals, and thus structure the incentives that determine economic behavior and performance. Second, property rights define the set of actors within an economic system by "assigning to specific individuals the authority to decide how specific resources may be used" (De Alessi and Staaf, 1989, p. 179). In doing so, property rights determine the distribution of wealth and power within an economic system. Different property rights structures thus give rise to differential opportunity sets and differential allocations of benefits and costs among economic agents and thereby affect economic choices through their respective structures of incentives and constraints.

To understand the role played by property rights within an economic system, we must begin by conceptualizing a situation in which (private) property rights are absent, that is, where individuals "lack exclusive, transferable rights to the use of [a] resource" (De Alessi, 1980, p. 5). Early analyses by H. Scott Gordon (1954), Demsetz (1967), Hardin (1968), and Cheung (1970) of such common pool situations reveal that, except where supply exceeds demand at a zero price, the absence of property rights generates common pool losses owing to overexploitation of the common pool resources, as the absence of private rights reduces the incentives of individuals to consider the full social costs of their actions. Consider, for example, a situation of agricultural land over which no private rights are assigned. If Farmer A were to allow land that he cultivates to lie fallow for a year, so as to let the soil regenerate, then, under a common property rights structure, Farmer B would likely step in and cultivate that land himself, thus frustrating A's purpose. Farmer A has no incentive to let the land lie fallow, and the productivity of the land will eventually be reduced, to the detriment of society. And indeed, Anthony Bottomly's (1963) analysis of land use in Tripolitania suggests that lands held in common had lower crop yields on average than privately held lands. Similarly, Richard Agnello and Lawrence Donnelley (1975) show that oyster harvests are substantially higher in common property rights situations than under private property rights structures, an effect that will, in the long run, lead to lower yields in the commonly held beds. In addition, a reduced incentive to invest in the development of these common pool resources (due to the inability of the investors to capture sufficient returns from their investments in a common pool situation), the difficulty, if not impossibility, of attempting to transfer such resources to higher-valued uses, and excessive expenditures on loss-preventing activities (e.g., trying to prevent others from appropriating your crops, which are not protected by private property rights), all contribute to the losses associated with common property rights (Libecap, 1989a, pp. 12–13).

The question that emerges, then, is one of why we observe common pool situations in the first place, or, why we do not observe well-defined, fully specified property rights over all of society's resources. Part of the answer, due to Coase (1960), is that there are costs to establishing and enforcing property rights, and individuals or groups will only devote resources to securing the establishment of or a change in property rights when they perceive that the benefits from such a change will outweigh the costs. Thus, although common property rights result in common pool losses, they save the costs of specifying and enforcing private property rights. Alternatively, although private property rights minimize common pool losses, they involve costs of specification and enforcement which may be sufficiently large that a society is either unable or unwilling to incur them in order to bring private property rights into existence (Cheung, 1992, p. 59). As explained in chapter 2, common pool problems would not exist in a world of zero transaction costs, since parties could costlessly bargain to realize the gains that would accompany a more fully developed rights structure. The point to be made here is that high transaction costs may serve to preclude the realization of the gains that accompany the establishment of private property rights.

Taking this a step further, we recognize, following Becker (1965) and Lancaster (1966), that individuals derive utility, not from goods and services per se, but from the various attributes of a good or the various separate activities that go into the performance of a service. Thus, a plot of land is not just a plot of land per se, but a bundle of attributes including the extent of its agricultural productivity, aesthetic qualities, or potential for commercial development of various kinds. Similarly, the automobile is a bundle of attributes that includes power, fuel economy, comfort, quality, and even image, and these attributes and their extent function prominently in determining resource value. The result is that exchange is not merely the transference of goods and services, but of bundles of diverse attributes and activities.

Given the presence of imperfect information, individuals must incur measurement costs in attempting to determine the nature of these valuable attributes or activities, or, more specifically, the rights over them, and these attributes must be defined and measured in order to be transferable in exchange. That is, a resource can be defined not only by its technical properties, but also by the bundle of rights of which it is made up. As the number and variety of attributes or activities increases, so too do the costs of measurement and thus the complexity of exchange (North, 1990b, p. 29). Other factors, such as the degree of observability of a resource or the extent to which a resource is migratory, will also influence measurement costs (Libecap, 1989a, p. 26). Given that these attributes have value, measurement problems will contribute to the costliness of exchange by causing the parties to a potential exchange to expend resources in the attempt to determine these attributes and their values. And because measurement costs are positive, rights will never be fully specified over all attributes, as the expected benefits of more fully specified rights will at some point be outweighed by the expected costs of measurement (North, 1990a, pp. 191–92; Barzel, 1989, pp. 64–65). Thus, the greater are the costs of measurement of attributes/rights associated with a given resource, the less well-defined will be the property rights associated with it, and thus the greater will be the extent to which the development or exchange of that resource is inhibited.[7]

Because of the problematic nature of measuring certain attributes, and because of the incentives for individuals to engage in opportunistic behavior—attempts to, in various ways, increase one's benefits from an exchange agreement by, for example, shirking or concealing information—the problem of enforcement also comes into play in the exchange process. Although instantaneous transactions over unidimensional goods would be easy to enforce, with exchange relationships over multidimensional goods and/or relationships that occur over time and space, there is the risk that self-interest-seeking individuals will fail to live up to the agreement, and thus some enforcement mechanism is necessary to induce individuals to form such exchange relationships (North, 1990b, p. 33; 1993b, p. 247). The difficulty, of course, is that enforcement, although having the benefit of reducing uncertainty in the exchange environment, is costly. In addition to the costs of having an enforcement mechanism in place, enforcement costs arise due to the costs of detecting and measuring violations and of imposing penalties on the violators (North, 1990b, p. 58). Even then, however, the fact that enforcement is costly and may be carried out by agents whose well-being is impacted by the outcomes will mean that certain rights are left unspecified, and that enforcement of some specified property rights will be less than perfect. Because of this, certain valuable attributes/rights will remain in the public domain, and individuals may have an incentive to expend resources in the attempt to capture this value, as well as to defend against its capture by others. Because of these potential conflicts, individuals have an incentive to structure contracts in such a way that these adverse incentive effects are minimized.

The extent to which complex exchange can proceed within a society is a function of the ability of agents to transact within a contractual framework which minimizes the degree of uncertainty about contractual performance (North, 1990b, p. 34). In order to have complex exchange (i.e., for the benefits of such exchange to outweigh the costs), it is necessary that some institutional mechanisms exist which induce potential parties to exchange to incur the relevant transaction costs and/or agree to exchange in the presence of imperfectly delineated property rights. Because of the difficulty of designing self-enforcing contracts for complex exchanges, it is in the interests of the parties and/or society to develop enforcement institutions.[8] One sees this evidenced among private parties through mechanisms such as private third-party mediation or arbitration. However, historical evidence suggests that a well-organized system of complex exchange within a society cannot proceed without a political order (North, 1990b, pp. 34–35, 54; Libecap, 1989a). Eggertsson (1990, p. 317) expresses this point forcefully: "Without the state, its institutions, and the supportive framework of property rights, high transaction costs will paralyze complex production systems, and specific investments in long-term exchange relationships will not be forthcoming." Even more to the point is North (1993b, p. 245), who says that the effectiveness with which agreements are enforced "is the single most crucial determinant of economic performance." The state, says North (1981, p. 27, quoted in Eggertsson, 1990, p. 320), seems to have a comparative advantage in the sort of enforcement institutions that facilitate exchange: "The economies of scale associated with devising a system of law, justice, and defense are the underlying source of civilization." The formal rules of the state work with and/or in place of informal constraints (custom, reputation, etc.) and, by lowering the various transaction costs associated with exchange, promote the formation of more complex exchange agreements.

Based on the foregoing, then, we can say that transaction costs arise primarily due to information costs, which consist of the costs "of contracting and negotiating, . . . of measuring and policing property rights, of engaging in politics for power, of monitoring performances, and of organizing activities" (Cheung, 1992, p. 51). A study by John Wallis and North (1986) shows that transaction costs made up 45 percent of gross national product in the United States in 1970. Because of the magnitude of these costs, the proponents of the NIE approach argue that many otherwise wealth-creating transactions will not take place, with the result that resources will not necessarily flow to their highest-valued uses. The legal/social/economic system plays an important role in determining the allocation of resources in society, in part through its impact on the cost of transacting. Specifically, new legal arrangements can affect production and exchange by reducing transaction costs, thereby allowing resources to flow to higher-valued uses (North, 1990b, p. 31). There is an additional issue here, which North does not touch on: Exchange is costly, but the cost of transacting falls both on the traders and on "society" or the state. Therefore, those who transact do not consider all the costs involved, and information costs prevent the state from knowing the efficient amount of state enforcement. As a result of the foregoing considerations, the net gains from exchange are the standard gains of neoclassical economic theory, less the costs of measurement, enforcement, and those costs that arise because measurement and enforcement are imperfect (North, 1990b, p. 31).

De Alessi's (1990, p. 8) characterization of the bundle of rights that attends a resource is indicative of how property rights affect the use of, income streams from, and transferability of resources: "The bundle of rights associated with a particular resource typically is partitioned; some rights may be held in common with open access (i.e., are non-exclusive and non-transferable), some may be limited to usufruct (i.e., are exclusive but non-transferable), and still others may be private (i.e., are both exclusive and transferable)." By so defining the constraints facing the owner, the property rights bundle affects the individual choice process and the uses to which resources are ultimately put.[9] As one moves across the spectrum from private to usufruct to common property rights, the incentives to economize on resource use in socially optimal ways becomes weaker, and thus the associated welfare losses tend to rise (De Alessi, 1980, p. 40).

Thus, the analysis of property rights formation and transformation demands an awareness of individual and group preferences (which govern perceived benefits) and economic and social factors that create opportunities and incentives for establishing or altering property rights, and those factors that contribute to the costs of establishing and enforcing a particular property rights regime. In addition, we must investigate "the general mechanism through which changes in cost-benefit calculations are translated into the development of property rights" (Furubotn and Richter, 1991, p. 16).

Property Rights Establishment and Change: Incentives and Politics

We have seen, in the above discussion, how the establishment of or changes in property rights can promote wealth-enhancing exchanges. How, then, are property rights established or changed? Furubotn and Richter (1991, p. 16) provide a succinct answer to this question: New property rights and changes in property rights come about "because certain individuals or groups within an economy believe it profitable to restructure the system and are willing to bear the costs of bringing about such change."[10] That is, the current property rights structure and/or associated informal constraints (e.g., custom) may be incapable of supporting newly developed opportunities for wealth-creating exchanges, leading to a demand for new or revised rights. This may occur due to changes in relative prices, in production or enforcement technology, or in individual preferences or certain political parameters (Libecap, 1989a, p. 16). For example, Demsetz (1967) shows how the evolution of the commercial fur trade in Canada, which increased the value of beaver pelts, and thus the amount of hunting, was followed within fifty years by the establishment of private property rights in beavers within the Indian communities. Similarly, Terry Anderson and P. J. Hill (1975) have examined how the development of economical means of fencing off lands—largely with barbed wire fencing—made the enforcement of private rights more economical and thus helped to stimulate the development of private land rights in the western United States. However, although such changes bring about the economic benefits associated with private property rights structures, they do not come without cost, which, aside from the costs of enforcing rights, include the bargaining costs associated with seeking change through the "political" process (broadly defined to encompass the efforts to reach bargains over rights structures within a community). Yet, if expected benefits are large, it will often pay to devote resources to lobbying efforts, including the establishment of formal lobbying organizations, in the attempt to effect change through the "political" process.

In modern economic systems, the establishment or change of property rights institutions is a contracting process that takes place within, and thus reflects the preferences of and constraints upon those operating within, the political arena. Pressures supporting and opposing new or changed rights structures will be brought to bear by those who stand to gain or lose under the proposed system, and the greater is the share of society's resources impacted by the proposed change, the greater will be the expenditure on offensive and defensive efforts by affected parties (North, 1990b, p. 87). The result is a bargaining process wherein each group seeks as large a share of the potential gains as it can get and wherein it will give its approval attendant outcome only if it expects to be at least as well off as under the status quo. Given a situation in which institutional change will result in net gains to society, the barrier to change is the problem of devising a method (which may include compensating losers) to allocate these gains in a way that will result in the adoption of the change, while still maintaining, to the greatest extent possible, the productive (wealth-enhancing) advantages of the change. This latter issue arises because different distributions alter the nature of property rights and thus the size of the potential gain from their establishment or change (Libecap, 1989b, pp. 215–16). That is, if, to secure agreement, those who gain are forced to compensate some of those who lose from the proposed change, it may be that the resulting net gains to the winners are reduced sufficiently to cause them to withdraw their support for the endeavor. The result, then, is that a wealth-enhancing change is not accomplished.

The ability to reach such an agreement through the political process is a function of (1) the size of the expected gain (larger expected gains increase the likelihood of being able to reach agreements); (2) the number of bargaining parties and (3) the extent to which their interests converge (fewer bargaining parties and more convergent interests increase the likelihood of agreement); (4) the extent to which information is imperfect (which affects the ability to accurately ascertain gains and losses and thus structure the appropriate side-payments to compensate powerful "losing" interests for supporting the change, as well as affecting the potential for deception among the various bargaining parties); and (5) the distribution of the gains (the extent to which benefits are broadly versus narrowly concentrated, with more narrow concentrations reducing the likelihood of reaching an agreement because too many interests will be harmed) (Libecap, 1989a, pp. 21–26).

The political process exists, at least in part, to facilitate exchange between various interest groups. As such, this political bargaining process reflects the pressures brought to bear by interest groups supporting the maintenance of the status quo or various changes in the status quo. Legislators, who wish to maximize their reelection potential, will endeavor to respond to the interests of those groups who can most greatly impact their reelection possibilities. Because of the divergence of interests that often occurs within society, a clear majority for or against a proposal may not emerge, forcing legislators who strongly favor certain causes to attempt to strike deals with other legislators who have different favorite causes. A legislator will attempt to strike bargains which induce others to vote for projects that provide relatively large benefits for his constituents, while offering in exchange to vote for things that impose low costs on his constituents, the end result being that, if the exchange is consummated, he will have provided a net gain (hopefully substantial) to his constituents. This may sound similar to the logrolling process of Public Choice theory, but the NIE approach is in fact different in that it recognizes that such bargains, which are made at a given point in time, in fact are carried out over time; that is, one action is given today with a promise, or commitment, for a reciprocal action in the future. The time element raises the potential for opportunistic behavior by legislators (e.g., refusing to vote as promised or attempting to reverse legislation voted for as part of a promise) or for altered performance by legislators which constitutes an honest response to altered circumstances (e.g., alterations in voter preferences or certain political circumstances) rather than opportunistic behavior.[11] What we have here is a process through which legislators are trading rights (North, 1990b, p. 50).

Given the existence of imperfect information, the question then becomes: "How does credible commitment evolve to enable agreements to be reached when the payoffs are in the future and on completely different issues?" (North, 1990b, p. 51). Although both self-enforcement and reputation effects play a role here, North suggests that they are of limited effectiveness because of the costs of measurement and enforcement. More generally, Eggertsson (1990, p. 71) suggests that "[i]n exchanges between politicians, transaction costs tend to be high because there is no powerful third party that helps to enforce contracts in these areas, unlike the situation in the marketplace." The result is the development of political institutions which resolve these enforcement problems, or, as Eggertsson (1990, p. 72) puts it, which serve as "capital structures designed to produce a flow of stable policy outcomes." North (1990b, p. 50) says that we see "political institutions [which] constitute ex ante agreements among politicians. They reduce uncertainty by creating a stable structure of exchange. The result is a complicated system of committee structure, consisting of both formal rules and informal methods of organization." The organizational structures of political bodies are adopted in an effort to reduce transaction costs that may impede consummation of political changes. Although not eliminating transaction costs, the agenda rules and committee structures of legislatures assign defined committee jurisdictions (in effect, property rights) over certain types of legislation, making outcomes less subject to the vagaries of majoritarian processes (Weingast and Marshall, 1988).

The property rights structure that exists at any given point in time, or that develops through the political bargaining process, will thus be determined by these political bargaining issues and their resolution, along with the technological issues surrounding the ability to define, measure, and enforce property rights claims (Libecap, 1989a, p. 12). Because of heterogeneity among competing interest groups and the often-sizable stakes of the game, it is likely that there will often be substantial conflict over changes in property rights, and, as a result, "institutional change is likely to be an incremental process with modest adjustments from status quo conditions" (Libecap, 1989b, p. 220). Moreover, although exchange leads to efficiency in the frictionless (zero transaction cost) Walrasian world, and although the above discussion suggests that property rights will be created or altered when it is efficient to do so (i.e., when the benefits exceed the costs), we do, in fact, see inefficient property rights arrangements in the real world. There is no guarantee that the outcomes of political exchange will be efficient property rights institutions. In fact, although the political rules are designed to facilitate exchange by lowering transaction costs, we frequently see inefficient property rules. Such inefficiency, says North (1990b, pp. 51–52), is a manifestation of inefficiency within the political exchange process, inefficiency which exists due to, for example, agency problems between legislator and constituent or between legislator and bureaucrat, rational ignorance on the part of constituents, a desire not to offend powerful interests by enacting rules which, although efficient, go against their interests, or a preference by politicians for an inefficient rights structure because it generates more tax revenue. Thus, although low transaction costs and accurate information will result in the adoption of efficient property rights structures, the frequent lack of such conditions makes inefficient rights structures a condition of economic life. As Eggertsson (1990, p. 317, quoting North, 1981, p. 20) suggests, "the state is a two-edged sword: 'The existence of a state is essential for economic growth; the state, however, is the source of man-made decline.'"

THE LEGAL-ECONOMIC ANALYSIS OF INSTITUTIONAL ARRANGEMENTS

We have seen from the above discussion that formal rules, and enforcement mechanisms generally, are costly to establish and maintain, and, in many cases, the costs of further formal mechanisms may exceed the gains, meaning that, even in the presence of the state, enforcement will be less than perfect.

Because formal and informal rules/constraints will not be sufficient to ensure contractual performance, the only way to ensure performance—and thus provide the greatest possible incentive to engage in wealth-enhancing exchange relationships—is to make it in each party's interest to live up to the agreement. That is, the institutional environment can only do so much; institutional arrangements become important relative to specific cases.

Whereas the institutional environment provides a set of rules, or a framework, within which production, exchange, and distribution go on, institutional arrangements, or governance structures, determine the specific set of functional relations between parties to a production, exchange, or distribution process. For example, whereas the basic rules of contracting help determine the contractual environment, specific contractual agreements constitute the institutional arrangements or governance structures, which determine production, exchange, and distribution. Within the evolving literature on institutional arrangements, the most extensive research has gone into the governance processes of production—that is, firm relationships, and thus the major emphasis of this discussion will be on the contracting processes of firms.[12]

The importance of contracting/institutional arrangements is well described by Cheung (1992, p. 56), who says that "[a]lmost every individual in our society is a contractor, or a sub-contractor, or a sub-sub-contractor, and we all compete. Subject to enforcement costs, the written and unwritten terms of contracts dictate how production and exchange activities are organized and .conducted. It is the observed contractual or institutional arrangements that require explanation." Contracts are the vehicles that facilitate exchange, which can run the gamut from simple market exchange to the internal exchange of the vertically integrated firm, and different exchange mechanisms require different forms of contractual arrangement. One of the central concerns of the NIE is the logic of the various contractual arrangements that are observed in the real world, and why particular types of contractual arrangements dominate others in a given context. This topic will be given extensive treatment below. The choice of contractual arrangements is a function of several factors, including transaction costs, risk, legal/political arrangements, social customs, and the technical attributes of the assets involved in the contracting process. The NIE posits that the goal of the agents involved in the contracting process is to select or devise contractual forms (within the limits allowed/enforceable by law) that minimize transaction costs. Two distinct (although related) approaches to contracting can be identified within the NIE—the property rights/agency approach and the transaction cost approach.

Whereas neoclassical economics assumes that contracts are fully defined, instantaneously consumated, and perfectly enforced by the courts, making the identity of the contracting parties essentially irrelevant, the property rights/ agency and transaction cost approaches recognize both that these assumptions are often not reflective of real-world contracting processes—and attempt to deal with the fact that observed contracts are often incomplete and are carried out over time—and that judicial enforcement is both imperfect and, in many instances, bypassed by the contracting parties in favor of alternative dispute resolution mechanisms. Each of these approaches casts the analysis of the contracting process in a somewhat different light, and we will examine them in turn.

Property Rights, Agency, and the Contracting Process

Although much of the literature within the property rights approach focuses on the analysis of institutional environments, this approach has also been fruitfully applied to the analysis of institutional arrangements and, specifically, the contracting process. This is only natural given that contracts function as a mechanism to transfer property rights between economic agents. Cheung (1970, p. 50) describes this in a way that clearly links the issues of contracting to the importance of property rights: "Combining resources of several owners for production involves partial or outright transfers of property rights through a contract. A contract for the partial transfer of rights, such as leasing or hiring, embodies a *structure*. The stipulations, or terms, which constitute the structure of the contract are, as a rule, designed to specify (a) the distribution of income among the participants, and (b) the conditions of resource use."

As Cheung goes on to point out, prices are often only one of many terms specified within the contract. Other terms may deal with the timing of deliveries, quality assurance, and mechanisms to deal with the risks of nonperformance. Moreover, as North (1990b, p. 52) suggests, the institutional environment, of which property rights are a central component, plays a fundamental role in setting the parameters for the contracting process by establishing the incentives and constraints which individuals face. The contracts that we observe, then, will reflect the opportunity sets and incentives embedded in the existing property rights structure.

The vast majority of contracting in modern capitalist economies is effectuated with firms as buyers and/or sellers, and often within the firm itself. Because of this, the NIE literature on contracting—and thus the discussion in this section and in the subsequent section on transaction cost economics—focuses primarily on the firm.[13] The NIE view of the firm posits the firm as a nexus of contractual relationships. The firm's contracting relationships exist with the suppliers of various input goods and services to the firm, including the employment relation and production relationships internal to the firm, and those to whom the firm sells the goods and services that it produces. Given the extent and diversity of potential contracting relations, the law of contracts and the form of contractual relationships play a crucial role in determining the organizational structure of the firm. Specifically, the NIE hypothesis is that "business firms exist to reduce postcontractual opportunistic behavior by lowering the cost of monitoring exchange (including effort) and directing the allocation of joint cooperating units" (De Alessi and Staaf, 1989, pp. 180–81).

An important problem that arises within the transacting (or contracting) process is that of agency: "An agency relationship is established when a principal delegates some rights—for example, user rights over a resource—to an agent who is bounded by a (formal or informal) contract to represent the principal's interests in return for payment of some kind" (Eggertsson, 1990, pp. 40–41). Agency relationships exist in many forms, including owner-manager, manager-worker, voter-legislator, legislator-bureaucrat. The central problem of agency is that the goals of the agent may not correspond exactly to those of the principal, which necessitates some sort of monitoring to ensure that the agent's behavior reflects the principal's interests. Because monitoring is costly, however, it is usually unfeasible or impossible for principals to perfectly monitor agent performance, thus giving rise to the possibility of opportunistic behavior, such as shirking, on the part of the agent when the principal's and agent's interests diverge. This opportunistic behavior imposes two types of costs on the principal: the direct agency cost that arises due to opportunistic behavior on the part of the agent, and the monitoring cost that accompanies attempts by the principal to monitor agent performance. Because monitoring is costly, the principal will incur additional monitoring costs only as long as the reduction in direct agency cost is greater than the additional monitoring cost. The result which obtains will almost certainly include some (and often some substantial) amount of direct agency cost.

For example, whereas the utility of a firm's owner (the principal) is a direct function of the firm's profits, the employee's (agent's) utility, which is a function of, among other things, income and leisure, may be maximized through behavior on the job which does not serve to maximize the firm's profits. That is, the worker may have an incentive to shirk because the reduction in work effort (which lowers the firm's profits) does not result in a corresponding reduction in the worker's income. Thus, the owner will wish to monitor the employee in an attempt to ensure that the employee's behavior furthers the owner's interests—that is, maximizes the firm's profits. However, the inability of the owner to fully monitor employee performance leads to a scenario in which the worker has some incentive to shirk. These monitoring and incentive issues are especially important where production is organized on a team basis.[14] If the contribution to team output generated by each member of the team is difficult to measure, each member of the team has an incentive to shirk. Moreover, if the monitor (or manager) is unable to capture the full returns to monitoring, the monitor too has an incentive to shirk.[15] Given this, and the costliness of monitoring, the issue becomes one of establishing an incentive system whereby shirking is discouraged.

It will sometimes be the case that the forces of competition are sufficient to vitiate these types of monitoring problems. For example, competition among teams or for "membership" on teams may be sufficiently powerful to induce forthright efforts on the part of teams or team members. Similarly, competition in the market for monitors/managers may be sufficient to largely eliminate monitor/manager shirking. In many instances, however, an absence of sufficient competition or information about performance may make such solutions problematic.[16]

In the absence of efficacious competition or low-cost information provision that facilitates effective control of agent performance, principals can attempt to reduce agency costs through appropriately structured contracts—that is, contracts that attempt to align the agent's interests with those of the principal. One prominent manifestation of such incentive-alignment schemes in modern employer-employee contracts is the profit-sharing arrangement. Here the employer offers the employee a share of the firm's profits as a performance bonus. The employee's income, then, is tied not just to the wage, but also to overall firm performance, to which the worker contributes through his or her work effort. The effect is that the incentives of the employee are aligned more closely to the employer's interests, thereby inducing the employee to perform in a manner that corresponds more closely to the employer's interests.

Alternatively, consider the situation of an owner-manager who decides to sell a portion of his equity in the firm.[17] Because he now owns less than the full equity value of the firm, the cost to him of expending firm resources on various perquisites, as well as the benefits to him from seeking out new, profit-enhancing activities for the firm, are correspondingly reduced. However, the ability of prospective shareholders in the firm to anticipate these incentives leads them to recognize that resources will have to be expended to monitor the manager's performance. The shareholders, in turn, will reduce the price that they are willing to pay for ownership shares, thereby increasing the cost to the owner-manager of raising capital in equity markets. These effects (on the owner-manager's incentive to indulge in perquisites and to increase firm profitability, and hence on the level of monitoring costs and the reduction in willingness to pay for a given equity share) will be greater, the lower is the share of the owner-manager's equity in the firm.

One method by which agents may attempt to guarantee their performance is through bonding, which is a situation where, within the contracting process, the agent offers the principal some collateral as security against the agent's opportunistic behavior (Eggertsson, 1990, p. 42). Within the shareholder-manager example above, this bonding may take the form of "contractual guarantees to have the financial accounts audited by a public accountant, explicit bonding against malfeasance on the part of the manager, and contractual limitations on the manager's decision making power" (Jensen and Meckling, 1976, p. 325). However, these bonding activities impose costs on the firm by increasing the cost of contracting and/or by imposing direct costs on the firm through, for example, the hiring of auditors or the foregone profit opportunities that arise because the manager cannot always take full advantage of these opportunities due to the restrictions on his behavior.

These agency problems may also be seen in contracts between firms, such as where one firm contracts to supply inputs to another firm. Here we have, in essence, a reciprocal principal-agent problem wherein neither party can be absolutely certain that the other party will perform as agreed in the contract. For example, the buyer may have concerns about on-time delivery, whereas the seller may have concerns about potential modification or cancellation of the order by the buyer. When at least one party has a strong interest in performance that accords with the specific contractual terms, it may be in the interest of the parties to insert, say, penalty clauses into the contract for failure to perform in accordance with the agreement. Although the insertion of such clauses entails additional bargaining costs, the parties will be willing to bargain over such clauses if the expected incentive-alignment benefits outweigh the expected bargaining costs.

More generally, because of imperfect measurement and enforcement, one party may be able to affect the value of certain attributes of the resource in question. The solution is to structure the contract so as to make this party a residual claimant over those attributes, thus giving this party an incentive to maximize the value of these attributes. More specifically, the greater is the extent to which an individual can influence the value of an asset, the greater should be the extent of their claim over the value of, or the income from, that asset (Barzel, 1989, p. 41; North, 1990a, pp. 187–88). For example, by structuring the monitor's contract so as to give him some residual claim over the returns to the monitoring function, one reduces the monitor's incentive to shirk.[18] In the realm of quality assurance in goods markets, since manufacturers have relatively more control over the short-term quality or durability of an asset, the warranty or guarantee places on them the responsibility for making good on defects that occur over short time horizons and thus gives the manufacturer an incentive to take cost-justified quality-assurance steps. In the longer term, however, the buyer's use of the asset has an important effect on its continued quality or durability. The fact that some or all of the warranty terms expire after a comparatively short period gives the buyer relatively more responsibility for those factors that he can affect and frees the producer from being victimized by opportunistic behavior on the part of the buyer.

These same issues also influence the organizational structure of the firm—that is, the decision to contract with an outside supplier or organize a set of transactions internally.[19] When a contract is incomplete, the right to determine outcomes regarding the missing elements of the contract lies with the agent who has property rights over the nonhuman assets in question (that is, residual rights of control). For example, suppose that A contracted with B for B to deliver X units of a good to A. However, A later determines that it needs X + e units of the good instead. However, B has the residual rights of control here (it controls the manufacture of the good) and will only sell these additional units to A if A meets its price (or not at all if B has more pressing matters). The situation is very different if A owns B, however. In that case, A has the residual rights of control and can compel B to sell to A at A's desired price. If A owns B and B's managers do not want to sell to A, then A can fire B's managers and hire new ones which will sell to A, provided the production of the good is dependent on nonhuman as opposed to human (that is, specific knowledge that only B's managers possess) capital. The benefit of A owning B is that A can compel performance and hence purchase the good at a lower cost than if B was independent. Furthermore, A will have a greater incentive to invest in the relationship because of the reduced threat of B expropriating A's return. B's workers are also likely to be more attuned to A's interests when A owns B because it is in the workers' self-interest—they will not see some of their return to increased productivity siphoned off by the owners of B. On the cost side, B's mangers may have a reduced incentive to come up with advances if B is owned by A, since they are unlikely to be able to extract as much of the surplus from these advances as they would if B were independent. Since B has no residual rights of control, bargaining power is greatly reduced (Hart, 1990, pp. 162–63).

The solution here, says Oliver Hart, is to have common ownership in cases of extreme asset complementarity. If agents have access to both sets of assets, then they are able to benefit from increases in their marginal productivities (Hart, 1990, p. 163). This, in turn, generates the firm relationship, with the extent of asset complementarity in various directions determining the extent of integration versus long-term contractual arrangements. For example, if the unified A and B (A-B) transacts with C, but this relation constitutes only a small portion of the total business of both A-B and C, then long-term contracting is preferred to vertical integration. The reasoning here is that integration increases hold-up problems (as A-B expropriates the surplus of C, much of which is not related to C's dealings with A-B), thereby reducing the incentives of the workers and mangers of C.

The extent to which these types of incentive-alignment mechanisms are incorporated into contracts is a function of the size of the relevant transaction costs—the costs of including such terms in the contract (mainly, bargaining costs) as compared to the costs of additional monitoring of agent performance, and both of these as compared to the direct agency costs anticipated by the principal. Within the firm, one might expect that, as firm size increases (or, more generally, with the emergence of the large modern corporation), both the expected direct agency costs and the costs of monitoring will increase, leading the firm's owners to attempt to devise incentive-alignment schemes that can be incorporated into contractual agreements. The contracts (and hence firms and their structures) that have emerged over time "are the products of a historical process in which there were strong incentives for individuals to minimize agency costs" (Jensen and Meckling, 1976, p. 357). However, as we have seen in our discussion of the institutional environment, increasing contractual complexity is costly, with the result that the optimal contract, like optimal monitoring, will result in some positive optimal direct agency cost.

Transaction Cost Economics

Transaction cost economics (TCE)[20] is part of the NIE tradition and draws on the literatures of law, economics, and organization to study governance institutions within the economic system. TCE begins with the insight, owing to John R. Commons (1934), that the transaction is the basic unit of economic analysis. Using this insight, along with Ronald Coase's (1937, 1960) seminal analyses of transaction costs, Chester Barnard's (1938) work on organization theory, and the law of contracts, the transaction cost approach analyzes the emergence of governance structures within the economic system and does so largely from the perspective of economizing on transaction costs. Within this general approach, the law of contracts and the contracting process are seen to play an important role in determining the form of economic organization.

Neoclassical economic theory assumes that contracts are fully defined, instantaneously consumated, and perfectly enforced by courts. Because of this, the identity of the contracting parties is essentially irrelevant. The transaction cost approach, however, recognizes that, although these assumptions may apply in certain circumstances, it is more often the case that contracts are incomplete, that contractual performance is carried out over time, and that court enforcement is imperfect and is indeed bypassed in many instances in favor of private dispute-resolution mechanisms. Because of these phenomena, the identity of the contracting parties matters. And, although the property rights/agency approach to the contracting process often focuses on *ex ante* arrangements and assumes perfect contract enforcement by (and only by) the courts, TCE focuses on the execution stage of contract and emphasizes *ex post* arrangements and the design of extrajudicial mechanisms (often set up within the contract) to resolve disputes between contracting parties.

The three pillars of TCE are (1) the bounded rationality of economic agents—behavior that is, according to Herbert Simon (1961, xxiv), "*intendedly* rational, but only *limitedly* so"; (2) opportunistic behavior, which Williamson (1985, p. 30) defines as "self-interest seeking with guile"; and (3) asset specificity—the idea that investments in transaction-specific assets often accompany the contracting or transacting process. These three features of the transacting process serve to differentiate the perspective on contracts within TCE from the perspectives of mainstream economic theory and the property rights/agency approach. Specifically, when bounded rationality, opportunism, and asset specificity exist simultaneously, we have an environment wherein "[p]lanning is necessarily incomplete (because of bounded rationality), promise predictably breaks down (because of opportunism), and the precise identity of the parties now matters (because of asset specificity). This is the world of governance. Since the efficacy of court ordering is problematic, contract execution falls heavily on the institutions of private ordering. This is the world with which transaction cost economics is concerned" (Williamson, 1985, p. 32). The role of these governance structures (i.e., "the institutions of private ordering") in TCE is twofold—to resolve conflicts that arise over the course of the contractual relationship, and, more importantly, to head off or attenuate potential disputes (Williamson, 1984, p. 55; 1985, p. 29).

SAFEGUARDING CONTRACTUAL RELATIONSHIPS

Although not denying the importance of the *ex ante* incentive alignment issues raised by the agency and property rights approaches, the transaction cost approach focuses on the "hold-up" problems that can arise over the course of the contractual relationship due to *ex post* opportunistic behavior by one of the contracting parties. This hold-up risk refers to "the probability that transactors may violate the intent of their contractual understanding by expropriating quasi-rents from the specific reliance investments that have been made by the contracting parties" (Klein, 1992, p. 150).[21] The potential for hold-ups is made possible by the long-term nature of a contract and the presence of specific investments in the contractual relationship. These investments cannot be recouped if there is a defection from the contractual agreement. This may give one of the parties an incentive to attempt to capture some of the other party's surplus from the contract, knowing that the other party's incentive to defect from the contract will be minimized by its nonrecoverable specific investment in the relationship. However, excessive concern about potential hold-ups will weaken the incentive for parties to invest in long-term contractual relations that require specific investments, causing the parties to substitute less efficient, short-term contracts for more efficient, long-term contracts. With this in mind, the TCE view of contracts is one of arrangements put into place in an attempt to minimize hold-up risks in a long-term cooperative relation characterized by reliance investments by one or both parties that are specific to the venture at issue, in order that parties can form mutually beneficial exchange relationships in which both parties have confidence.

Because of the transaction costs that accompany the contracting process, most importantly, the costs of attempting to anticipate future events and haggling over related contractual contingencies that may or may not come into play over the life of the contract, parties will often elect to leave gaps in the contractual arrangement. These gaps can then be dealt with as circumstances evolve over the course of the contract through processes that entail lower expected costs than would obtain if the parties attempted to explicitly specify terms dealing with all relevant contingencies within the contract itself. In addition, since courts are likely to enforce clearly spelled-out contractual terms, parties have an additional incentive to leave certain terms out of the contracts to avoid committing themselves to potential future courses of action that may impose substantial costs. Thus, in a situation where events arise such that efficiency and profit maximization would dictate that Party A opt out of some or all of its contract with Party B, Party B may have an incentive to engage in hold-up activity that makes breach extremely expensive for A, as B recognizes that the threat that the court will order specific performance means that it can extort substantial rents from A in return for allowing A to opt out of the contract. In contrast, contractual gaps leave certain aspects of intended performance unspecified, and thus unenforceable by courts.

Although the above paragraphs discuss specific investments in terms of the resulting threat, or hold-up, potential, these specific investments can also be used to secure contractual commitment.[22] Specifically, specific investments can function to make contractual agreements self-enforcing.[23] This process works as follows. In the presence of specific investments, the parties can leave certain contractual terms unspecified and handle hold-up threats by recourse to various private enforcement mechanisms, one of which is the attempt to secure credible commitments. The party contemplating engaging in hold-up behavior will recognize that the threat of the termination of the contractual agreement by the other party—made easier by the contractual gaps—raises the possibility of the loss of specific investments and, in addition, reputation (the latter raising others' expected costs of doing business with this party, which will cause them to demand more favorable contractual terms in their dealings with this party to account for hold-up risks). The hold-up decision, then, becomes one of weighing expected benefits against expected costs, and if the expected costs are sufficiently high, there is a range of conditions over which the contractual arrangement will be self-enforcing (Klein, 1992, pp. 153–57).

From this perspective, the presence of specific investments made in reliance on (or in support of) the contract functions to establish "hostages" (Williamson's [1983, 1985] term) or "private enforcement capital" (Klein's [1992] term) that aids in making contracts self-enforcing. These investments serve to bond one to the contractual relation by raising the costs of defections and signaling to the other party one's commitment to the contractual relationship. By offering to invest specific assets in the exchange relation (perhaps in return for reciprocal investments by the other party), one can signal one's commitment to the continuance of the relationship and mitigate, in the eyes of the other party, the potential that one might engage in hold-up activity. This private enforcement capital functions as both substitute for and complement to explicit contractual terms. That is, private enforcement capital can be substituted for explicit contractual terms as a mechanism to increase the probability of performance when using it is cheaper than the expected costs of including additional explicit terms in the contract. In addition, the private enforcement capital works along with the court-enforceable specific terms to define the self-enforcing range of the contract *ex post*. The distribution of this private enforcement capital among the contracting parties is also important, in that it affects the hold-up incentives of each party and thus the range of conditions over which the contract is self-enforcing (Klein, 1992, pp. 159, 161–62). As Williamson (1985, p. 30) notes, these arrangements, by effecting adaptability and promoting continuity, create economic value. Of course, it will happen that, in certain cases, the actual conditions that emerge will diverge from expected conditions to such an extent that hold-ups become worthwhile.[24]

The use of hostages is only one mechanism through which parties may deal with the uncertainty that attends long-term contractual relationships. Because the time element introduces uncertainty into the picture, parties will often choose to forego costly efforts to make contracts more explicit in favor of a situation where the contract sets up some formula or governance structure through which contractual terms can be adjusted over time.[25] As Victor Goldberg (1976a, p. 432) has pointed out, the longer that parties expect their relationship to continue, and the greater is the complexity and uncertainty of the environment in which they are dealing, the smaller will be the emphasis on the use of explicit contractual terms of exchange; rather, "The emphasis will instead be on establishing rules to govern the relationship: rules determining the appropriate length of the relationship; rules determining the process of adjustment to unexpected factors that arise in the course of the relationship; and rules concerning the termination of that relationship" (Goldberg, 1976a, p. 432). For example, many long-term contracts specify, not the price at which goods will be purchased over time, but rather a pricing rule (e.g., cost-plus pricing). Such a pricing rule serves to minimize the occurrence of disputes when the supplier wishes to alter the price being charged because its input costs have risen. Alternatively (or complementary to this), the parties may set up, within the contract, mechanisms, such as recourse to mediation or binding arbitration, which will be used to resolve disputes that the parties are unable to settle among themselves. These arrangements may function in place of or along with the use of hostages in the contracting process.[26]

Thus, whereas the *ex ante* transaction costs of the property rights/agency approach consist of those costs associated with drafting, negotiating, and devising safeguards for contracts, the *ex post* transaction costs emphasized within TCE include maladaption costs (those costs that arise when disturbances expose gaps in long-term contracts that necessitate gap-filling and realignment of the contractual relation, during which time the transaction will likely be maladapted to the environment), certain haggling costs, setup costs for governance structures to effect dispute resolution, and bonding costs that may be necessary to secure credible commitments. Although *ex post* transaction costs draw attention to the different aspects of the contracting process than do those costs incurred *ex ante*, it bears keeping in mind that *ex ante* and *ex post* transaction costs are interdependent (Williamson, 1985, p. 21).

CONTRACTS, GOVERNANCE STRUCTURES, AND CONTRACT LAW

The transactions of firms can take three organizational forms: market, hybrid, or hierarchy, each of which will be discussed below. Drawing in part on the work of Ian Macneil (1974, 1978, 1981), Williamson (1991) suggests that three basic forms of contract law—classical, neoclassical, and forbearance—work to determine the organizational structure of the firm's transactional activities. Specifically, classical contract law supports market contracting, neoclassical contract law supports hybrid modes of contracting, and forbearance law supports hierarchical modes of contracting.

As described above, the view of contract in mainstream economic theory is one where discrete, autonomous market exchange is instantaneously consummated under the aegis of fully specified contracts, with monetized commodities being exchanged for money payments, and where contracts are perfectly enforced by courts. Here, relational considerations are absent and the identity of the contracting parties is irrelevant. Even where contractual performance is not instantaneous, future considerations are dealt with in the present (e.g., through specific contingency clauses specified in the contract) so that relational considerations are absent. Such contracts are not merely theoretical fictions, but are, in fact, observed in the real world, particularly in "thick" market situations where, for example, a firm has many alternative sources of supply for a given input, among which it can switch at negligible cost, and acquires that input through a series of short-term contracts executed over time with the supplier offering the lowest price on that input at that point in time. The combination of short-term contracts and the multiplicity of alternative suppliers secures the firm from the hazards of opportunistic behavior on the part of its counterparts.

These discrete market transactions are facilitated/supported within a framework of classical contract law in several ways having to do with the characteristics of classical contract law. Classical contract law (1) treats the identity of the contracting parties as irrelevant, (2) emphasizes clearly spelled-out contractual terms and provides rigorous court enforcement of these terms (including giving things that are written down precedence over things communicated orally) and emphasizes that offer and acceptance commit one to a contractual relation and the attendant risks, (3) limits the scope of remedies primarily to specific performance or expectation damages, which makes the end-value of the contract predictable, (4) discourages the introduction of third parties (including arbitrators or mediators) into the relation, and (5) provides a well-defined body of law to deal with matters not specifically covered in the contract (Macneil, 1978, pp. 862–65). As such, classical contract law functions to preclude the types of relational problems discussed above and facilitates contractual situations where specification of the relevant contractual terms and the performance of the contract are nonproblematic. That is, classical contract law facilitates market organization.[27]

Although discrete market organization/contracting plays an important role within the modern capitalist economic system, increasing situational complexity and the pervasiveness of uncertainty will often require that, for reasons of transaction cost economies, contracts be made over long time periods and be less than fully specified. As we have seen, this will manifest itself in intentional contractual gaps and/or the establishment of formulas or governance mechanisms through which parties can adapt their relations to changing circumstances or fill contractual gaps. These factors become more important the longer is the time horizon of the contract and the greater is the extent to which the parties invest specific assets in the relationship. The relation itself, then, takes on value, and continuity (and thus party identity) assumes a substantial degree of importance. It should be clear from the above discussion that classical contract law is not well-suited to this sort of relational contracting because of its emphasis on specific terms, its discouragement of third-party resolution mechanisms, and its limited range of dispute-resolution options. The forces of contractual gaps, time, uncertainty, and specific investments can raise the specter of opportunistic behavior and thus contractual disputes. These disputes may be more efficiently dealt with through extrajudicial mechanisms such as arbitration or mediation because of both the relatively lower costs of these mechanisms and the greater latitude that an arbitrator or mediator has in attempting to come to grips with the facts at issue in a dispute. As a result, contracts may set up these types of hybrid (Williamson's term) or relational (Goldberg's term) governance structures as a first resort in the dispute or gap-filling process.

Neoclassical contract law offers a much more fertile framework for these hybrid forms of organization because, although built on the basic framework of classical contract law, it diverges from the classical framework by virtue of its enhanced flexibility.[28] At the most basic level, neoclassical contract law recognizes the fact that contractual incompleteness is often an optimal response to uncertainty, and as such allows that gaps and adjustment mechanisms put into place by the contracting parties should be recognized as contractual terms within certain limits. Whereas, under classical contract law, dispute resolution is effected through the judicial system, neoclassical contract law gives a great deal of credence to the governance structures that attend hybrid forms of organization. Karl Llewellyn (1931, p. 737, quoted in Williamson, 1991, p. 272) describes this contractual framework as " 'a framework highly adjustable, a framework which almost never accurately indicates the real working relations, but which affords a rough indication around which such relations vary, an occasional guide in cases of doubt, and a norm of ultimate appeal when the relations cease in fact to work.'" In addition, neoclassical contract law embodies a set of excuse doctrines—including impossibility of performance, frustration of purpose, mistake, and unconscionability—which allow contracting parties to avoid excessively costly adaptations. The flexibility of the courts to excuse contractual performance functions as a curb on opportunistic behavior and promotes adaptive efforts on the part of the contracting parties (Williamson, 1991, p. 273).

As evidence of the elasticity of neoclassical contracts, Williamson (1991, p. 272) offers the following example, taken from a thirty-two-year coal supply agreement between the Nevada Power Company and the Northwest Trading Company:

> In the event an inequitable condition occurs which adversely affects one Party, it shall then be the joint and equal responsibility of both Parties to act promptly and in good faith to determine the action required to cure or adjust for the inequity and effectively to implement such action. Upon written claim of inequity served by one Party upon the other, the Parties shall act jointly to reach an agreement concerning the claimed inequity within sixty (60) days of the date of such written claim. An adjusted base coal price that differs from the market price by more than ten percent (10%) shall constitute a hardship. The Party claiming inequity shall include in its claim such information and data as may be reasonably necessary to substantiate the claim and shall freely and without delay furnish such other information and data as the other Party reasonably may deem relevant and necessary. If the Parties cannot reach agreement within sixty (60) days the matter shall be submitted to arbitration.

Williamson goes on to note that this contract is distinguished from a classical contract in that it "(1) contemplates unanticipated disturbances for which adaptation is needed, (2) provides a zone of tolerance (of ± 10%) within which misalignments will be absorbed, (3) requires information disclosure and substantiation if adaptation is proposed, and (4) provides for arbitration in the event voluntary agreement fails" (Williamson, 1991, p. 272).

In spite of the increased flexibility of hybrid organizational forms and neoclassical contract law, they still may not be sufficiently elastic to promote continuity and adaptation in the face of extreme deviations between actual and expected circumstances. The self-interested bargaining that occurs to fill gaps or resolve disputes may involve significant costs. For example, when circumstances become such that the contract is maladapted to existing conditions, the costs that result from this maladaption and attempts to resolve it through the extrajudicial mechanisms of hybrid organization may be severe (Williamson, 1991, pp. 278–79). That is, the costs of the mechanisms necessary to maintain the relation may be prohibitive, or the mechanisms may simply be insufficient to preclude wholesale defections from contractual agreements, and thus even more flexible organizational/contractual arrangements are necessary. Such arrangements are to be found in hierarchy, or internal organization, which, according to Williamson (1991, p. 279), functions as the organizational form "of last resort" when market or hybrid modes fail or are expected to fail.

Hierarchical organization substitutes administrative control for the formulas or third-party governance mechanisms of hybrid organization. As such, hierarchy economizes on transaction costs in several ways, ways which are driven by the ability to resolve disputes by fiat rather than through arbitration or the courts. These include the ideas that, within hierarchy, information is more easily acquired, less formal documentation is necessary, direct costs of using more formal mechanisms (e.g., lawyer, court, or arbitration costs) can be avoided, disputes can be resolved in a more timely fashion, and the potential for defection within a hierarchical relationship is reduced (Williamson, 1991, p. 280). At the same time, however, hierarchical organization can impose substantial bureaucracy-related costs on the firm, costs that will not be worth incurring if one does not anticipate that adaptation problems will become severe, and thus costly.

Williamson (1991, pp. 274–76) suggests that hierarchical organization is supported by forbearance law, which facilitates the use of administrative fiat as a dispute resolution mechanism. Williamson describes this as follows: "whereas courts routinely grant standing to firms should there be disputes over prices, the damages to be ascribed to delays, failures of quality, and the like, courts will refuse to hear disputes between one internal division and another over technical issues. Access to the courts being denied, the parties must resolve their differences internally. Accordingly, hierarchy is its own court of ultimate appeal" (Williamson, 1991, p. 274).

Were the courts to grant standing to the parties to such internal disputes, or were the law to mandate third-party arbitration, the working of the hierarchical system would be undermined, robbing it of much of its useful function. By recognizing hierarchy as an individual authoritative relation, forbearance law has the effect that parties to an internal dispute must resolve the dispute among themselves or, upon failure to do so, appeal to higher authorities within the hierarchy for final dispute resolution. By granting hierarchies fiat power, then, forbearance law allows for adaptive mechanisms that are not allowed under classical and neoclassical contract law and thus are not present within market or hybrid forms of organization.

The effects of changes in the institutional environment on institutional arrangements, and the efficiency of such changes, are illustrated by an examination of how changes in the structure of contract law affects the relative costs of alternative contractual/governance arrangements.[29] For example, the broadening or narrowing of excuse doctrine in neoclassical contract law will, respectively, increase or decrease the opportunities for agents to defect from contractual relationships, and thus impact the costs of hybrid modes of organization. If excuse doctrine is drawn too broadly, parties may be reluctant to make specific investments in a contractual relationship because of the relative ease with which the other party may be able to defect from the contract. Similarly, if excuse doctrine is too strict, parties may be reluctant to make specific investments because of the high costs that may result if the other party insists on performance in accordance with the terms of the contract in the face of adverse conditions that would render such performance excessively costly for the former party. The evaluation of a given structure of excuse doctrine, or of changes therein, should thus proceed on the basis of its effects on the costs of hybrid modes of contracting. In like manner, changes in forbearance doctrine affect the relative costs of hierarchical modes of organization. Should courts, for example, resolve to grant standing to intrafirm disputes, the costs of hierarchy would increase. Thus, the evaluation of changes in forbearance doctrine should proceed on the basis of their effects on the costs of hierarchical modes of organization.

In some of the early writing on coordination, F. A. Hayek (1945) and Chester Barnard (1938) emphasized that adaptation to changing circumstances is a central problem of economic coordination. Yet, whereas Hayek finds the mechanism for adaptation in the market, Barnard finds it in internal organization, or hierarchy. The seeming incongruence between these two views is resolved in the above discussion. Although markets serve as efficacious adaptation mechanisms for certain types of contractual relations, the increasing severity of adaptation problems requires more expansive modes of coordination—perhaps hybrid, perhaps hierarchy. Because classical contract law, which sets up an environment that is well-suited for market organization, is ill-suited to hybrid and hierarchical organization, other forms of contract law—neoclassical and forbearance—have developed to facilitate these other forms of organization.[30] We have seen, then, that three different types of contract law, or contractual environment—classical, neoclassical, and forbearance—support, respectively, three different types of governance structure—market, hybrid, and hierarchy. There will be a single type of governance structure which economizes on the cost of organizing a particular transaction. The prescription for organization that emerges from this analysis is to "align transactions (which differ in their attributes) with governance structures (the costs and competencies of which differ) in a discriminating (mainly, transaction cost economizing) way" (Williamson, 1988, p. 73), or, stated slightly differently, "*[o]rganize transactions so as to economize on bounded rationality while simultaneously safeguarding them against the hazards of opportunism*" (Williamson, 1985, p. 32, emphasis in original).

These processes are illustrated very nicely by the *make* versus *buy* decisions faced by firms in securing production inputs. The firm can choose to produce

CHAPTER 6

Critical Legal Studies

> Critical legal studies . . . is a movement in search
> of a theory, but at the same time it is a movement
> which has not agreed that such a theory is either
> possible or desirable.
> *(Hunt, 1987, p. 5)*

INTRODUCTION

The conference on Critical Legal Studies (CLS) was originally established in 1977 as a national organization of law practitioners, professors and students, social scientists, and others committed to the development of a critical theoretical perspective on law, legal practice, and legal education (Klare, 1979, p. 123). The movement stemmed from the prevailing dissatisfactions and grievances over (1) the general state of legal education, (2) the purported conservatism of legal education, and (3) the failure of orthodoxy and doctrinalism to truly come to grips with what advocates of CLS saw as the real problems in society and the attendant role of the law in dealing with those problems (Hunt, 1987, p. 5). Two distinct functions are fulfilled by CLS:

> First, [CLS] insists that there is an orthodoxy that needs to be and can be challenged and that the debates and disputes which take place within [traditional] legal scholarship are arguments within a more or less monolithic tradition, . . . [thus] the need for continuing debate about both the nature of orthodoxy and how much of it should be jettisoned. A second function of reactive scholarship is to draw attention to the very real difficulties involved in mounting a challenge to a well-established orthodoxy. A primary characteristic of critical legal theory lies in insistence that it is both possible and necessary to think differently about law. (Hunt, 1987, p. 6)[1]

Today, CLS can be interpreted, in part, as a reaction to what it eclectically terms *liberalism*, which includes the standard liberal and conservative orthodoxy.[2] From a slightly different vantage point, CLS can also be seen as a reaction to both the formalistic,[3] doctrinal legal reasoning that constitutes much of today's traditional legal scholarship and the underlying tenets of the Chicago school of law and economics.[4] CLS rejects the notion that either formal, doctrinal, traditional legal reasoning and scholarship or Chicago school law and economics are apolitical or value neutral, the latter's respective claims to the contrary notwithstanding.

CLS has been described as an attempt to demolish liberalism, which it regards as a mask for exploitation and injustice (Schwartz, 1984, p. 422), and its ultimate ambition is to demonstrate the political and philosophical bankruptcy of the liberal dialogue (Hutchinson and Monahan, 1984b, p. 1477). Although CLS does not embrace a single, formal, constructive alternative political program, the movement is marked by a continuing commitment to some conception of praxis—the continuing interaction of legal/political theory and practice—in short, a commitment to activism.[5]

It must be underscored that, as it has developed, CLS has become quite heterodox. It does not have a definitive methodological approach (Note, 1982, p. 1669 at note 3), nor does it embrace or constitute itself as a common alternative school of thought. As described by Hutchinson and Monahan, "CLS is *not* a homogenous or monolithic movement. Its proponents unite in rejecting mainstream legal thought, but *they do not possess* a common diagnosis of the liberal-legal patient's ailment, much less a remedy" (Hutchinson and Monahan, 1984b, p. 1483, emphasis added). The following review of CLS recognizes the various overlapping philosophies, arguments, and concerns of those within CLS. However, given the space limitations here, we must necessarily overlook the individual differences of various contributors with respect to both subject matter and modes of expression.[6]

EARLY PREDECESSORS TO CLS: ITS ORIGINS

The CLS literature typically credits Legal Realism, American Historiography, and elements of Marxism as providing the early origins of many of its ideas.[7] It is useful to briefly explore how each of these movements has influenced the development of CLS.

Legal Realism

As established in chapter 1, much of the work within all the schools of thought outlined here is, in part, a follow-up or reaction to the void left by Legal Realism in the 1920s and 1930s. The work of CLS shares in the Realists' contention that it simply is not accurate to suggest that legal results or outcomes can be deduced or intuited by an understanding of a relatively few fundamental, underlying abstract doctrines or concepts (Tushnet, 1986, pp. 505–10). Following on the work of the Realists, CLS advances a rejection of formalism—a rejection of the Langdellian doctrinal conception that the study of law is the science of discovering legal principles from the careful scrutiny and examination of common law cases. In this, CLS attempts to advance the Realist enterprise of rebelling against the view that legal and social arrangements are in any way natural or inevitable. As should be evident, the schools of thought described in earlier chapters and CLS by and large share in this characteristic. However, unlike the other schools of thought within Law and Economics, CLS—with its radical tradition—remains distinctive in its hostility to positivist explanatory frameworks that suggest that law can be understood as the consequence of phenomena that are purported to be empirically verifiable.[8]

American Historiography

A second point of origin for CLS lies in the work of American Progressive historiography during the early twentieth century. Within this tradition, American history was interpreted with an emphasis on the causal and deterministic nexus between sets of external influences and legal phenomena. For example, Progressive historians examined the relationship between (1) economic interests and the prevailing interest groups and (2) American politics and policies.

American Progressive historiography has its roots in the works of scholars such as Frederick Jackson Turner, Vernon L. Parrington, and Charles A. Beard.[9] The Progressive movement within which they wrote was born in the days of conflict, hardship, and economic and political despair, and gradually became a broad-based campaign for the economic, political, and social reform that took place in the United States from the 1890s to 1917. As has been extensively documented, this movement resulted from a widespread public disapproval of the growth of big business and of restrictions on political and economic freedom for which large corporations were held either directly or indirectly responsible. It was during the course of the Progressive movement that America experienced the increased regulation of business, the enactment of federal antitrust laws, the establishment of the Federal Trade Commission, and the adoption of the federal income tax.[10]

Within the context of the Progressive movement, American Progressive historiography is best understood in light of the dominant mode of relating history prior to the 1890s. This tradition held that history (which was once a branch of literature) consisted largely of "the objective retelling of a narrative" and was "a discipline dominated by well-to-do gentlemen-amateurs inspired by a literary ideal and writing grand narrative history" (Hofstadter, 1968, pp. 37, 35). However, at the turn of the century, scholars such as James H. Robinson and Carl Becker promulgated the idea of "the New History" (Saveth, 1965, p. 17). Just as politics, anthropology, sociology, and economics were attempting to strengthen their status in the academy by affirming whenever possible their scientific character, so too was the New History, in its attempt to provide a greater profundity of thought. The New History represented the historian's call to answer questions about events rather than retelling a narrative (Hofstadter, 1968, p. 37). In this, the New Historians studied the techniques of progress and concentrated on those aspects of the past that were the most relevant to domestic democratic reforms and to the public policy issues of the day. The work of Turner, Beard, and Parrington attempted to link history to the "scientific" endeavors of anthropology, sociology, politics, and economics (the latter all now within the Darwinian mainstream).

In particular, Turner's "The Significance of the Frontier in American History" (1920), Parrington's *Main Currents in American Thought* (1930), and Beard's *An Economic Interpretation of the Constitution of the United States* (1913) gave what may be termed "a connected meaning to the multiple events of American history" (Hofstadter, 1968, p. 41). Practitioners of the "New History" were disposed to think more directly and critically about the economic issues of society, about the ruling forces, and about the powerful plutocracy that had emerged during the previous three decades. Building on the notion that Turner's concepts of the "frontier" and "natural economic groupings," together with Parrington's view of "economic forces serving as cultural determinants," were fundamental to understanding American political history, Beard explicated the economic and class forces at work—men's material interests—in determining the historical events surrounding the framing of the U.S. Constitution.

Thus, it was with the development of American Progressive historiography that the scientific monograph replaced the objective narrative; the role of politics, social forces, and, especially, economics was fixed as part of recounting history; and material causation and economic determinism were taught to young scholars (Commager, 1950, pp. 303–4). To a generation of materialists, American Progressive historiography made clear that the stuff of history was material—a convenient take-off point for CLS Scientific Marxism.

Neo-Marxism

In order to understand the neo-Marxist strands of CLS, it is necessary to comprehend the so-called two Marxisms. The neo-Marxist strands of CLS are partially divided over the split between Scientific Marxism and Critical Marxism.[11] Scientific Marxism emphasizes the *determinative* importance of class-based ownership of the means of production and the determination of the content of political, legal, and other ideas (the superstructure) by the social relations and structures (the base) that follow from ownership of the means of production. In this sense, it is committed to the elaboration of intelligible laws of historical change.

Critical Marxism, in contrast, stresses the *radical indeterminacy* in social circumstances and thus the impossibility of deriving intelligible laws of historical change, be they political, legal, or otherwise. They reject the distinction between base and superstructure. They view alienation, ideology, historical contingency, and the role of human agency in history, together with the relations of production, as conceptually separate (though in fact inseparable) parts of the total socioculture of capitalism.[12]

We should note that although the neo-Marxist strands of CLS unite in the Marxist tradition of railing away at liberalism, formalism, and capitalism, CLS formally rejects the arguments of orthodox Marxism. Typically, the position taken by CLSers is that "like liberalism, Marxism has reached an advanced stage of scientific decline" (Hutchinson and Monahan, 1984a, p. 220). Indeed, Hutchinson and Monahan (1984a, p. 221) continue by stating that "Marxist theory is now in a self-proclaimed state of crisis," and, quoting G. Lukacs, they provide a characteristic CLS assessment of orthodox Marxism: "One may say that Marxism, conceived as it should be conceived, as a general theory of society and of history, no longer exists, that it came to end some time ago." And, as Schwartz (1984, pp. 423–24, 426, 433) has observed, unlike orthodox Marxist analysis, "there is little discussion [within the neo-Marxist CLS tradition] of the core socialist goal of ending the private ownership of capital," "how far to suppress private property is hardly mentioned," and "they reject the traditional Marxist notion that law embodies the crude coercion of the ruling class."[13]

FUNDAMENTAL ELEMENTS OF CLS ANALYSIS

This section, which describes the fundamental elements of CLS, rests on the notion that neo-Marxist CLS can be described as generally following two (not entirely distinct) contours: (1) the "Critical Marxist–indeterminacy" contour and (2) the "Scientific Marxist–deterministic" contour. This is not to suggest that there is a one to one correspondence, but, for the purposes of this brief review, much (though not all) of the CLS scholarship that emanates from the Critical Marxism is primarily concerned with the concept of *indeterminacy* as related to the contradictions inherent in the social structure. On the other hand, the alternative line of CLS scholarship has as its base the work of the Scientific Marxists and relies more on the ideas of false consciousness and illegitimate hierarchy together with domination and exploitation. Moreover, unlike Critical Marxism, it remains *deterministic*, espousing the view that fundamental laws govern the social world and that these laws give society its deep logic and exist irrespective of our wills (Trubek, 1984, p. 579).

The underlying debate between the two Marxisms essentially concerns the issue as to whether one can determine the precise relationship between the material conditions of life—including the processes of production in society and the relationships that arise from them, such as the organization of work and the distribution of profits (Hutchinson and Monahan, 1984a, p. 218 at note 89)—and the form and content or the structure and substance of legal doctrine.[14] As should be evident from the above characterization of the two Marxisms, the strand of CLS that rests on the ideas of Critical Marxism argues that this nexus is indeterminate. As stated by Kennedy, "The outcomes of struggle are not preordained by any aspect of the social totality, and the outcomes within law have no 'inherent logic' that would allow one to predict outcomes 'scientifically'" (Kennedy, 1990, pp. 38, 47). In contrast, those proponents of CLS who are oriented toward the Scientific Marxist approach maintain that the nexus is both identifiable and crucial to understanding the development of law, and that, in many respects, this nexus is the determinative engine of social history.

In an attempt to describe the main elements of CLS, we have opted to break down the analytical structure along the following lines: Law as a Social Institution, CLS at Work—including the Nature of Scientific Marxist CLS Discourse and the Nature of Critical Marxist CLS Discourse—and the CLS Agenda. The following sections do not attempt to maintain a strict demarcation between the two Marxisms and the corresponding two general contours of CLS thought. We will, as necessary, provide such distinctions when they are essential to clarify the characterizations set forth. As will become evident, many of the ideas connected with each of these notions are interwoven throughout the others.

Law as a Social Institution

Both strands of CLS view law as simply one aspect of the larger social structure, with the political dimension of the law serving to structure mass consciousness and contribute to the reproduction of the social and political structures of society. It must be clear from the outset that CLS rejects the "idea that a bright line can be drawn between the study of legal doctrine and the study of social behavior" (Trubek, 1984, p. 596). CLS thus attempts to incorporate some vision of the external forces and influences—be they social, economic, political, and/or psychological—that affect the development of law in society (Note, 1982, p. 1677). Proponents of CLS argue that the study of law should focus on law as a social institution, with particular attention paid to (1) the roles it plays in society, (2) how it fulfills those roles, and (3) how it interacts with the other prevailing social institutions (Kornhauser, 1984, p. 365). As described by Trubek (1984, pp. 588–89), "CLS scholars seek to expose the assumptions that underlie judicial and scholarly resolution of such issues, to question the presuppositions about law and society of those whose intellectual product is being analyzed, and to examine the subtle effects these products have in shaping legal and social consciousness." To this end, members of CLS see themselves as working out the implications of radical indeterminacy and contradiction (for the Critical Marxists) or the implications of false consciousness and the illegitimate hierarchy (for the Scientific Marxists). But for both, the work of CLS is contoured, colored, and conditioned by the belief that law is subordinate to social theory (Hutchinson and Monahan, 1984a, p. 213).

In addition, the work of neo-Marxist CLS has attempted to lay the foundations of a Marxist jurisprudential culture in the United States. The political vision of the advocates of CLS rejects the idea of social engineering and liberal reforms under the belief that justice cannot be attained merely by tinkering with the existing legal system.[15] CLS takes the position that to the extent to which injustices exist within society, they are essentially irremediable absent dramatic changes in the social structure (Kornhauser, 1984, p. 351). In this regard, CLS focuses attention upon the need to conceive and anticipate the institutional forms necessary for political expression, collective decision making, resource allocation, and dispute resolution.[16] Their political vision is one of participatory democracy, civic republicanism, and decentralized socialism—institutional forms which, once appropriately structured, would embody or constitute a free and democratic society (Klare, 1979, p. 124).

It is precisely because of the neo-Marxist CLS focus on alternative ways of thinking about the law and on alternative institutional legal/political structures and, ultimately, the potential impact of those alternatives (both ideas and legal structures) on resource allocations, that CLS is presented here as one of the schools of thought that will have a direct bearing on the continuing development of Law and Economics. Indeed, as presented, CLS is a vital, necessary, and valuable player in the marketplace of ideas.

CLS at Work

THE NATURE OF SCIENTIFIC MARXIST CLS DISCOURSE

It should be noted that the Critical Marxist-radical indeterminacy approach is the more prevalent of the two approaches (Note, 1982, p. 1677 at note 58). Nonetheless, Scientific Marxist CLS is explored briefly here before we move on to a more comprehensive review of Critical Marxist CLS.

The work of Scientific Marxist CLS is quite similar in style to the work of the progressive tradition of American historiography. Within the Scientific Marxist tradition, there is a tendency to analyze the development of American law in the context of the deep structure of the prevailing modes of production and the resultant material relations, the latter being the central motivating force of history. The analysis often includes a discussion of the staged-development of capitalism and emphasizes the substantial deterministic congruence between the material relations in society and the legal system.

Proponents of Scientific Marxist CLS are committed to the idea of a structured social world and the view that law is informed by the ideology or logic
of that structure. As such, there is a deterministic nexus between material relations and the legal outcomes. CLS undertakes to both reveal the logic underlying legal decisions and demonstrate that the legal decisions legitimate the logic
used in reaching the result. One of the essential roles of Scientific Marxist CLS
is to help unmask exploitation, based on the idea that, inter alia, the phenomena of economic and political power inherent in liberal ideology underlie an
accurate, deterministic understanding of both the political and legal outcomes
that obtain in society. In short, the thesis is that class and managerial elites set
the terms upon which others are to lead their lives (Hutchinson and Monahan,
1984a, p. 209). To provide the reader with a sense of the nature of the arguments set forth under the Scientific Marxist–determinacy thesis, we will use
three examples to provide a very brief characterization of a sample of the
contributions to the literature.

Morton Horwitz, building on his earlier work in "The Emergence of an
Instrumental Conception of American Law, 1780–1820" (1971), authored a
pathbreaking work entitled *The Transformation of American Law: 1780–1860*
(1977), which went beyond many past historians who concentrated on legislative policies, and, in an exhaustive examination of the decisions of American
courts, found that courts, like the legislative branch, made decisions that promoted the interests of American corporate enterprise and industrialization at
the expense of other group interests in society.

Richard Abel (1990), in an article entitled "Torts," describes contemporary
tort law as intimately related to the rise of capitalism, as both cause and effect.
He argues that capitalist tort law exploits and alienates accident victims by
separating the victims from the means of redressing their wrongs. In tort law,
as in production, a fraction of the dominant class mobilizes the power of the
state in its own interests, namely, to protect the property of the capitalist and
the monopoly of expertise of the lawyer and physician.[17]

Jay M. Feinman and Peter Gabel (1990), in an article entitled "Contract Law
as Ideology," trace the relationship between the history of contract law and the
three-stage development of capitalism over some two hundred years. Moving
from economic life premised on status and social responsibility, through free
market capitalism, and into the twentieth-century structure of integrated, coor-
dinated monopoly dominance, they assert that each period is marked by ideological images that justified the prevailing hierarchy as well as divisions in the
social world. What judges and lawyers did over this period of time can be
explained in terms of a process through which they came to identify with the
structure of the economic order and thereby became imbued with the logic of
the system. The results reached in arguing and deciding cases both conform to
the logic and legitimize it.[18]

THE NATURE OF CRITICAL MARXIST CLS DISCOURSE

Social Historical Contingency: Contradiction[19] and Indeterminacy

As noted above, most of CLS scholarship follows the critical path. In this regard, much of the work of Critical Marxist CLS demonstrates the manner in which traditional legal doctrine presents historically contingent, deeply political assumptions as *rational, natural, necessary, inevitable, and just* (Sarat, 1989, p. 10). In direct opposition to the traditional approach, CLS contends that "reality" is a cultural and social construction, and that legal relations possess no intrinsic meaning and ultimately become comprehensible and significant only within the shared construction of reality. As described by Hutchinson and Monahan (in part, quoting Mannheim), "Truth is seen as relative to any particular social or historical group. Insofar as it is impossible to conceive of truth existing independently of the values, social position, and historical location of the subject, 'it lies in the nature of certain assertions that they can not be formulated absolutely, but only in terms of the perspective of a given situation'" (Hutchinson and Monahan, 1984a, p. 215). Hutchinson and Monahan make the more general and perhaps more fundamental point that although the symbolic universe has a subjective origin insofar as it exists only in people's minds, individuals (based on particular abstract sets of categories, beliefs, and assumptions) perceive it as an objective fact about the world. They go on to say that the background sets of beliefs become the so-called "gatekeepers of the mind" (Hutchinson and Monahan, 1984a, p. 214 at note 66, quoting Wood, 1971, p. 35).

Proponents of Critical Marxist CLS deny that there is a rational determinacy in legal reasoning. They assert that because (1) no distinctive mode of legal reasoning exists that differs from political analysis, (2) law, like politics, operates in an historical context and within a political setting of competing individual ideologies, and (3) law cannot generate determinant results in concrete cases, the reality is that *law is politics*. This is the central tenet of CLS[20] and the element of CLS that represents the greatest perpetual threat to traditional legal teaching and scholarship (Note, 1982, pp. 1677–78). Given the historical social contingency of society and law, CLS attempts to identify the role played by law in the process through which social structures acquire the appearance of being inevitable, natural, or just. By demonstrating the fundamental contradictions within the legal structure of liberalism, CLS is seen to be committed to exposing both the indeterminacy of the legal order and the political facets underlying the adjudication process (Hutchinson and Monahan, 1984a, p. 212). In this, the CLS "analyses of legal doctrine emphasize its incoherence and its espousal of contradictory values," from which comes the view that "law is not so much a rational enterprise as a vast exercise in rationalization" (Hutchinson and Monahan, 1984a, pp. 223, 206).

Legal Ideology: Liberalism, Masking, and
False Consciousness

In Critical Marxist CLS, legal ideology is taken to be the sets of beliefs, ideas, and values embodied in legal institutions and legal materials (including cases, regulations, and statutes). Ideas, in particular, ideas about the law—what it is, what it does, why it exists—provide the basic notions about human and social relations that comprise society's shared "worldviews." These ideas, legal and otherwise, can be said to constitute society (Trubek, 1984, p. 589). CLS argues that legal reasoning is indeterminate, but at the same time believes that actual judicial decisions are heavily conditioned by a pervasive liberal legal ideology (Hutchinson and Monahan, 1984a, p. 201). According to CLS, the dominant legal ideology is not only an expression of values but also directly (perhaps incompletely) works to shape the values of individuals.[21]

Within CLS, liberal legal ideology has a pejorative connotation; it is condemned (together with formalism) not because it is morally wrong or inappropriate, but because it provides a false consciousness,[22] lending an appearance of coherence to the otherwise indeterminate legal system. The underlying legal ideology that provides the foundation of liberalism serves to disguise an individual's motivations from him- or herself. This might come about because one misperceives one's own interests or because one misperceives the world in which one acts. In either event, the ideological deceit ultimately comes about by virtue of the manner in which the individual came to embrace those beliefs. Kornhauser (1984, p. 375) describes the role of ideology in CLS as follows: "Ideology disguises one's motivations from oneself and thereby permits action that one might otherwise eschew as against one's own interests or beliefs about the world. . . . [I]deology leads an individual to act contrary to his interests because he misconceives the nature of the world and the likely consequences of his acts."

Liberalism is understood to mask the unidentified forces and roles within traditional legal studies. The basic charge against liberalism is that it provides the illusion that it is concerned with freedom and the rights of individuals. In doing so, liberalism lends a certain legitimacy to the legal structure and, thereby, the capitalistic system. But as CLS takes great pains to point out, the liberal conception of law (and capitalism) presents itself in a manner which masks the underlying exploitation that is actually taking place. As described by Schwartz (1984, pp. 424, 433) in an essay critical of CLS, "Liberalism lulls the victimized masses and 'coopts' them into supporting the very system that oppresses them. . . . By 'masking' exploitation with apparent fairness so as to enlist the exploited in support of the 'system' and of their own oppression, it 'legitimates' the class structure."

Legitimation and the Illegitimate Hierarchy

The concept of legitimation is central to CLS analysis and is, in fact, closely linked with the concepts of ideology and historical contingency. The position here is quite straightforward: Society's shared ideas about human and social relations that are embedded in legal consciousness *legitimate* unjust social relations by making these relations seem either necessary or desirable (Trubek, 1984, p. 597). Thus, CLS views law as deceptive: "law clothes power and interest in an elaborate robe of legitimate authority" (Kornhauser, 1984, pp. 352–53). As described by Kennedy (1979, p. 212), "Through our existence as members of collectives, we impose on others and have imposed on us hierarchical structures of power, welfare, and access to enlightenment that are illegitimate, whether based on birth into a particular social class or on the accident of genetic endowment."[23]

With respect to this conception of the illegitimate hierarchy, advocates of CLS do not believe that the law furthers the goals that legal actors consciously seek to advance. Further, they deny that the law primarily affects the behavior of individuals in the society by the link between changes in law and altered incentives or prices. The fundamental point here is that the oppressive and coercive nature of law is inherent in the ideology of law. The legal outcomes are not the conscious by-products of lawmakers or those seeking to influence lawmakers (Kornhauser, 1984, pp. 370–71); the nature of the coercive process is more complex and not so obvious to the uninitiated. Thus, CLS research seeks to discover the false but legitimating worldviews hidden in complex bodies of rules and doctrines and in legal consciousness in general (Trubek, 1984, p. 597). As described by Kornhauser (1984, p. 373), "If people believe the social structure they inhabit is natural and necessary, rather than social and contingent, they will, perforce, accept it; if they think the world can not be changed, they will not change it."

At a very fundamental level, Critical Marxist CLS attempts to demonstrate or make evident to the traditional scholars of the legal community both the problematic character of the underlying political assumptions within law and the social, political, and cultural constructions that mask or underlie the contingency of events in law. In the standard narrative of the legal system, presocial, inevitable, natural, or just conditions are presented in the context of voluntary associations among individuals (whose beings are alleged to be presocially or asocially determined) that yield an institutional order. This is followed by a clarifying analysis that identifies the underlying deep legal structure and, thereby, the discordant and open-ended legal practices that obtain in the system. This *open-ended character* implies that when, for example, a statute is passed, there is an indeterminacy of both the meaning of the text and the political circumstances surrounding the passage of the law. Thus, there is no coherent set of principles that can provide the judiciary with a conclusive guide to the law's interpretation, and, as such, the judiciary imposes its own emerging legal consciousness in its interpretation of the law. CLS typically derides the notions of compromising and the balancing of interests and thereby dismisses the concomitant concepts of bargaining and contract on the grounds that the latter are masks for domination that results from the initial disparity of power in society. Given this initial disparity, no deference is paid to settlements that may be reached.[24] Thus, as described by Schwartz (1984, p. 441), "In the CLS discourse 'contradictions' and 'incoherence' are dismissive references to the existence of opposing interests in society. Liberalism seeks to accommodate such tensions by compromise and balancing; CLS sees them instead as fundamental defects portending the end of capitalism and of liberalism."

Within the many historical and contemporary studies of Critical Marxist CLS,[25] each doctrinal dispute is reduced to contradictory claims, typically those between communal security and individual freedom, with each study concluding that the legal process is fundamentally indeterminate and manipulable.[26] Thus, given the inherent contradictions in the dualities within liberal thought, assertions of legal rights created under liberal theory cannot diminish the oppressive character of the social relations (Sparer, 1984, p. 517). To provide the reader with a sense of the nature of the arguments set forth under the Critical Marxist–indeterminacy thesis, we will provide four brief examples that characterize the contributions to the literature.

Duncan Kennedy (1976), in an article entitled "Form and Substance in Private Law Adjudication," analyzes the insoluble conflict between two contrasting orientations: the "individualistic" and the "altruistic." The use of rigid *rules* in the context of individualism (as related to liberalism and subjective values) is juxtaposed with the use of generalized *standards* in the context of altruism (as related to collectivism and inherently superior guides to justice). Both doctrines "ring true" in modern legal discourse, thereby requiring a political choice for disposition.

Roberto Unger (1983), in an article entitled "The Critical Legal Studies Movement," identifies legal principles of contract law that each have matching counterprinciples used to resolve doctrinal ambiguities. He further identifies a small group of ideas that underlie the principles and explains how these ideas represent two rival visions of human association (generally, individual versus communal). Modern legal doctrine is described as masking the existence of the conflict inherent in these two visions.[27]

Karl Klare (1981), in an article entitled "Labor Law as Ideology: Toward a New Historiography of Collective Bargaining Law," identifies the contradictory principles encoded in labor law doctrine, including the ambivalent distinctions between "public" and "private" and the ambivalent conceptualizations of workers' rights, which are alternatively treated as "individual" or "collective," "inalienable" or "waivable."[28]

Finally, Mark Kelman (1981), in an article entitled "Interpretive Construction in the Substantive Criminal Law," examines the standard doctrinal arguments made by judges and commentators on the substantive facet of criminal law in the United States. He exposes both the universally held false beliefs that underlie the case results and the false sense of rationality (and hence complacency) that those results impart.[29]

The common thread running throughout the work of this strand of CLS is that within each substantive dichotomy, *individualism* is pejoratively associated with liberalism, whereas *collectivism* inherently incorporates the virtues of altruism and/or justice.[30] As described by Johnson (in part, quoting Kennedy): "The task of Critical thought is to pierce through accepted intellectual categories to the reality of the fundamental contradiction that lies behind them. As our thinking becomes more sophisticated, we will understand that every legal issue can be reduced to a 'single dilemma of the degree of *collective as opposed to individual* self-determination that is appropriate'" (Johnson, 1984, p. 254, emphasis added). Thus, for the Critical Marxist strand of CLS, contemporary legal doctrine and analysis is understood to reveal an endless series of ad hoc, fragile compromises between inevitable, contradictory ideals (Hutchinson and Monahan, 1984a, p. 226), between opposing and inassimilable worldviews, and between self and other, private and public, and state and society.

Textual Explication

To more fully appreciate the work of Critical Marxist CLS, it is also important to understand one of the primary modes of analysis that it embraces—the explanation of judicial decisions through an exploration of the way legal decisions work as texts. Textual analysis seeks to expose the underlying structure of social relations contained in legal doctrines and documents, and, consistent with the CLS mission, is intended to explicate how assumptions about self and other, private and public, and state and society—the essentials that underlie traditional legal thought—are encoded in law (Sarat, 1989, p. 10).

The explication of legal texts is largely accomplished by borrowing the interpretive techniques of literary criticism,[31] a method by which advocates of CLS can go beyond the surface meaning of legal texts to explore the structure and the ideological content of the text to unmask or reveal the underlying truths about the legal order.[32] Most CLS structuralists would assert that one cannot study human activity from outside the activity itself. Consequently, one must choose some internal perspective from which to examine the phenomena being studied, noting that the objects being observed are largely defined by their relations to one another (Kornhauser, 1984, p. 368 at note 57). In this undertaking, CLS seeks not so much to discover from the text of cases what values the law *ought* to implement, as it does to search for the values expressed by the law. As so clearly stated by Kornhauser,

To understand society, a theory must explain not only external phenomena but also the conscious acts of humans, in particular the acts that generate the social theory in question. . . . While structuralism does not necessarily share the view that the method of social science differs radically from that of natural science, *it shares the perception that theories do not explain social reality so much as constitute it.* (Kornhauser, 1984, p. 368, emphasis added)

The CLS Agenda

At one level, we have seen that CLS seeks to expose the relationships between (1) the ideology (or "worldviews") embedded in modern legal consciousness—its contradictions, its incoherence, and its masking—and (2) the domination within hierarchical structures in a liberal, capitalistic society. However, at a deeper level, there is more to it than exposing contradictions. In CLS there is a continuing commitment to *change* the legal consciousness and the imbedded relationships, and it is the transformative politics that provides the *critical* element of CLS (Trubek, 1984, pp. 590–91). The political purpose of demonstrating that current traditional legal doctrines allow for contradictory and incoherent results is ultimately to energize "the motors of social transformation" on the belief that "criticism would challenge complacency" (Note, 1982, pp. 1684–85); that is, CLS attempts to locate those categories of traditional legal analysis which are laced with contradictions and complexities and then to explain why so many individuals—under a false consciousness—do not recognize their own self-interest and undertake "real" political change. As articulated by Thomas C. Heller (1984, pp. 132, 174), "Such false consciousness is to be expected precisely because an individual's phenomenal or experienced sense of 'self' is a material product serving the collective reproduction of a social order. If one can overcome the conceptual difficulty of the analyst seeing behind the structure in which he or she lives, the strategy for pursuing political change becomes visible."

All this is an attempt to "liberate the individuals in society" (Hutchinson and Monahan, 1984a, p. 217) and to "free citizens to imagine a different and better social and legal order" (Sarat, 1989, p. 10). "When this is done," says Trubek (1984, p. 593), "the blinders will fall from our eyes, and we will be free to create new systems of meanings and thus new relationships." Perhaps Trubek sums up this position the best when he says that "[i]f society is in some sense constituted by the world views that give meaning to social interaction, then to change consciousness is to change society itself. . . . For if [CLS] scholarship can change consciousness, it is not merely a move towards an ultimate transformation: It *is* the real thing" (Trubek, 1984, p. 592).

CHAPTER 7

Continuous Development and Continuing Concerns

> [T]he rules of just conduct which the lawyer studies
> serve a kind of order of the character of which the
> lawyer is largely ignorant; . . . this order is studied
> chiefly by the economist who in turn is similarly
> ignorant of the character of the rules of conduct
> on which the order that he studies rests.
> *(Hayek, 1973, pp. 4–5)*

CONTINUOUS DEVELOPMENT

In his recent book, *Patterns of American Jurisprudence*, Neil Duxbury
stated that

> [t]oday, law and economics is a subject over which controversy and confusion
> reigns. Defining the subject is like trying to eat spaghetti with a spoon. Law and
> economics can be positive, normative, neoclassical, institutional, Austrian—quite
> simply, the subject is weighed down by a multitude of competing methodologies
> and perspectives which are not always easily distinguishable. However one con-
> ceives it, one finds that, between promoters and detractors, misunderstandings
> abound. (Duxbury, 1995, p. 314)

It was in 1897 that Oliver Wendell Holmes, in his seminal essay "The Path of
Law," predicted that "[f]or the rational study of law the blackletter man may be
the man of the present, but the man of the future is the man of statistics and the
master of economics" (Holmes, 1897, p. 469). Although the Legal Realist
movement brought to law a certain economic perspective (among others, and
perhaps only for a time), it would seem that Holmes's future is beginning to be
realized in late-twentieth-century American legal culture. Economics has by no
means come to dominate the law. Indeed, there are some who would say that the
economic analysis of law has "peaked out as the latest fad in legal scholarship"
(Horwitz, 1980, p. 905).[1] A recent study by Landes and Posner disputes this
claim, however, suggesting that "[t]he influence of economics upon law was
growing at least through the 1980s (it is too early to speak about the 1990s),
though the rate of growth may have slowed beginning in the mid-1980s; that
the growth in the influence of economics on law exceeded that of any other
interdisciplinary or untraditional approach to law; and that the traditional ap-

proach ... was in decline over the period relative to interdisciplinary approaches in general and the economic approach in particular" (Landes and Posner, 1993, p. 424). And Anthony Kronman—a less than fully sympathetic contributor—has labeled the economic analysis of law "the most powerful current in American law teaching today. . . . [It] now completely dominates some fields and is a significant presence in most others" (Kronman, 1993, p. 226).[2]

Holmes (1897, p. 474, emphasis added) also argued, with respect to the law, that "every lawyer *ought to* seek an understanding of economics" owing to the light that it can shed on "the ends sought to be attained and the reasons for desiring them." More recently, Posner (1995, p. 90) has echoed this sentiment, asserting that "[l]egal training and experience equip lawyers with a set of essentially casuistic tools and a feel for legal doctrines, but not with the tools that they need in order to understand the social consequences of law." As Edmund Kitch has reminded us, it was the Realists who first taught legal scholars that the study of law as it works in practice ought to include and use the contributions from the social sciences, particularly economics (Kitch, 1983b, p. 184). Since that time, economists, as well as other social scientists (especially those in political science and sociology), have learned that Law and Economics is a useful discipline to help understand the social consequences of law and legal change. In sum, the various approaches to Law and Economics discussed in the previous chapters help several disciplines to understand the interrelations between law and the economy as well as the impact of legal change and the development of law.

There are a great many factors which suggest that any predictions of the demise of Law and Economics are extremely premature. And, even if, as a discipline within a discipline (economics or law), it has reached its zenith (and we contend that it has not), any talk of its demise fails to consider the enormous impact that Law and Economics already has had on the law and legal analysis. If Law and Economics seems less threatening now, it may be due to the fact that a number of its basic insights have become more or less a part of orthodox legal thinking. Indeed, part of the message of this book is that Law and Economics, viewed as a body of thought that recognizes and probes the interrelations between law and economy (from Chicago to CLS—indeed, any of the schools of thought), is now an entrenched part of the legal landscape. For this and other reasons, law is no longer an autonomous discipline.

Furthermore, the influence of Law and Economics on the discipline of economics has been growing substantially for some three decades. Although Holmes asserted that lawyers should understand economics, it is equally the case that economists need to understand law. Ronald Coase suggested that to do economics without understanding the role played by institutions, such as the law, is akin to studying "the circulation of blood without having a body" (Coase, 1984, p. 230). Speaking in terms of the law, Coase has argued that what is traded, and how much, depends upon "what rights and duties individuals and organizations are deemed to possess—and these are established by the legal system" (Coase, 1988, p. 656). Because of this, "the legal system will have a profound effect on the working of the economic system and may in certain respects be said to control it" (Coase, 1992a, pp. 717–18). Even so, there has long been a tendency within economics to take as given the institutional environment—including the structure of law—and to undertake analysis on that basis.

As described in several earlier chapters, some economists of the 1930s, 1940s, and 1950s did engage in significant work on the economic implications of antitrust law, corporations law, public utility regulation, and tax law; however, much of the legal-economic environment remained unexamined.[3] As such, economic analysis largely failed to get at the role that law plays in structuring incentives, influencing behavior and, thus, economic activity; that is, it failed, first, to generate a thorough understanding of the forces affecting the working of the economic system and, second, to provide a basis for evaluating the effects that law and legal change will have on this system. In the 1960s, there was a serious effort to deal with some of the deficiencies within mainstream economics, particularly through the efforts of those members of the Chicago school, as well as the Institutionalists who had long been preoccupied with many aspects of the interrelations between law and economy. Each of these endeavors did much to begin to bring out certain important features of the influence of law on economy. The more recent work by the New Institutional economists has indicated a resurgence of these types of concerns within economics. Needless to say, the influence of Law and Economics on the discipline of economics continues (having started much more slowly than within law) and has yet to achieve its full potential.

Each of the approaches described in the preceding chapters brings something different to Law and Economics—sometimes competing views on important questions or on the method of analysis, sometimes a focus on different aspects of the interrelations between law and economy. Chicago law and economics is, by and large, the economic analysis of law. As such, it employs the tools of neoclassical economic theory to the law to make both positive and normative evaluations of legal rules. In doing so, it is concerned with the "price" incentives embodied within legal rules; how rational utility-maximizing and profit-maximizing agents will respond to these rules; and the need to appreciate the *ex ante* nature of incentives, as well as their *ex post* impact. The concern is with whether legal rules promote the efficient allocation of resources by individuals, and hence within society generally, with such allocations placing rights and resources in the possession of those who value them most highly and where costs are incurred by those for whom costs are lowest.

The Public Choice approach to Law and Economics brings a rather similar set of tools to the table, but is focused primarily on the process of lawmaking within the political (as opposed to judicial) arena. Agents operating within the political process are seen to be rational maximizers of their satisfactions within the rules imposed by the political process. Within this framework can then be analyzed the decisions of individual voters and elected representatives, as well as the behavior of bureaucrats who interpret and carry out the legislation in force. This analysis at once generates insights into both the legal/social rules that emerge from the political process and the effect of (and implications for potential reform of) the rules that govern the political process itself. The goal, again, is primarily to assess the foregoing from the perspective of economic efficiency or the outcome of catallactics.

The Institutionalist and Neoinstitutionalist approaches to Law and Economics reflect a rather different perspective from Chicago and Public Choice. Although still concerned with the study of law and lawmaking, these approaches embody a greater emphasis on the study of the effect of law on the working of the economic system. Moreover, both approaches contemplate agents who have limited ability to process information and are procedurally rational and learning. Institutional law and economics is one manifestation of the greater concern within Institutional economics to uncover how the influence of social institutions shapes the structure and performance of the economic system over time. Because it determines the structure of rights within society, law is seen as one of the sources through which control or power is effectuated, and the primary concern of Institutional law and economics is with understanding and describing how these forces influence the economic system and how the economic system influences the evolution of these forces. In doing so, the Institutionalists hope to come to grips with the interrelations between law and economy—to an understanding of the legal-economic nexus—which in turn will allow for the analysis of the potential effects of legal-economic change that play so important a role in governing social life. In the process of explicating the nexus, the Institutional approach rejects the emphasis on efficiency on the grounds both that it cannot serve as a standard to render unambiguous judgments regarding rights and that it is an overly narrow and presumptive basis upon which to make normative evaluations of law, since it forecloses the political working out of conflicting interests.

Like Institutionalism, the Neoinstitutional law and economics confronts the issue of how law influences the economic system. It does so both at the macrolevel—considering the effect of the rules that make up the environment within which economic activity takes place—and at the microlevel—analyzing how institutional arrangements between economic agents govern and influence their relations. In doing so, the NIE places particular emphasis on the structure of property rights and the rules governing the contracting process, their effects on the costs of transacting, and the resultant implications for the efficiency with which society's scarce resources are allocated.

The two primary neo-Marxist strands of CLS unite in the Marxist tradition of railing away at liberalism, formalism, and capitalism along with its attending institutions. The neo-Marxist strands of CLS have at their foundation the so-called two Marxisms: Scientific Marxism—the "deterministic" contour of CLS, and Critical Marxism—the "indeterminacy" contour of CLS. Scientific Marxism emphasizes the determinative importance of class-based ownership of the means of production and the determination of the content of political and legal ideas and the social relations and structures that follow from ownership of the means of production. In contrast, Critical Marxism stresses the radical indeterminacy in social circumstances and thus the impossibility of deriving intelligible laws of historical change, be they political, legal, or otherwise.

Both contours of CLS attempt to incorporate some vision of the external forces and influences, be they social, economic, political, and/or psychological, that affect the development of law in society and believe that the study of law should focus on law as a social institution. For this group, law is politics. Particular attention is paid to (1) the roles that law plays in society, (2) how it fulfills those roles, and (3) how it interacts with the other prevailing social institutions. To this end, members of CLS see themselves as working out the implications of radical indeterminacy and contradiction (for the Critical Marxists) or the implications of false consciousness and the illegitimate hierarchy (for the Scientific Marxists). In their combined undertaking, CLS focuses attention upon the need to conceive and anticipate the institutional forms necessary for political expression, collective decision making, and resource allocation. Consequently CLS has a direct bearing on Law and Economics because of the continuing neo-Marxist CLS focus on alternative ways of thinking about the law and on alternative institutional legal/political structures and, ultimately, the potential impact of those alternatives (both ideas and legal structures) on resource allocations.

Notwithstanding the across-the-board success of the various approaches to Law and Economics, it remains the case that, as noted by Posner (1975, pp. 772–73), many critics and detractors persist, insisting, among other things, that since Law and Economics is not at once a complete and perfect science, that is, a model of logical perfection, it should be summarily dismissed. Such critics, of course, miss the point.

Legitimate critiques of Law and Economics can only come from comparing competitive methodologies or approaches. In contemplating the usefulness of Law and Economics, thoughtful consideration must take place at two different levels within the marketplace of ideas. At one level is the question of whether Law and Economics, as broadly used here, helps us to better describe the interrelations between law and the economy and better enables us to predict the impact of legal change and the development of law than do alternative social science paradigms. At the second level is the question as to which of the schools of thought within Law and Economics provide us with the more useful perspective, tools, and insights to enable us to better understand these aspects of the law. At this point in time, we can safely say that law is not so well understood that one can confidently assert that *the way* to improve the law is by relying solely on one or more of the schools of thought within Law and Economics as opposed to either the principles and doctrines of conventional legal theory or perhaps some alternative paradigm set forth by another social science. One can further argue that neither is it unambiguously clear that the way to improve the law is to enhance the economic sophistication of judges and attorneys as opposed to allowing them to remain obedient to the traditions, precedents, and precepts of conventional legal theory and practice. These are open questions.

However, as we stated in the opening chapter, we believe that as the schools of thought comprising Law and Economics develop, a new conventional wisdom—a more eclectic received doctrine—will take hold in law. As we have tried to make clear throughout this book, law has important implications for economic structure, behavior, and performance; thus we contend that it is inevitable that the more eclectic received doctrine in law will have an important economic component—and that it will incorporate a healthy dose of the principles and ideas of Law and Economics.

By presenting the reader with a noncritical description of the various perspectives on Law and Economics, it has been our goal to explicate some of the distinctions among the schools of thought, and, in the process, to get at what it is that each of these alternative approaches has to offer in helping us understand the relationships between the formation, structure, and processes of law and legal institutions and their impact upon the performance of the economy. Our purpose is not to pick "winners" and "losers," although that is not to deny the dominance of the Chicago school of law and economics discourse over the past thirty years as well as the popularity of both CLS and public choice theory throughout the 1980s. What remains is to highlight some of the important issues that are unresolved within Law and Economics. The purpose of the closing section of this chapter is to describe these issues to further indicate the many-layeredness of Law and Economics and to probe the concerns that have direct implications for legal-economic policy.

CONTINUING CONCERNS IN LEGAL-ECONOMIC POLICY

The Level of Analysis

One of the most difficult issues confronted by all schools of thought in Law and Economics is trying to decide what is the appropriate level of analysis from which to analyze the impact of legal-economic policy. Typically what transpires is that a regulation or piece of law is culled out for investigation from a configuration of law arbitrarily chosen and then subjected to some version of efficiency analysis. But much more is involved here.

The vehicle of analysis that will be used here to explicate the issue of "the appropriate level of analysis" is the takings issue as it arose in *Pennell v. City of San Jose*. The case deals with a rent-control ordinance adopted by the City of San Jose, California, in 1979 that included a so-called "tenant hardship provision." In this case, the Supreme Court Justices were required to determine whether the "harm to tenants" provision of this rent control ordinance constituted a taking of private property without just compensation under the Fifth and Fourteenth Amendments to the U.S. Constitution.[4] We begin with a brief outline of the facts of the case.[5]

In 1979 the City of San Jose, California, enacted a rent control ordinance stipulating that a landlord may annually set a "reasonable rent" comprised of an increase of as much as 8 percent, plus an increment based on seven factors that are subject to review by the mediation hearing officer. If a tenant objects to a greater than 8 percent increase in rent, a hearing is required before the hearing officer to determine whether the landlord's proposed increase is reasonable under the circumstances.

Of the seven factors to be considered, the first six factors were described by the Court to be *objective* in that they were derived from (1) the history of the premises, (2) the physical condition of the units, (3) any changes in the provided housing services, (4) the landlord's costs of providing an adequate rental unit, (5) the cost of debt servicing, and (6) the prevailing status of the rental market for comparable housing. Application of the first six factors resulted in an objective determination of a reasonable rent increase. The seventh factor included in the ordinance was termed the "tenant hardship provision" which, in part, read as follows:

> In the case of a rent increase . . . which exceeds the standard set [in the ordinance], with respect to such excess and whether or not to allow same to be part of the increase allowed . . . the Hearing Officer shall consider the economic and financial hardship imposed on the present tenant(s). . . . If the Hearing Officer determines that the proposed increase constitutes an unreasonably severe financial or economic hardship . . . he may order that the excess of the increase . . . be disallowed.[6]

It was the potential denial of the incremental rent increase on grounds of the tenant's financial hardship that was at issue in this case. Richard Pennell (owner of 109 rental units) and the Tri-County California Apartment House Owners Association sued in Superior Court of Santa Clara County seeking a declaration that the ordinance was, on its face, constitutionally invalid inasmuch as application of the tenant hardship clause violated the takings clause of the Fifth and Fourteenth Amendments. They argued that the potential reduction (solely attributable to the application of the provision regarding the tenant's hardship), from what otherwise would have been a *reasonable* rent increase based on the other six specified *objective* factors, constituted a taking in that it transferred the landlord's property to individual hardship tenants.

The Superior Court of California entered a judgment on behalf of Pennell and the association. The California Court of Appeal affirmed the lower court's ruling. However, the Court of Appeal's decision was subsequently reversed by the Supreme Court of California which found the ordinance was not in violation of the takings clause. The case was then appealed to the U.S. Supreme Court.

The U.S. Supreme Court[7] noted that the ordinance made it mandatory to consider the hardship to the tenant. That is, under conditions specified in the ordinance and when requested by an aggrieved party, the hearing officer was required to consider the economic hardship imposed on the present tenant. If the proposed increase constituted an unreasonably severe financial or economic hardship, then the officer could order that some or all of the excess of the increase (beyond 8 percent) be disallowed, although the officer was not required to do so. However, the Supreme Court noted that there was no evidence that this provision had ever been used, and thus found the two lower-court rulings to be premature.

However, the Court went on to consider the substantive merits of the case. In doing so, the Court recognized the legitimate goal of price regulation within the context of the police powers of the state. Specifically, it found the purpose of the ordinance—that of preventing unreasonable rent increases caused by the city's housing shortage—to be legitimate. Furthermore, the Court found the ordinance to represent a rational attempt to accommodate the conflicting interests of protecting tenants from burdensome rent increases and at the same time ensuring that landlords were guaranteed a fair return on their investment. The Court went on to find that the ordinance, which so carefully considered both the individual circumstances of the landlord and the tenant before determining whether to allow an additional increase in rent over and above certain amounts that are deemed reasonable, did not, on its face, violate the Fifth and Fourteenth Amendments' prohibition against taking of private property for public use without just compensation.

In his dissent, Justice Scalia disagreed with the Court's finding that the appellants' taking claim was premature, and asserted that the tenant hardship provision did indeed effect a taking of private property without just compensation. Justice Scalia maintained that the bounds of excessive versus reasonable rent increases were properly set by the first six factors alone. He argued that the tenant hardship provision served a different purpose, that being a poverty program for poor tenants. He contended that putting the burden of resolving a public problem—poverty—on one class of individuals—landlords—constituted a taking because it forced a small group of private individuals to bear a burden that should have been borne by the public at large, as is typically done through social welfare programs.

This is a useful case because it so clearly illustrates that the assessment or analysis of legal-economic policy necessitates "picking up a camera," so to speak, to frame the issue. It is clear that the majority of the Court framed the issue more broadly than did Justice Scalia. Donald Schön (1979, pp. 264–65) has labeled this process "naming and framing," and describes the process and its effects as follows: "Things are selected for attention and named in such a way as to fit the frame constructed for the situation. . . . Through the processes of naming and framing, the stories make . . . the 'normative leap from data to recommendations, from facts to values, from is to ought.' It is typical of diagnostic/descriptive stories such as these that they execute the normative leap in such a way as to make it seem graceful, compelling, even obvious."

The parties of interest, the court, and the legal-economic analyst may all frame the issue differently; that is, in arguments, the parties of interest in attempting to make their case will select a level of analysis that best suits their case. In addition, the court in deciding the case will set forth its rationale at one level of analysis or another in making its determination in a particular case. In sum, (1) the legal-economic analysis, (2) the arguments of each party of interest, and (3) the court's determination in a case are significantly helped by subjectively couching the issue at the "appropriate" level.

In cases such as *Pennell*, the strategy is typically the same: to isolate and focus on a single regulation (or provision) and place it into a legal relief—that is, against the appropriate background law—that best supports one's arguments (here either the legal-economic analyst's, a party of interest's, or the court's) by selecting the appropriate background law. One key to understanding case analysis and court decisions is to first uncover the subtle choices made as to what will constitute the appropriate background law in deciding a case. Thus, the purpose of this section is to suggest that the selection of the level of analysis has implications for analyzing and therefore developing legal-economic policy.

In rent control cases there are typically three levels of analysis from which to analyze, argue, or decide the case. First, in the narrowest context, one can concentrate solely on the particular contested provision of an ordinance; that is, following Scalia, one can cull out this one provision (here, the tenant hardship provision) of the larger piece of relevant legislation (or regulation) and subject it to legal-economic scrutiny. It is incontrovertible that such scrutiny will always bring into the sharpest relief the fact that some individuals will benefit while others will bear a burden consequent to the enactment of such a provision; that is, virtually any provision, when narrowly viewed, will be shown to allocate economic benefit *and* harm. Indeed, if this were not the case, there would be no legal dispute in the first place. This observation is perfectly consistent with the appellants' more narrow contention (as recognized by the U.S. Supreme Court) that "the provision accomplishes a transfer of the landlord's property to individual hardship tenants" (*Pennell*: 856). It is clear that this one isolated provision will serve to benefit one party of interest (the tenants) over the other (the landlords). Thus, the Court's upholding of the ordinance, in one sense, "takes" from the landlords. However, an opposite ruling declaring the ordinance unconstitutional (such as the two California lower-court decisions) would have "taken" from the tenants to and for the direct benefit of the landlords. As recognized throughout Law and Economics, in deciding cases, courts determine rights between competing interests, and the inevitable result is that someone will gain and someone will lose. Viewed narrowly, when a single provision is scrutinized against one particular frame of otherwise unquestioned, and hence legitimated background law, one can expect to find that this frame provides a pattern of benefit *and* harm, with the latter providing a potential claim for a taking.

But neither the analyst, the parties of interest, nor the court need have such a narrow focus. From a slightly broader perspective, one could examine the "harm to tenants" provision as just one facet of the rent control program, a program that remains part of San Jose's (indeed, California's) housing policy. From this broader perspective that focuses on rent control programs and housing policy in general, it requires a certain selective perception by the analyst, the parties of interest, and the Supreme Court (in this case, Justice Scalia in dissent) to single out this one harm to tenants provision as *the one* causing a taking. San Jose and California's housing policy is a maze of (1) federal and state public tax and expenditure programs, (2) state and local housing regulations, and (3) municipal building codes. Each of these categories has its own differential economic impacts—impacts that benefit some parties at the expense of others. None of them provide only benefits; all involve some costs, and therefore, when viewed in this somewhat broader relief, each could provide a potential claim for a taking. As was evident in this case, it was at this level that the Court's majority analysis took place, and, consequently, the Court's decision reflects the selective perception that is specific to this level of analysis.

Finally, one can look at the "harm to tenants" provision in the broadest context possible, that is, as a singular instance of legal change across society. Viewed from this perspective, one sees that since, in modern government, legal change is ubiquitous, so too are the differential economic benefits and the economic burdens both ubiquitous (the latter each potentially a taking) (Samuels and Mercuro, 1979, 1980). This is not to suggest that all legal changes are part of a zero-sum game. We do contend, however, that few legal changes are win-win situations; and further, we pragmatically contend that the vast majority of legal changes are win-lose situations, where the gains to the winners may or may not exceed the losses to the losers. The fundamental point here is that in modern mixed-market economies, society is constantly redetermining rights between competing sets of interests. The inevitable result is that some will gain and some will lose. Since rights are continually being created and re-created, against this background, against this legal relief, there will be a vast number of losers who will (and must) for fiscal reasons go uncompensated.

Thus, with respect to takings litigation, in Law and Economics the questions to be answered are (1) Who will have rights? and (2) Whose losses will be compensated? These questions may be answered differently depending upon the level of analysis chosen. The level at which the analysis is conducted drives the results generated by making some elements of the analysis central and fundamental while others are pushed into the background. Given the win-lose nature of legal-economic policy, and given the motivations of plaintiffs who are prepared to contend that a cost brought on by a legal change constitutes a taking, a deeper understanding of the fundamental issues in such cases is garnered by appreciating from which level of analysis—from which perspective—the discourse is being conducted, and, ultimately, legal policy and court decisions are being made.

The Place of the Rational Actor Model in the Analysis of Individual and Social Behavior

One of the important questions for Law and Economics, and indeed for the whole spectrum of attempts to apply economic analysis outside of its traditional boundaries, is that of whether, and to what extent or in what cases, people behave in the way suggested by economic analysis. Or, put a different way, to what extent can economics apply its toolkit to legal-political behavior? Although there is no unanimity among the schools surveyed here on the behavioral idea, the rationality postulate is strongly evident at least within the Chicago, Public Choice, and NIE approaches. The understanding of the forces motivating the individual responses to law and legal change has implications for both positive and normative law and economics.

One need not accept the rational actor model to understand that law influences individual and group behavior—that, for example, a law requiring polluters to pay compensation for harm caused (or absolving them from harm) is likely to have an impact on the behavior of polluters, and, perhaps, on those deciding whether or not to locate residences, businesses, farms, and other entities near polluting factories. When an activity becomes more costly, people will tend to engage in less of that activity; when it becomes less costly, that activity is likely to be pursued to a greater extent. One can observe the responses of individuals, but it is more difficult to understand what it is that motivates these responses. There are numerous theories of human behavior, of which the rational actor model is only one; the reason, of course, is that human behavior is a very complex phenomenon. Perhaps not even the most ardent proponent of the rationality-based approaches believes that the economic model of rational utility maximization explains all facets of human behavior or that it is the sole motivation governing any given choice. However, although the depiction of human agents as rational actors is one of the major criticisms that has been leveled against the enterprise of Law and Economics (and especially the Chicago school) by both its friends and its critics,[8] there is a more or less general agreement within many quarters of Law and Economics that, in the large, the responses of people to changes in constraints, be they dollar prices or the law, comport with the dictates of utility maximization. And, as Cooter and Ulen (1988, pp. 11–12) have pointed out, the predictions from Law and Economics as to how individuals will respond to the law are often mirrored very closely in the reasonableness standard that depicts human beings under the traditional approach to law.

This having been said, evidence continues to accumulate—even in work by individuals rather sympathetic to Law and Economics—that, in important ways, the utility maximization model fails to account for many aspects of individual behavior, and in ways that have important implications for Law and Economics. Robert Ellickson (1989) argues that Law and Economics would be greatly enriched by devoting attention to the psychological and sociological influences on human behavior, and thus individuals' responses to law. Regarding psychological factors, he contrasts the standard assumption within Law and Economics that agents "both know and honor legal rules" (Ellickson, 1989, p. 40) with the evidence that, in many contexts, agents do not know or understand well the laws to which they are subject. The influence of these cognitive limitations is evidenced in the tendency in certain situations to rely on norms or rules of thumb, rather than the law itself, to resolve disputes. The presence of various types of cognitive limitations (among which uncertainty is only one) raises questions about certain fundamental results derived within Law and Economics, such as the equivalence of particular remedies or the nonequivalence of others, and the results that follow from these presumed equivalences or nonequivalences. One example of such behavior is found in a study of cattle trespass disputes by Ellickson (1991). He discovered that changes in the laws governing cattle trespass had virtually no effect on the resolutions of these disputes—not because the Coase theorem mechanisms were at work, but because individuals continued to rely on the same set of norms to resolve their disputes, despite the fact that the changes in law had changed the respective legal rights of the parties. In fact, contrary to the assumption of the Coase theorem, transaction costs were not low in this case, which leads one to expect that the law would indeed influence resource allocation. However, Ellickson asserted that these norms essentially served to assist in the overcoming of transaction cost–related difficulties, but as such led to a different outcome than would be suggested by rational-actor-based Law and Economics. The presence of such behavior thus raises questions about the ability of Law and Economics to usefully predict the influence that legal change will have on individual actions (Ellickson, 1989, pp. 40–42).

Ellickson suggests that the model of individual behavior can be further enhanced by relying on the insights found in sociology and, in particular, by analyzing the effects of social or cultural influences on individual tastes. The utility maximization approach assumes that tastes are exogenously given, yet there is ample evidence to support the claim that tastes are, in fact, endogenous, and that one of the factors influencing tastes and preferences is legal rules. Beyond this, Ellickson suggests that there are larger social forces at work that influence individual tastes and preferences away from the selfish, noncooperative outcomes that are often implied by economic theory (Ellickson, 1989, pp. 43–54).

None of this is to deny that the forces of self-interest are at work in the decision-making process. To the extent that human behavior, at least within certain contexts, exhibits a certain means-ends consistency, the economic approach to law generates insights into how individuals and groups will respond to law and legal change, whether or not one wishes to go to the extent of fully applying the rational actor model. However, there remains much dispute over what the forces are that influence the individual response to law, and there is much work to be done to uncover these influences and thus advance the enterprise of Law and Economics.

In some sense, the question is one of domain: The type of response that is predicted by economic analysis may well apply more accurately to more overtly economic areas of the law—property, contract, tort, and corporations, for example—than to family or criminal law, where noneconomic motivations might be expected to play a more critical role.[9] Indeed, this now is being recognized within Law and Economics, as reflected in the recent attempts to probe the effects of psychological and sociological influences on the predictions it generates.[10] The ability of Law and Economics to theorize and to be forward-looking (i.e., to assess impacts of potential legal changes) depends very much on having an understanding of individual behavior in response to legal change.

Mixing Normative Law and Positive Economic Analysis

One of the major issues that remains to be resolved within Law and Economics, and between Law and Economics and legal theory generally, is in deciding what is the proper domain of efficiency both in positive analysis and normative application. It is beyond dispute that the emphasis on efficiency as a legal norm, evidenced particularly within the Chicago-oriented approaches, has been the cause of much of the hostility to Law and Economics.[11] But even across the schools of thought comprising Law and Economics, the role of efficiency—in both its positive and normative uses—is decidedly unsettled.

The less controversial aspect of efficiency analysis is its *positive* variant—the assessment of the extent to which the law promotes an efficient allocation of society's scarce resources. In the positive realm, answers are sought to such questions as the following: Does the rule of negligence in force induce those who can undertake precautionary activities at the lowest cost to do so? To what extent does the law of contracts facilitate or inhibit the movement of resources into areas where they are most highly valued? Do environmental regulations or the application of common law nuisance rules generate benefits (generated through pollution abatement) in excess of their costs? Do the judicial and/or legislative processes facilitate efficient legal change? And so on. These are just typical questions within the realm of positive economic analysis, here applied to the law. It must be underscored that in this respect, the analysis is no different from the traditional economic analysis of the efficiency of alternative market structures, farm subsidies, minimum wages, capital gains taxes, and tariffs on imports (which, in themselves, really fall within the bounds of Law and Economics, as broadly defined here).

Even in its positive, descriptive form, however, efficiency analysis is not without controversy. Two open questions persist with respect to the positive approach. The first concern is with the question: How much does the positive, descriptive, economic approach, namely, the use of efficiency, drive the way we think about the law? The second concern is with the circularity argument that is inherent in the use of efficiency to analyze the law.

It has been argued that the very enterprise of applying economics to law—that is, a purely positive efficiency analysis—shapes legal thought and language by determining what we look at and therefore what we see. The efficiency analysis of law frames the law a certain way and thereby frames the objectives of law (Johnston, 1990; Schön, 1979). Simply put, how can one regularly labor through precise analyses of the efficiency of laws X, Y, and Z and then not think of efficiency as an objective of law? This is a recognized, inherent limitation of all purported positive analysis of law. One response to this enduring critique from a thoughtful commentator is that while "law and economics helps to illuminate and enrich our understanding of the law . . . as an instrument of analysis which inevitably shapes the legal world it analyzes, the economic model alone is not enough: It must be enriched by a broader understanding of the social and cultural context within which law and economics operates" (Johnston, 1990, p. 1221).

The second concern is with the ability of economists to render meaningful efficiency judgments[12] on the grounds that, since wealth itself is a function of rights, there is no unique wealth-maximizing result; any such result is relative to the initial distribution of entitlements—thus, efficiency analysis takes for granted what is at issue. Since prices, costs, quantities, and so on are partially a function of rights, and efficiency is a function of prices, costs, and quantities, can efficiency be employed to evaluate one assignment of rights against another? Within wide areas of Law and Economics, the answer given to this question continues to be in the affirmative. However, more and more scholars are beginning to point to the difficulties that this circularity poses, particularly for the analysis of legal changes that are expected to have "large" impacts on prices, costs, and other factors. Thus, a question remains as to the ability to make meaningful efficiency comparisons between two different values, sometimes derivative of significant legal change, at other times the consequence of legal changes that have only small impacts on these variables.

Having outlined two of the major concerns with positive analysis, we now turn to the more controversial issue—the *normative* application of the efficiency criterion. Here we also confront two concerns. The first includes the question: To what extent do individuals in society behave in a manner that comports to legal-economic models that purport to describe their behavior? The second question concerns the desirability of selecting one law over another based on the efficiency criterion.

With respect to the first concern, the issue is quite straightforward. Prescribing a particular legal change, rule, or remedy on instrumental grounds—that it will promote a particular desirable outcome, be it efficiency or something else—assumes that individuals will respond in such a way that the desired end will be achieved. Certainly, most individuals will obey the law, but there is more to it than this. For example, the adoption of a particular tort liability rule on efficiency grounds—a rule that generates the efficient levels of precaution on the part of the potential injurers and the potential victims—assumes that these individuals will in fact respond by taking such precautions. Indeed, it may be in their self-interest to do so, in order to minimize their expected costs. On the other hand, as noted above, since the evidence suggests that people do not necessarily behave in this manner, for cognitive or other reasons, the case for being able to confidently apply the efficiency criterion is correspondingly weakened. This is not an indictment of the utility-maximization/efficiency theory alone, for it remains an open question whether any of the approaches to Law and Economics have the sort of generalized notion of individual behavior that will allow them to take account of the actual individual response to law.

The second concern over the normative application of efficiency is the more controversial one. Here we confront the question as to the desirability of prescribing one legal arrangement over another "because it is more efficient"; that is, to what extent should efficiency be *the* or *one of the* criteria employed in selecting among alternative legal rules? The normative use of the efficiency criterion may take two forms: a "first-order" rule, in which efficiency is one of several goals or is the goal in making legal-economic policy, and a "second-order" rule, in which efficiency is used to determine the means by which non-economic goals are pursued.[13] The use of the "first-order" rule will yield the optimal or efficient level of an activity—one that maximizes net benefit to society. For example, the efficiency norm would suggest that the level of pollution allowed by law be that level which is efficient, in the sense of maximizing the net-value of pollution abatement to society. The use of the "second-order" efficiency norm would suggest minimizing a cost function subject to a constraint that the desired levels of an activity be provided such that a given total benefit is achieved. For example, once society has determined (on, say, ethical grounds or for political reasons) the appropriate level of pollution reduction, the desired level of pollution reduction should be achieved in the least-cost, most efficient manner. Apart from questions as to the uniqueness of any such efficiency judgments, the criticisms raised against the use of such efficiency norms are primarily ethical and political.

One fundamental issue is over the defensibility of labeling as an improvement (either in the first-order or second-order sense) instances where gains do exceed losses but losers are not compensated (i.e., wealth maximization). CLS, and to some extent Institutional law and economics, argue that the wealth maximization criterion reifies the existing distribution of wealth (i.e., that wealth maximization favors those who already have the wealth); consequently, the invocation of the efficiency norm merely serves to reinforce the existing power relations within the economic system and makes the market system the arbiter of rights.

A second issue is whether efficiency should play any role at all in the determination of what constitutes justice. This has become the arena of one of the most widespread arguments regarding the Law and Economics movement. Whereas Posner, for example, has argued eloquently that efficiency is moral and comports with the dictates of justice, others are equally adamant in their views that the use of the efficiency criterion in making law is antithetical to the idea that law should reflect some sense of justice.[14]

Avery Katz has rightly pointed out that part of the source of the difficulty over locating the jurisprudential niche of efficiency in legal theory lies in the culture clash between economics and law: "Within their own culture, economists can safely restrict their attention to means—that is, to efficiency—knowing that some other actor or institution will see to the content of ends. Lawyers may not feel they can abdicate responsibility for these other goals, and citizens and public officials surely cannot adopt such an approach" (Katz, 1996, p. 2264). Katz is correct. Economists have been known to frequently make normative pronouncements, such as, for example, on questions of taxes or of tariffs on imports. Although economists are sometimes questioned on other— perhaps distributional—grounds, generally they have been given a voice, if for no other reason than that such questions are generally acknowledged to be on the economists' home turf. However, the more widespread application of the efficiency criterion into areas such as the constitution, the making of common law rules, the internal workings of the political process, and so on represents a vast extension of the application of the economist's toolkit, and into areas where many believe it does not belong, at least in the normative sense.

With respect to its normative component, law is not simply a set of commands; it is a principle for ordering society. The open question here is thus one of whether efficiency is the, or one of the, principles to be used in determining the basic ordering of society. If it is to be one of the principles employed, then the ancillary question goes to the appropriate weight to be given to it when it conflicts with other (ethical and/or political) principles. This is a question that remains to be worked out, within Law and Economics, within law generally, and within society at large. But it is worth noting that even Posner, who is often painted as the embodiment of the Chicago-efficiency approach, does not believe that efficiency should be the sole basis for making law: "I do not believe that the economist holds all the keys to legal theory. Rather, I believe that economics is one of the keys. The others are pragmatism, shorn however of postmodernist excesses, and liberalism, especially that of the classical tradition" (Posner, 1995, viii).

But critics of Posner and Chicago who would seize upon the emphasis on efficiency, label the entire enterprise of Law and Economics as immoral, and dismiss it on those grounds miss the boat, for this does not remove the issue that $\triangle$ law $\rightarrow \triangle$ economy. Even if one holds to the view that efficiency should play no role (or a limited, albeit an ambiguous, role) in the making of legal-economic policy, this does not vitiate the fact that there are choices to be made among competing ends, that tradeoffs accompany these choices, that certain of these tradeoffs are economic, and that an understanding of economics is thus an important component of understanding the impact of law. The same point can be made about another set of critics—those who argue that law can necessarily select the interests which become costs to other actors. Any given set of laws incorporates a set of moral values, and thus markets do as well. The issue then is not efficiency versus other values, but, rather the values which efficiency chooses to include (see chapter 4, above).

A Change in Law Affects Both Allocation and Distribution

It was highlighted at the end of chapter 1 (quoting Hirsch) that a change in law typically has an effect on both the allocation and the distribution of resources—respectively, the manner in which resources are employed (more or less efficiently) and the determination of who gets what.[15] One of the questions left open within the field of Law and Economics is: Is there a consensus approach as to how Law and Economics should report out the allocation and distribution effects of legal-economic policy? More specifically, should, and if so, *how* should, Law and Economics systematically and formally treat these two impacts that most contributors to the various schools of thought stipulate to be of paramount importance?

It is clear from the thrust of the "economic side" of Law and Economics that the efficiency with which resources are allocated consequent legal change is a major concern. Indeed, much of the contributing economic theory brought to bear on analyzing legal change focuses directly on the relative efficiency of the allocation of resources. On the other hand, from the "law" side, the traditional concerns are often with questions of distribution under the guise of legal doctrines built on the precepts of justice and fairness.

If the world were as simple as that described by the perfectly competitive market, then as counseled by Kneese, all we need do is to set in place the just and fair initial property rights structure and, baring problems with information, externalities, and public goods, the market would provide us with an efficient allocation of resources—the *optimum optimorum*.[16] However, no one in Law and Economics believes that, in modern, mixed-market economies, legal change or legal-economic policy is confined merely to the initial starting points. Government policy—indeed all legal change—is ubiquitous, both its doing and undoing, perhaps more appropriately described as in regulating, then in deregulating, and then in reregulating.

The major reason for the emphasis on efficiency within Law and Economics is very simple: The received paradigm within economics takes as one of its primary goals the assessment of the efficiency of economic outcomes. As a glance at almost any text in economic theory will tell you, economists tend to believe that making distributional judgments is a matter for the politicians, not for the economists. What the economist offers, rather, is an assessment of the relative efficiency of various states of the world. One might well ask how a discipline that pays so little attention to distribution would come to achieve such prominence in a discipline, such as law, where distributional issues (in various guises) have traditionally played such a central role. Reuven Brenner's (1980) description as to why the economic approach to the study of law has dominated other social science approaches is instructive here. He argued that its dominance is attributable to two reasons. First, economics has a received paradigm, a mature, uniform framework built on first principles that each legal-economic analyst knows and can confidently assume the other contributors know—they have a common takeoff point. Brenner argued that the other present-day social science paradigms lack such uniformity and broad acceptance within their own discipline and therefore require each social science observer of law to start anew building his or her own theory from its foundations. Second, he argued that part of the success of the economic approach is owed to the fact that the predictions made by the economic approach are more consistent with the facts than the predictions of other theories of social sciences. Whether or not Brenner is correct, it seems that this perception is widely held and has no doubt helped economics (as evidenced by its growing schools of thought) gain an upper hand in the wider social science marketplace of ideas. Given its success, economics was well placed to fill the void that existed in law in the 1960s. And given its inherent emphasis on efficiency, it becomes clear why, from the "economics side," allocation is at center stage within Law and Economics.

Such cannot be said for the legal doctrines built on the concepts of justice or fairness. From the "law side," fairness and corrective justice are directly related to distribution and thus put distribution at center stage. Whatever hold doctrines based on justice and fairness may have over the legal academy as evidenced in most of the conventional teachings of law, they appear to hold less and less sway for many of the legal scholars regularly contributing to Law and Economics. Indeed, one of the common themes of some of those contributing to Chicago law and economics is that "economic principles are encoded in the ethical vocabulary that is a staple of judicial language, and that the language of justice and equity that dominates judicial opinions is to a large extent the translation of economic principles into ethical language" (Landes and Posner, 1987, p. 23). As long as some continue to argue that law be transmitted from generation to generation under its proclaimed autonomy and rely on its first principles of justice and fairness, while others advocate a greater or lesser role for efficiency within the legal calculus, a tension will persist.

Our purpose here is not to argue the merits of whether law should incorporate more or less economics—we think it will include more, but that's not the point! The purpose of this section is simply to demonstrate that for a variety of reasons—due in part to what each economics and law bring to the table—no consensus exists on how to systematically and formally report out the combined issues of allocation and distribution. There appear to be two extreme positions, neither satisfactory. On the one hand, there are those contributors to Law and Economics who simply argue that society ought to go forward with those (and only those) legal changes that are determined to be efficient. To those in law who argue that efficiency should not be the primary social value, the burden is placed on them to demonstrate why a standard (based in justice or fairness) that imposes avoidable costs should nonetheless be adopted (Posner, 1973, p. 221). On the other hand from the "law side" there are those who believe that once questions of justice and fairness are brought to bear to evaluate legal change, there will be little, if any, room left for concerns regarding efficiency and, hence, eschew the efficiency approach. These are the extremes.

On the surface there appears to be a third alternative, one that may lay claim to some support inasmuch as, by occupying the middle ground, it does serve to lay some minds to rest. This is essentially the approach taken by Hirsch and many, many others in Law and Economics—basically to admonish one's colleagues to consider both allocation and distribution. Who among us would (indeed, could) reject it? Of course the obvious questions remain: Just what does this entail? How does one proceed? The reality appears to be that, although this admonition to consider both allocation and distribution is widely accepted in principle, it is most often honored only in the breach; thereafter one moves quickly (speed depending upon how brazen) into a detailed analysis of the allocation/efficiency considerations. There is as yet no consensus within Law and Economics as to how we are to systematically undertake an analysis that formally includes a combined description of allocation and distribution, to say nothing of what rules should be adopted to judge between outcomes on a combined basis—the relative weights to be given to efficiency vis-à-vis distribution. Much remains to be done—many questions remain.

The Need for More Empirical Work

As a number of scholars working within the field have pointed out, one of the greatest needs within Law and Economics is for more empirical work of both historical and contemporary varieties.[17] From a historical perspective, there is valuable knowledge to be gained from the study of the forces motivating changes in legal rules and the effects of these changes within the economic realm. Why, for example, have we observed such substantial changes in tort and products liability rules over the past century, and what have been the effects of these changes? Referring back to the above example from takings law, what has been the effect of the expansion of the definition of takings? There are a number of such important issues that are worthy of detailed examination, and such studies can provide valuable insights into present-day legal-economic issues, as well as enhancing our understanding of the interrelations between law and economy.

The benefits to be gained from more standard empirical work have been hinted at in the preceding discussion. What, for example, does the evidence show regarding the effect of changes in legal rules on individual behavior? Such evidence can be fed back into the theory to improve our ability to evaluate the consequences of alternative legal rules. Beyond the effects of rules on individual behavior, there is the entire issue of assessing the greater economic impact of alternative legal rules. These range from institutional studies of the contracting process to assessment of the impacts of particular product liability rules to attempts to get a handle on the nebulous concept of transaction costs, and, indeed, to the entire corpus of legal-economic relations. Although we have theories about many of these phenomena, there tends to be far too little evidence either to support, refute, or suggest refinements in the theories themselves, or to indicate the magnitude of effects. In other instances, particularly as to the economic impact of law, the theory itself is lacking and the development of theory can be enhanced by a strong empirical foundation. One of the difficulties that has stood in the way of such work is the difficulty of assembling data. Admittedly, some of these phenomena may be difficult to quantify. Yet, there is good reason to believe that the major reason for the absence of empirical work is simply the failure to undertake it, rather than the lack of data, the gathering of which may involve rather painstaking and innovative work. As Laplace is said to have put it, "What we know is not much; what we do not know is immense" (Bell, 1937, p. 172).

Notes

Chapter 1

1. Throughout this book, we use Law and Economics (capital L and E) as an eclectic title to refer to all of the schools of thought subsequently presented—schools that, in our view, deal explicitly with the interrelations between law and economy.

2. This book builds on and extends the discussion in Mercuro and Medema (1995).

3. This information is contained in the 1995 program brochure *Law and Economics Center's Institute for Law Professors*, 1995, Law and Economics Center, George Mason University School of Law, Arlington, Va.

4. In fact, one can go back much further than this, to Adam Smith, whose work is in some respects part of the Law and Economics tradition.

5. As Kornhauser (1984, p. 366) stated, "Everyone debates what law ought to be while quietly adhering to instrumentalism. The adherence to legal instrumentalism . . . has largely been implicit in traditional legal studies." See also Summers (1981). We recognize that this belief is not universally held among legal scholars. On the idea that law maintains its autonomy and has its own internal, coherent logic, see, for example, Weinrib (1995).

6. We regret that space limitations do not allow us to include the work of two groups, both of which present highly relevant approaches to legal or legal-economic studies. The first is the work of the "rights-based theorists," including jurisprudential scholars such as Ronald Dworkin (1977, 1986), Charles Fried (1978), John Rawls (1971), and Robert Nozick (1974). The second is work of that group of scholars in the Austrian or Hayekian tradition, including F. A. Hayek (1973), Randy Barnett (1992), Mario Rizzo (1980, 1985), Dieter Schmidtchen (1993), and the early work of Richard Epstein (e.g., 1980). A bit of the flavor of this perspective can be found in the brief discussion of Epstein in chapter 2, below. See also Linda Schwartzstein (1992).

7. The appendix to this chapter provides a detailed analysis of the three primary concepts of economic efficiency.

8. See, for example, Bodenheimer (1974, chs. 1–7).

9. This discussion of the common law is based largely on Cotterrell (1989, pp. 21–37).

10. See, for example, Langdell (1871). The following discussion of Langdell draws on Friedman (1973, pp. 530–36). See also Thomas C. Grey (1983).

11. As Duxbury (1995, pp. 10, 32–64) has aptly noted, however, neither these scholars nor the Realists who followed them were able to totally shed formalistic elements from their thought. Nor did they necessarily attempt to do so. Holmes, for example, saw an important role for logical analysis within legal thinking.

12. See also Hall (1947).

13. See also Holmes (1897, p. 469).

14. It should be noted that there is no settled position as to the boundaries and contours of Legal Realism. For surveys of various issues related to the Realist movement, see Fischer, Horwitz, and Reed (1993) and Duxbury (1995, ch. 2).

15. From these ideas was derived the caricature that legal decision making has less to do with logic, rules, and precedent than with what the judge ate for breakfast. See Minow (1987, p. 93).

16. For surveys of the intersection between Realism and economics, see Samuels (1993) and Duxbury (1995, ch. 2).

17. See, for example, Llewellyn (1925), Litchman (1927), and Holdsworth (1927–28).

18. See Llewellyn (1925, pp. 678–81) and the discussion in Samuels (1993, pp. 247–48).

19. This affinity turned very much on the pessimism reflected within both Realism and Institutionalism regarding laissez-faire legal-economic policy and the inequalities of power and position that were masked under the laissez-faire emphasis on individual liberty. For a discussion of the links between Realism and Institutionalism, see Duxbury (1995, pp. 97–111). A discussion of the Institutionalist position, which traces its roots to this earlier era, is found in chapter 4, below.

20. See, for example, Monahan and Walker (1990, p. 28), Woodward (1968), and Duxbury (1995, ch. 4).

21. Again, we note that this tendency is by no means universal among legal scholars. See Weinrib (1995).

22. See also Gordon (1990, p. 413).

23. See, for example, Feldman (1980, pp. 47–58) and Pindyck and Rubinfeld (1992, p. 584).

24. This tabular approach to depicting the efficiency conditions is based on Wonnacott and Wonnacott (1979, pp. 178–94).

25. The line of literature that comprises the core elements of compensation principle analysis includes the works of E. Barone (1908, translated into English in 1935), Nicholas Kaldor (1939), John R. Hicks (1939), and Tibor Scitovsky (1941–2).

26. The original formulation of status rights was provided by Dales (1972, pp. 152–54).

Appendix to Chapter 1

1. The graphical analysis regarding general equilibrium theory and welfare economics is consistent with its usual treatment in standard intermediate price theory textbooks, such as Pindyck and Rubinfeld (1992). The original graphical formulation was by Francis M. Bator (1957); we have generally followed the presentation by Gould and Ferguson (1980). A more advanced treatment is contained in Feldman (1980).

2. The following discussion of consumer and producer equilibrium is presented in the context of a pure exchange model. For a treatment of these issues in a competitive market framework, see, for example, Boadway and Wildasin (1984) and Pindyck and Rubinfeld (1992).

3. The following analysis is parallel to the above Edgeworth box discussion of consumer exchange.

4. A detailed discussion of real-valued social welfare functions (also known as Bergson-Samuelson welfare functions) is provided by Mueller (1989, pp. 373–83). For the original formulations, see Bergson (1938) and Samuelson (1947, ch. 8; 1955, 1956).

5. The analysis can also be carried out by reference to the Scitovsky community indifference curves in output space. For example see Rowley and Peacock (1975, pp. 46–51).

6. These four cases are variously presented in Price (1977, pp. 19–30). For an alternative graphical treatment, see DeSerpa (1988, pp. 468–72).

7. See, for example, Price (1977, p. 23).

Chapter 2

1. Coase, Calabresi, Manne, and Posner were honored as the "four founders" of law and economics at the Plenary Session of the American Law and Economics Association on 24 May 1991.

2. This is also the approach to law and economics that is reflected in the major texts in the field, including Posner (1992), Cooter and Ulen (1988), and Hirsch (1988).

3. The use of the "old" and "new" terminology is evidenced in Posner (1975, p. 759) and Kitch (1983a).

4. This brief survey of the Chicago school of law and economics prior to 1960 draws on the work of Reder (1982), Duxbury (1995, ch. 5), Kitch (1983a), and Coase (1993). See also Hovenkamp (1995).

5. Frank Knight's students included, among others, Milton Friedman, James M. Buchanan, Aaron Director, and George Stigler, all of whom, with the exception of Director, have received the Nobel Prize in Economics (as has Gary Becker, who was a student of Viner).

6. In his review of the history of law and economics at Chicago, Coase stated that "[w]hat can, I think, be said with confidence is that Simons . . . played little or no part in the development of the ideas which make up the modern subject of law and economics" (Coase, 1993, p. 242).

7. See, for example, Director (1933).

8. For wide-ranging discussions of the Chicago school of economics, see Bronfenbrenner (1962), Coats (1963), Miller (1962), Samuels (1976), and Reder (1982). It should be noted that, even today, the Chicago school is not nearly as homogeneous as some would make it out to be.

9. James M. Buchanan, an early Chicago economist, has not been reluctant to castigate the methodological thrust of "economic science" as practiced in the 1980s and exemplified by many of the positivists working within the Chicago tradition. His reference to "economic science" is purely pejorative, and he argues that the modern economists' focus on tools and mathematical prowess has rendered them illiterate as to fundamental ideas and principles of economics and, further, has turned them into ideological eunuchs. Most academic programs in economics, he says, are "now controlled by rent-recipients who simply try to ape the mainstream work of their peers in the discipline" (Buchanan, 1986, pp. 14–17).

10. On the imperialism of economics, see Brenner (1980) and Posner (1993a).

11. See, for example, Alchian (1961), Demsetz (1967), Alchian and Demsetz (1972), and Furubotn and Pejovich (1974). For a concise overview of the early economics of property rights literature, see Furubotn and Pejovich (1972).

12. Two recent extensions of the property rights approach into Neoinstitutional law and economics are found in the work of Barzel (1989) and North (1990b). See chapter 5, below, for further discussion.

13. See, for example, Demsetz (1967), North (1968), Cheung (1970), Umbeck (1977), and De Alessi (1980), which are but a few examples of the empirical research that explore the emergence and development of property rights.

14. See Cooter and Ulen (1988, p. 1) and Posner (1990, p. 354). Note that this definition of rationality does not imply the necessity of conscious deliberation.

15. See Kreps (1990, ch. 2) and Varian (1992).

16. However, as Becker (1976, pp. 151–58) has shown, we may expect an increase in price to lead to a reduction in quantity demanded even when people are not rational.

17. And thus the winners could, hypothetically, compensate the losers for their losses and still be better off, creating a hypothetical (or potential) Pareto improvement.

18. See, for example, Coleman (1980), Dworkin (1980), Kronman (1980), and Michelman (1978).

19. Posner does, however, rule certain wealth-maximizing ideas out of bounds. See generally Posner (1983, chs. 3 and 4) and Posner (1990, pp. 374–87).

20. For an elaboration of these ideas, see Posner (1983, pp. 88–115). See also Mercuro and Ryan (1984, p. 125).

21. The first Chicago study that advanced the efficiency hypothesis in in-depth form was Posner (1972b). See also Rubin (1977), Priest (1977), and Goodman (1978). An overview of the efficiency theory of the common law can be found in Posner (1992, chs. 8, 19–21) and in Cooter and Ulen (1988, ch. 10). Landes and Posner (1987) present an extensive analysis of the efficiency theory of the common law as applied to the area of torts.

22. Of course, this analysis generalizes to differing expectations of judgment value and differing subjective probabilities of prevailing at trial between plaintiff and defendant. The assumed symmetry within this example serves only to simplify the discussion.

23. There are important parallels between this idea and the Coase theorem, which is discussed below.

24. See, for example, Landes (1971).

25. See, for example, Gould (1973) and Shavell (1982).

26. The Posnerian distinction between the efficiency properties of common law and those of statutory law has been challenged by Rubin (1982). See also the essays in Hirshleifer (1982).

27. See, for example, Posner (1992, part II), Posner (1990, ch. 12), Cooter and Ulen (1988), and Landes and Posner (1987).

28. See also Posner (1992, p. 255).

29. Of course, since the cost to the polluter of abating is $600,000, the downstream landowners would not be willing to offer the polluter a "bribe" sufficient to induce him to undertake the abatement.

30. For surveys of the vast literature on the Coase theorem, see Zerbe (1980), Cooter (1982a), Medema (1994, ch. 4; 1995), and Medema and Zerbe (forthcoming). One of the most controversial aspects of the Coase theorem is what is known as the invariance proposition—that the *same* efficient outcome will be reached regardless of the initial assignment of rights. It is widely accepted that the presence of income effects is suf-

ficient to invalidate the invariance claim; that is, *an* efficient outcome will be reached regardless of the assignment of rights, but these efficient outcomes will not give *identical* allocations of resources. This issue is dealt with in detail in the above-cited surveys.

31. This is analogous to movements from positions off to positions on contract curves in the Edgeworth Box analysis of microeconomic theory. See Varian (1993, pp. 484–507).

32. Again, this is subject to the qualifications dealt with in note 30, above.

33. For an in-depth analysis of the concept of transaction costs, see Allen (1991).

34. More specifically, where transaction costs exceed the economic surplus from a bargain.

35. We are assuming, for simplicity, that the potential victim cannot take precaution here. However, the example easily generalizes to a situation in which both potential injurer and potential victim can take precaution. See Cooter and Ulen (1988, chs. 8, 9) and Posner (1992, ch. 6).

36. Comprehensive treatments of the economics of contract law include Craswell and Schwartz (1994), Cooter and Ulen (1988, chs. 6, 7), Goldberg (1989), Kornhauser (1986), Kronman and Posner (1979), and Posner (1992, ch. 4).

37. Craswell and Schwartz (1994, p. 54) illustrate the ubiquitous reliance on Coasian thinking throughout the economics of contract law in their assertion that "[w]henever a remedial rule requires conduct that seems inefficient, you should consider whether the party who would lose the most from that inefficiency will be able to pay the other party to abandon his or her insistence on the inefficient remedy."

38. On the limits of expectation damages, see Goetz and Scott (1983).

39. There are two additional efficiency issues that arise in the discussion of the appropriate form of damages. These relate to the effect of the damage remedy employed on (1) the potential breacher's incentive to undertake precaution against breach and (2) the potential victim's incentive to undertake expenditures in reliance on the contract. See, for example, Cooter and Ulen (1988, pp. 304–19) for discussion.

40. See, for example, Cooter and Ulen (1988, pp. 320–23) and, more generally, Schwartz (1979).

41. This is parallel to the argument made by Calabresi and Melamed (1972), discussed above.

42. On the economics of liquidated damages, see, for example, Goetz and Scott (1977), Cooter and Ulen (1988, pp. 293–96), and Polinsky (1989, pp. 63–65).

43. The following characterization is a bit premature. Some contributors to this area of Law and Economics have labeled it "the Legal Reformist school"; others call it "the Progressive school"; still others remain content with the "New Haven" label. Not knowing where it will all lead and recognizing that many of the contributors have (or have had) some affiliation with the Yale Law School, we follow Ackerman (1986, pp. 929–30) and Fiss (1986, pp. 7, 15) and opt for the "New Haven school" label.

44. Some of the works that underlie the ideas contained in the New Haven approach to law and economics include Rose-Ackerman (1989, 1992), Ackerman (1984), Ackerman and Stewart (1988), and Sunstein (1990).

45. This insight has been modified, qualified, and extended in more recent work by Polinsky (1979, 1980), Ayres and Talley (1995), and Kaplow and Shavell (1995a,b).

46. The contribution of Shavell (1987) marks a major extension of Calabresi's path-breaking work. Evidence of Calabresi's impact on the theory of tort law is explored in Komesar (1990).

47. As Calabresi and Klevorick (1985, p. 626) conclude, "Ultimately, the choice among . . . the [tests/rules] . . . is, as we have repeatedly said, profoundly empirical."

48. For an analysis of Calabresi's distributivist philosophy, see Attanasio (1988, 723–34).

49. Rose-Ackerman (1992, p. 20) calls the Chicago approach to law and economics "deeply flawed" as "a comprehensive view of the relationship of law to economic analysis." More generally, see Rose-Ackerman (1992, ch. 2).

50. See also Rose-Ackerman (1992, pp. 120–21).

Chapter 3

1. This review draws from Johnson (1991), Mueller (1989), McLean (1987), and Buchanan (1972, 1986).

2. Given space limitations here, we will not explore axiomatic social choice theory. Axiomatic social choice theory is an outgrowth of the theory of welfare economics and the literature on real-valued social welfare functions. Given the many difficulties in formulating real-valued social welfare functions, social choice theory sets forth various sets of axioms (based on specified value judgments) and attempts to determine the results of various collective choice processes (typically various voting schemes). For a concise review of the literature on real-valued social welfare functions and axiomatic social choice theory see Mueller (1989, pp. 373–407). As it has developed, social choice theory has become highly mathematical and abstract. On this latter point see Mitchell (1982, pp. 98–101).

3. Buchanan (1986, p. 25) has also referred to this as the "maximization-scarcity-allocation-efficiency" paradigm.

4. See Stigler (1976) and Peltzman (1976).

5. See Shughart and Tollison (1986), Faith and Tollison (1983), Stigler (1976), and Peltzman (1980).

6. Early works include Downs (1957) and Riker, *The Theory of Political Coalitions* (1962).

7. Early works include Tullock, *The Politics of Bureaucracy* (1965), Downs, *Inside Bureaucracy* (1967), and Niskanen, *Bureaucracy and Representative Government* (1971). See also the more recent treatment in Niskanen (1994).

8. Catallaxy is a term suggested by Hayek and is consistent with the earlier idea of "catallactics," the nineteenth-century science of exchanges. The concept of catallaxy is described in Buchanan (1986, pp. 19–27).

9. For a concise, critical review of both the positive and normative elements of public choice theory, see Farber and Frickey (1991).

10. For example, Judge Frank Easterbrook (1982) argued that because it relies on majority voting, the Supreme Court's opinions will necessarily be incoherent.

11. As documented by Buchanan, this movement toward closure has its roots in the work of Knut Wicksell and a group of Italian public finance scholars of the late nineteenth century including Antonio De Viti De Marco, Amilcare Puviani, Mauro Fasiana, and Matheo Pantaleoni. See Buchanan (1986, pp. 23–24) and Buchanan (1988, p. 7).

12. For a synoptic review of the nature of the analysis of politicians and bureaucrats see Reisman (1990, pp. 56–62).

13. An extensive discussion of alternative voting rules can be found in Mueller (1989, chs. 4–8).

14. See Wicksell (1896). The central portion of this work appears as "A New Principle of Just Taxation," in Wicksell (1967).

15. The most straightforward application of this is in the context of public goods. By adjusting individuals' tax shares ("Lindahl prices") to reflect the value that these individuals place on the public good in question, one can obtain unanimous consent on the provision and finance of the efficient amount of the public good.

16. There is an abundance of literature on the issue of multipeaked preferences and their implications for voting. Mueller (1989, ch. 3) provides a good discussion.

17. An important related question is whether there is any ethically acceptable scheme (i.e., voting method) for translating individual preferences into collective preferences. Arrow's impossibility theorem suggests that there is not. Arrow suggested that, in a democratic society, a collective decision-making rule should satisfy the following ethical criteria:

1. It can produce a decision whatever the configuration of voters' preferences. Thus, for example, the procedure must not fall apart if some people have multipeaked preferences.

2. It must be able to rank all possible outcomes.

3. It must be responsive to individuals' preferences. Specifically, if every individual prefers A to B, then society's ranking must prefer A to B.

4. It must be consistent in the sense that if A is preferred to B and B is preferred to C, then A is preferred to C.

5. Society's ranking of A and B depends only on individuals' rankings of A and B. Thus, the collective ranking of defense expenditures and foreign aid does not depend on how individuals rank either of them relative to research on a cure for AIDS. This assumption is sometimes called independence of irrelevant alternatives.

6. Dictatorship is ruled out. Social preferences must not reflect the preferences of only a single individual. (Rosen, 1995, p. 130, emphases omitted)

Arrow's impossibility theorem shows that there is no collective decision-making scheme that can satisfy these six reasonable ethical properties. However, if any one of these properties is dropped, it is possible to construct a decision rule that satisfies the remaining five.

18. These gaps may well be intentional, as legislators defer the difficult political choices to the bureaucrats in order to not overly damage their chances for re-election.

19. It is in this sense that Buchanan states that "[t]here are no lines to be drawn at the edges of 'the economy' and the 'polity,' or between 'markets' and 'governments,' between 'the private sector' and the 'public sector'" (Buchanan, 1986, p. 20).

20. Buchanan stresses that the catallaxy approach of public choice theory does not imply, infer, or suggest that the power elements of political relationships are squeezed out of what is transpiring in the field of politics or within the political process. He calls upon "the discipline of political science to concentrate more attention on political ar-

rangements and for that of economics to concentrate more attention on market arrangements" (Buchanan, 1986, pp. 19–20).

21. As described by Buchanan (1959, p. 129), the requirement for compensation is essential, "not in order to maintain any initial distribution on ethical grounds, but in order to decide which one from among the many possible social policy changes does, in fact, satisfy the genuine Pareto rule. Compensation is the only device available to the political economist for this purpose."

22. As Buchanan has stated, "In the subjectivist-contractarian perspective, 'efficiency' can not be said to exist except as determined by the process through which results are generated, and criteria for evaluating patterns of results must be applied only to processes" (Buchanan, 1986, p. 102).

23. Extensive discussions of rent seeking can be found in Buchanan et al. (1980), Mueller (1980, ch. 13), and Tullock (1993).

24. For critiques of this literature see Samuels and Mercuro (1984), and Medema (1991).

25. This characterization is set forth in the various contributions to the "Symposium on the Theory of Public Choice," *Virginia Law Review* (March 1988). For example, see the contributions by Geoffrey Brennan and James M. Buchanan, Dwight R. Lee, and, especially, the critical analysis of public choice theory by Mark Kelman.

26. An introduction to modern civic republicanism is provided in "Symposium: The Republican Civic Tradition," *Yale Law Journal* (July 1988). See especially the contributions by Frank Michelman (1988) and Cass R. Sunstein (1988). Elsewhere, see also Richard A. Fallon (1989), Frank Michelman (1986), and Cass R. Sunstein (1990).

27. This synoptic review of republicanism borrows heavily from Farber and Frickey (1991, pp. 42–47) and the several contributions to the "Symposium: The Republican Civic Tradition," *Yale Law Journal* (July 1988).

28. This historical account of Madison's revisions to classical republican thought is from Sunstein (1990, pp. 12–18).

29. This point is made by both Fitts (1988, p. 1651) and Bell and Bansal (1988, p. 1610).

30. These four principles are fully defined in Sunstein (1988, pp. 1541–42, 1547–58).

31. This point is made by Epstein (1988, p. 1633), who, in affirmatively describing civic republicanism, stated that "Politics offers a calling in which we can find the highest expression of individual worth and respect. Politics becomes a noble undertaking."

32. *Lochner v. New York*, 198 U.S. 45 (1905).

33. This section borrows heavily directly from Sunstein's (1988, pp. 1579–80) discussion of the Lochner era.

Chapter 4

1. For extensive surveys of Hale's contributions, see Samuels (1973) and Duxbury (1990).

2. This synoptic review of institutional economics is drawn from Bell (1967), Gordon (1964), Srivastava (1965), and Whalen (1996). For extensive overviews of institutional economics, see also Hodgson, Samuels, and Tool (1994), Samuels (1988), and Tool (1988, 1993).

3. It should be noted that Veblen placed substantial emphasis on the role of the state in giving effect to the power that he saw these business interests exerting and the manner in which this was done. Thus, although institutional law and economics has taken its cue primarily from Commons, there are certain aspects of Veblen's work that dovetail nicely with this tradition. See, for example, Duxbury (1995, pp. 108–16) and Samuels (1995).

4. The following discussion draws on Dorfman (1959), Samuels (1973), and Duxbury (1995).

5. As noted below, the work of Harry Trebing is exemplary of the contemporary Institutionalist analysis of public utility regulation.

6. Although Posner (1995, p. 3) contends that the Legal Realists had little influence on the contemporary law and economics movement, he does allow that Hale "anticipated some of the discoveries . . . of law and economics" as we know it today.

7. The following propositions were set forth by Gordon (1964, pp. 124–25).

8. This evolutionary facet of institutional economics underlies the name of the association—The Association For Evolutionary Economics—that has maintained some intellectual continuity and focus among this group of economists. The association publishes its own journal, the *Journal of Economic Issues*. The journal *Review of Political Economy* also publishes a great deal of work with an Institutionalist perspective, but with a somewhat more European flavor.

9. The drive for realistic assumptions led the early Institutionalists in particular to extensive data collection efforts. A pioneer in this regard was Wesley C. Mitchell, who is best known for his extensive studies of business cycles, and who also founded the National Bureau of Economic Research, which has become a major center for empirical work in economics.

10. See, for example, Trebing (1976, 1989) and Trebing and Estabrooks (1993).

11. See, for example, Solo (1967, 1974, 1982).

12. A concise statement of Schmid's approach to institutional law and economics is contained in his *Property, Power, and Public Choice: An Inquiry Into Law and Economics*, 2d ed. (1987), especially "Chapter 1: A General Paradigm of Institutions and Performance" (pp. 3–24); "Chapter 2: Property in a Social Context" (pp. 25–35); and "Chapter 3: Restatement of Paradigm" (pp. 181–96). For examples of empirical studies undertaken by Schmid, see Schmid (1987, pp. 257–91).

13. In addition to the essays found in Samuels and Schmid and the references cited herein, examples of the institutional approach to law and economics can be found in Schmid (1989, 1994), Mercuro and Ryan (1984), Liebhafsky (1987), Samuels (1992), Bromley (1989), Seidman (1973), Ostrom (1986), Parsons (1974), Kanal (1985), and Carter (1985).

14. See, for example, Field (1979, 1981) and Bromley (1989, ch. 2).

15. At the microlevel, the firm is seen as something more than a nexus of contracts. It is a community designed in part to suspend narrow, individualistic calculations of advantage and facilitate the learning of shared objectives. See, for example, Hodgson (1988), Eisenberg (1990), and Leibenstein (1987).

16. "Rights are whatever interests government protects vis-à-vis other interests when there is a conflict" (Samuels, 1974, p. 127). See also Samuels (1974, pp. 118–19).

17. See also Samuels (1989a, p. 1578).

18. See also Samuels and Mercuro (1979, pp. 160–63).

19. See Samuels (1971, p. 440), Samuels (1989a, p. 1565), and Schmid (1989, p. 67).

20. On this topic, see also Medema (1991).

21. The need for a comparative institutional approach has long been recognized. Other proponents—not necessarily coming from a perspective identical to that of the Institutionalists—of a comparative institutional approach include Harold Demsetz (1969), Neil Komesar (1981, 1994), Richard Stewart (1987), Kenneth Shepsle and Barry Weingast (1984), and, generally, those working under the banner of the New Institutional Economics (see ch. 5, below).

22. A sample of Institutionalist-oriented case studies include Carter (1985), Seidman (1973), Schmid (1985), and Wandschneider (1986).

23. See also Samuels (1989b).

24. See, for example, Bromley (1989), Calabresi (1985, 1991), Griffin (1991, 1995), Lang (1980), and Mishan (1972).

25. This example is drawn from Schmid (1987, pp. 263–66).

26. See, for example, Baumol and Oates (1988), Stewart (1988), and Ackerman and Stewart (1988).

27. As such, says Schmid, regulatory standards are not unlike the employment of the doctrine of reasonable use.

28. Taking this logic a step further, increases in the regulatory standard hold constant the relative ownership shares of the firms, but reduce the firms's ownership shares relative to those of the third-party environmentalists.

29. This is, according to Samuels (1971, pp. 444, 445), yet another illustration of the idea that "the issue is not government or no government but which interests, that is, whose interests the state is used to effectuate," and, at a deeper level, of the ultimate necessity and specificity of choice "which no reference to general or neutral principles will avoid." See also Mercuro and Ryan (1980).

30. For other treatments of the Institutionalist approach to the compensation issue, see Samuels (1974) and Samuels and Mercuro (1979, 1980).

Chapter 5

1. A useful overview of the early property rights literature is found in Furubotn and Pejovich (1972). A more recent treatment is contained in De Alessi (1980).

2. Oliver Williamson (1975, p. 3), a leading exponent of the NIE, acknowledges the influence of the Institutionalist John R. Commons on the NIE view of the centrality of transactions in economic activity.

3. Arrow (1969, p. 48) calls transaction costs the "costs of running the economic system"; Williamson (1985, p. 19) says that transaction costs are "the economic equivalent of friction in physical systems."

4. See also North (1989, 1993b).

5. Useful surveys of this literature are found in Furubotn and Pejovich (1972), De Alessi (1980), and Eggertsson (1990).

6. See Libecap (1989a, pp. 2, 10) and De Alessi and Staaf (1989, p. 179).

7. The rationale for the reduced incentives to develop and exchange resources when property rights are less well defined follows the line of argument developed in the discussion of common pool problems, above.

8. Issues related to the design of self-enforcing contracts will be discussed below.

9. For a discussion of common versus usufruct versus private property rights, see De Alessi (1980).

10. An empirical illustration of this line of reasoning is provided in Hayami and Ruttan (1984).

11. See Eggertsson (1990, p. 356) and Weingast and Marshall (1988).

12. The above discussion of the political contracting process is an illustration of the extension of these contracting ideas into the political arena. The fact that the political contracting process influences the development of social institutions exemplifies the multidirectional interrelations between institutional environments and institutional arrangements.

13. See, however, the discussion of contracting in the political process, above.

14. Production is organized in teams when the productive abilities of individuals working together in a team relationship exceed the sum of the outputs that could be produced with each individual working separately. See, for example, Alchian and Demsetz (1972) and Eggertsson (1990, ch. 6).

15. That is, who monitors the monitor? See Jensen and Meckling (1976) and the discussion below.

16. See Eggertsson (1990, pp. 134–35) and De Alessi and Staaf (1980, pp. 180–82).

17. This example is adapted from Jensen and Meckling (1976, pp. 312–13).

18. See, for example, Barzel (1985, 1987) and Eggertsson (1990, ch. 6).

19. The following discussion draws on Grossman and Hart (1986) and Hart (1990).

20. A note on terminology is in order here. The particular vein of NIE research discussed in this section goes by the name of "transaction cost economics," following the lead of Oliver Williamson. However, as should be apparent from the above discussion, the use of transaction cost analysis is pervasive within the NIE, and thus the ideas discussed below are just one manifestation of transaction cost analysis, in spite of the label attached to them.

21. For a discussion of hold-up problems and quasi rents, see Klein, Crawford, and Alchian (1978). Quasi rents are the difference between an asset's value in its current use and the value of that asset in its next best use.

22. Williamson (1983, p. 519) draws the following distinction between credible commitments and credible threats: "The former involve reciprocal acts designed to safeguard a relationship, while the latter are unilateral efforts to preempt an advantage." See also Williamson (1985, chs. 7, 8).

23. Lester Telser defines a self-enforcing agreement as one in which, if "one party violates the terms the only recourse of the other [party] is to terminate the agreement" (Telser, 1981, p. 27, quoted in Williamson, 1985, p. 168).

24. This discussion illustrates that the property rights/agency and TCE approaches to contracting are not mutually exclusive. That is, the hostages function as, in a sense, incentive-alignment mechanisms between the contracting parties. Where the hostages are offered within the confines of the contract, these approaches converge. However, the TCE approach recognizes that hostage offers may also exist outside of the confines of the contract (Klein, 1992, p. 159). See also Klein (1985).

25. See Goldberg (1976a,b), Macneil (1974), and Williamson (e.g., 1984, 1985, 1991).

26. This discussion is indicative of another major point of divergence between the property rights/agency and TCE approaches: The property rights/agency literature im-

plicitly or explicitly relies on the ability of courts to resolve any disputes that may arise, whereas TCE emphasizes that parties may choose to establish extrajudicial dispute resolution mechanisms to forestall recourse to litigation. See Klein (1992, p. 159) and Williamson (1985, pp. 26–32).

27. See, more generally, Macneil (1974, 1978, 1981) and Williamson (1985, 1991).

28. See Macneil (1978, pp. 870–80) from which the following discussion is drawn.

29. This discussion is based on Williamson (1991, p. 290).

30. See Williamson (1991, pp. 277–79; 1985).

Chapter 6

1. For a concise review of CLS, see Tushnet (1984). More elaborate reviews are provided in Kelman (1987), Hutchinson (1988), Altman (1990), and Boyle (1994).

2. In CLS, *liberalism* is broadly defined as the spectrum of scholarship outside of the range of ideas associated with Marxism and critical scholarship. As such, the work of John Stuart Mill, Richard Posner, John Rawls, Robert Nozick, and Ronald Dworkin, among others, is taken to comprise liberalism. See Hutchinson and Monahan (1984a, p. 209).

Elsewhere, Hutchinson and Monahan describe the "mansion of modern liberalism" as having two wings. One wing is based on the teleological approach, where, in the context of individual freedom, the justification of actions depends upon some future good to be achieved. This wing emphasizes that the "right" must be subordinated to the "good," that is, that the ends of actions count for more than the means. The other wing is based on the deontological approach, where, if an individual is to be treated as separate and independent, the individual must remain entirely sovereign in choice of actions. This wing emphasizes that the "right" must take priority over the "good," that is, that the source of an action is more important than its consequences. See Hutchinson and Monahan (1984b, p. 1480).

Sparer (1984, p. 516) describes *liberalism* as "the dominant Western ideology . . . seen as viewing the world in terms of a series of contradictory dualities and values such as reasons and desire; freedom and necessity; individualism and altruism; autonomy and community; and subjectivity and objectivity."

3. In CLS, *formalism* is used to convey the notion that law is a deductive and autonomous science; it is self-contained in the sense that particular decisions follow from the application of legal principles, precedents, and rules of procedure without regard to values, and outside of a social, political, or economic context. See Schwartz (1984, p. 431).

4. For a concise review of the CLS critique of (Chicago) law and economics, see Tushnet (1980, 1986, p. 508), Kelman (1979a,b; 1987, chs. 4, 5), and Kornhauser (1984, pp. 357–64). CLS is also critical of the work of the rights-based theorists. See Hutchinson and Monahan (1984b, pp. 1477–91) and Kornhauser (1984, pp. 364–66).

5. For a restatement of the issues surrounding the dispute as to whether CLS *ought* to advance a coherent, substantive working alternative theory, see Hunt (1987). The dispute as to whether a "grand theory" is desirable is evidenced in Kennedy and Gabel (1984). Levinson (citing Tushnet) describes the so-called "blueprint problem" as CLS's refusal to offer such "blueprints" on the grounds that one cannot really know how a

radically transformed society would or should operate (Levinson, 1989). On the question of CLS's commitment to praxis, see Sparer (1984, pp. 552–67).

6. Before proceeding we should note two points. The first is that most, if not all of the writings in CLS are characteristically "dense and difficult and often inaccessible" (Gordon, 1990, p. 415). The second point to note is that CLS has other strands beyond those reviewed here. One strand includes the work of some of the law and social science scholars whose origins lie in the work of the "law and development movement" of the late 1960s and 1970s. See, for example, Trubeck and Galanter (1974). This group of CLSers includes empirically oriented social scientists who were originally the central representatives of the Law and Society Association (founded in 1964). Much of this work is published in the *Law & Society Review*. See Note (1982, p. 1670 at note 5). In many respects, the law and society movement also represented an effort to fill the void left by the Legal Realists. See Friedman (1986). Although this group has often been characterized as part of CLS, especially in the early years, it may now be more accurate to consider the Law and Society circle as a separate entity. See Hutchinson and Monahan (1984a, p. 200) and Donohue (1988).

Although CLS continues to sputter along in various places with uneven intensity, two related movements—critical feminist theory and critical race theory—have emerged within CLS. In 1985, the critical feminists organized the Nineth annual Conference on Critical Legal Studies as the "CLS Feminist Conference," and, over the ensuing decade, their contributions—although delayed (see Schlegel, 1984, pp. 398 at note 24, 410)— have grown substantially. See, for example, Taub and Schneider (1990) and Olsen (1990). The critical feminists have now been joined by yet another movement within CLS, critical race theory, as exemplified in Williams (1987) and Delgado (1987).

7. See Note (1982, p. 1677). See also Tushnet (1986, pp. 505–7).

8. See Note (1982, p. 1681 at note 81). CLS also rejects both the instrumentalist and formalist approaches to the study of law. The instrumentalist approach denies that the legal order possesses any autonomy from the demands imposed on it by the actors within the capitalistic society; it conceives of law as a mere instrument or tool of the will of the dominant class of parties of interest. The formalist approach, in contrast, asserts an absolute, unqualified autonomy of the legal order from society; the legal order is a closed system whose meaning and development is to be understood exclusively in terms of its own internal dynamic. See Balbus (1977, pp. 571–72). As noted by Kornhauser (1984, pp. 361, 369), "Almost all American legal scholars, judges, and lawyers hold an instrumental view of the law. . . . Most lawyers in the United States, as legal instrumentalists, believe that laws should promote some desired conduct in the real world."

9. For a review of their works, see Hofstadter (1968).

10. For an historical account of this era, see Gould (1974).

11. On the distinction between Scientific Marxism and Critical Marxism, see Gouldner (1980). For a recount of the initial relationships between members of the "Law and Society" group and the CLSers as well as some of the philosophical debates internal to CLS—the so-called "three-corner catch" between the "law and social science crowd," the Scientific Marxists, and the Critical Marxists—see Schlegel (1984).

12. The Scientific Marxist tradition is more akin to the central premises of Marxist thought. This characterization of the two strands of Marxism is provided by Schlegel (1984, p. 393 at note 9). See also Note (1982, p. 1677 at note 58). The Critical Marxist

theory draws on the work of several schools of thought within continental philosophy, including (1) the Frankfurt School of Sociology, especially the work of Max Horkheimer, Herbert Marcuse, and Theodor Adorno; (2) the writings of Karl Mannheim, Michel Foucault, A. Gramsci, and Jürgen Habermas; (3) the structuralists, for example, F. de Saussure and Claude Lévi-Strauss; (4) the phenomenologists, such as E. Husserl, Martin Heidegger, and M. Merleau-Ponty; and (5) the hermeneutists, such as H. G. Gadamer and Paul Ricoeur. See Kornhauser (1984, p. 367 at note 53), Hutchinson and Monahan (1984a, pp. 215–16), and Schlegel (1984, p. 393 at note 9). See also David Kennedy (1985–1986).

13. Elsewhere, Hutchinson and Monahan (1984b, p. 1488) document "the distance between CLS and classical Marxism."

14. As Hutchinson and Monahan (1984a, p. 221) point out, orthodox Marxism has always been committed to defining the nature of the nexus between the material conditions of life and the superstructure of society.

15. See Note (1982, p. 1682), and Klare (1979, pp. 123–24).

16. As to the many reasons that have been offered explaining why a Marxist legal culture was so slow to develop in the United States, see Klare (1979, p. 124 at note 4).

17. Abel (1990), as described by Hutchinson and Monahan (1984a, p. 222).

18. Feinman and Gabel (1990), as described by Hutchinson and Monahan (1984a, pp. 222–23).

19. In CLS writings, the term *contradiction* is used in the manner of the Marxian dialectic to denote conflicting social forces, especially within advanced capitalism. See Schwartz (1984, p. 429).

20. In reviewing a 1982 lecture titled "What's Really Going on in the Law School Classroom?" presented by Horwitz to the students of Harvard Law School, Hudson quotes Horwitz as stating that "anyone who attempts to find a realm of neutral craft and law distinct from politics is lying to himself" (Hudson, 1982, p. 5). As described by Hutchinson and Monahan, "whether presented in terms of legal doctrine or policy analysis and no matter how skilled the advocate or judge is, *no objective correct results exist*—choosing between values is inescapable" (Hutchinson and Monahan, 1984a, p. 208, emphasis added). Within the tradition of CLS Enlightenment rationality, Peller (1985) has explored the socially-created metaphors that provide the mythical distinctions between law and politics.

21. See Fraser (1978, p. 147). In CLS, the concept of "legal ideology" is used in a manner similar to Gramsci's use of "hegemony," which is the term for the noncoercive control of oppressed classes in society by means of nongovernmental structures and activities. Thus, to the extent that legal ideology serves to falsely legitimate a social structure, the individual's relationship with the law can be characterized as one of "hegemony" (Kornhauser, 1984, p. 376).

22. As described by Kornhauser (1984, pp. 372–73), "Ideology is pejorative; it is something to see through and discard."

23. See also Tushnet (1986, pp. 506–7), who traces the importance to CLS of the idea of illegitimate hierarchy as an ordering institution in our society to both the Realists' and American historiography's emphasis on the importance of relations of power in the development and employment of law.

24. See Heller (1984, p. 173) and Schwartz (1984, p. 423).

25. For a concise review of the studies comprising this line of literature (mostly, though not exclusively, the work of Kennedy, Unger, Kelman, Brest, Klare, Singer, etc.), see Hutchinson and Monahan (1984a, pp. 223–26; 1984b, pp. 1482–85).

26. See Hutchinson and Monahan (1984a, p. 211). Sparer suggests that the "private/ public" distinction that remains at the core of CLS theory was originally espoused by Karl Marx (1958) in *On the Jewish Question* wherein, in a critique of Hegelian philosophy, Marx explores the difference between political and human emancipation, arguing that the modern state splits the human being between political life, which is public and communal in spirit, and civil life, with its individualistic pursuit of private gain. See Sparer (1984, pp. 527–35).

27. Unger (1983), as described by Hutchinson and Monahan (1984a, pp. 223–25).

28. Klare (1981), as described by Trubek (1984, p. 595) and by Hutchinson and Monahan (1984a, pp. 223–25).

29. Kelman (1981), as described by Schwartz (1984, p. 427).

30. This is of course consistent with the orthodox Marxist position that identifies the community as the paramount source of value. See Hutchinson and Monahan (1984b, p. 1488).

31. These include semiology, phenomenology, and structuralism. See Note (1982, p. 1683) and Tushnet (1986, p. 513).

32. See Note (1982, pp. 1682–83) and Kornhauser (1984, p. 366 at note 52).

Chapter 7

1. See also Fiss (1989).

2. On Kronman's skepticism regarding the economic analysis of law, see Kronman (1993, pp. 226–240).

3. This includes the greater body of common law, constitutional law, and statute law that has economic implications, as well as the role and behavior of the legislature and the bureaucracy.

4. The Fifth Amendment to the U.S. Constitution states "nor shall private property be taken for public use without just compensation." Although cases regarding regulatory takings are not new, the U.S. Supreme Court case that firmly established them as a distinctive class was *Penn Central Transportation Company v. City of New York*, 98 S.Ct. 2646 (1978).

5. The facts of this case are taken directly from the *U.S. Supreme Court Reporter.* This section draws directly from the case as reported. Our purpose in so stating this is to avoid what otherwise would be excessive citations within this brief review of the case.

6. This section of the ordinance is contained in *Pennell v. City of San Jose* (hereafter cited in the text as *Pennell*), 108 S.Ct. 849 (1988) at 854.

7. Chief Justice Rehnquist delivered the opinion of the Court. Justice Scalia, with whom Justice O'Connor joined, concurred in part and dissented in part. Justice Kennedy took no part in the decision of this case.

8. See, for example, Ellickson (1989), Kahneman, Knetsch, and Thaler (1990), and Hoffman and Spitzer (1993) from the sympathetic point of view, and Kelman (1979a,b, 1987) from the opponents' camp.

9. The application of economic reasoning to wide-ranging areas of law is confined almost exclusively to the Chicago approach, and the best general discussion of this is found in Posner (1992). A number of the essays in Posner (1995) also reflect the wide-ranging application of the Chicago approach.

10. For example, the 1995 meetings of the American Law and Economics Association included a number of papers probing these frontiers.

11. In passing we note that most critics of the economic analysis of law identify Law and Economics almost exclusively as Chicago law and economics; hence the critics' hostility toward efficiency is concentrated on Chicago.

12. As to this critique from the Institutionalists, see chapter 4, above. For other, similar critiques, see also Calabresi (1982, 1991) and the references cited in Duxbury (1995, p. 403 at notes 512–514).

13. The *first-order rule* is consistent with solving an unconstrained maximization problem, whereas the *second-order rule* is consistent with solving a constrained maximization problem.

14. See the discussion of this point in chapter 2, above.

15. See the quote from Hirsch at pp. 23–24, above.

16. See the quote from Kneese at p. 18, above.

17. See, for example, Ulen (1989, pp. 223–24) and Coase (1992, pp. 718–19).

Abel, Richard. "Torts." In *The Politics of Law: A Progressive Critique*, edited by David Kairys, 326–49. New York: Pantheon Books, 1990.

Abrams, Kathryn. "Law's Republicanism." *Yale Law Journal* 97 (July 1988): 1591–1608.

Ackerman, Bruce A. *Reconstructing American Law*. Cambridge, Mass.: Harvard University Press, 1984.

———. "Law, Economics, and the Problem of Legal Culture." *Duke Law Journal* 6 (December 1986): 929–47.

Ackerman, Bruce A., and Richard B. Stewart. "Reforming Environmental Law: The Democratic Case for Market Incentives." *Columbia Journal of Environmental Law* 13, no. 2 (1988): 171–99.

Adams, Henry C. *Relation of the State to Industrial Action and Economics and Jurisprudence*. Edited by Joseph Dorfman. New York: Columbia University Press, 1954.

Agnello, Richard J., and Lawrence P. Donnelley. "Prices and Property Rights in the Fisheries." *Southern Economic Journal* 42 (October 1975): 253–62.

Alchian, Armen A. "Private Property and the Relative Cost of Tenure." In *The Public Stake in Union Power*, edited by P.D. Bradley. Charlottesville, Va.: University of Virginia Press, 1959.

———. *Some Economics of Property*. Santa Monica, Calif.: Rand Corporation, 1961.

Alchian, Armen A., and Harold Demsetz. "Production, Information Costs, and Economic Organization." *American Economic Review* 62 (December 1972): 777–95.

Allen, Douglas W. "What Are Transaction Costs?" *Research in Law and Economics* 14 (1991): 1–18.

Altman, Andrew. *Critical Legal Studies: A Liberal Critique*. Princeton: Princeton University Press, 1990.

Anderson, Terry L., and P. J. Hill. "The Evolution of Property Rights: A Study of the American West." *Journal of Law and Economics* 18 (April 1975): 163–79.

Arrow, Kenneth J. *Social Choice and Individual Values*. New York: John Wiley, 1951.

———. "The Organization of Economic Activity: Issues Pertinent to the Choice of Market versus Nonmarket Allocation." In *The Analysis and Evaluation of Public Expenditures: The PPB System*. Joint Economic Committee, 91st Cong. 1st sess., 44–64. Washington, D.C.: U.S. Government Printing Office, 1969.

Attanasio, John B. "The Principle of Aggregate Autonomy and the Calabresian Approach to Products Liability." *Virginia Law Review* 74 (May 1988): 677–750.

Ayres, Clarence E. *The Theory of Economic Progress*. Chapel Hill: University of North Carolina Press, 1944.

Ayres, Ian, and Robert Gertner. "Filling Gaps in Incomplete Contracts: An Economic Theory of Default Rules." *Yale Law Journal* 99 (October 1989): 87–130.

Ayres, Ian, and Eric Talley. "Solomonic Bargaining: Dividing a Legal Entitlement to Facilitate Coasean Trade." *Yale Law Journal* 104 (March 1995): 1027–1117.

Balbus, Isaac D. "Commodity Form and Legal Form: An Essay on the 'Relative Autonomy' of the Law." *Law and Society* 11 (winter 1977): 571–88.

Barnard, Chester. *The Functions of the Executive.* Cambridge, Mass.: Harvard University Press, 1938.

Barnett, Randy. "The Function of Several Property and the Freedom of Contract." *Social Philosophy and Policy* 9 (winter 1992): 61–84.

Barone, E. "The Ministry of Production in the Collectivist State." In *Collectivist Economic Planning*, edited by F. A. Hayek, 245–90. London: Routledge, 1935.

Barzel, Yoram. "Transaction Costs: Are They Just Costs?" *Journal of Institutional and Theoretical Economics* 141, no. 1 (1985): 4–16.

———. "The Entrepreneur's Reward for Self-Policing." *Economic Inquiry* 25 (January 1987): 103–16.

———. *Economic Analysis of Property Rights.* Cambridge: Cambridge University Press, 1989.

Bator, Francis M. "The Simple Analytics of Welfare Maximization." *American Economic Review* 47 (March 1957): 22–59.

Baumol, William J., and Wallace E. Oates. *The Theory of Environmental Policy.* 2d ed. Cambridge: Cambridge University Press, 1988.

Beard, Charles A. *An Economic Interpretation of the Constitution of the United States.* New York: Macmillan, 1913.

Becker, Gary S. *The Economics of Discrimination.* Chicago: University of Chicago Press, 1957.

———."A Theory of the Allocation of Time." *Economic Journal* 75 (September 1965): 493–517.

———. "Crime and Punishment: An Economic Approach." *Journal of Political Economy* 76 (March/April 1968): 169–217.

———. *The Economic Approach to Human Behavior.* Chicago: University of Chicago Press, 1976.

Becker, Gary S., and Robert J. Barro. "A Reformulation of the Economic Theory of Fertility." *Quarterly Journal of Economics* 103 (February 1988): 1–25.

Becker, Gary S., Michael Grossman, and Kevin M. Murphy. "Rational Addiction and the Effects of Price on Consumption." *American Economic Review* 81 (May 1991): 237–41.

Becker, Gary S., and Kevin M. Murphy. "The Family and the State." *Journal of Law and Economics* 31 (April 1988a): 1–18.

———. "A Theory of Rational Addiction." *Journal of Political Economy* 96 (August 1988b): 675–700.

Bell, Derrick, and Preeta Bansal. "The Republican Revival and Racial Politics." *Yale Law Journal* 97 (July 1988): 1609–21.

Bell, E. T. *Men of Mathematics.* New York: Simon and Schuster, 1937.

Bell, John F. "Institutional Economics." In *A History of Economic Thought*, 539–71. New York: Ronald Press, 1967.

Bergson, Abram. "A Reformulation of Certain Aspects of Welfare Economics." *Quarterly Journal of Economics* 52 (February 1938): 310–34.

Berolzheimer, Fritz. *The World's Legal Philosophies.* Boston: Boston Book Company, 1912. Reprint, Rothman Reprints, 1968.

Black, Duncan. *The Theory of Committees and Elections.* Cambridge: Cambridge University Press, 1958.

Blaug, Mark. *Economic Theory in Retrospect.* 3d ed. Cambridge: Cambridge University Press, 1978.

Boadway, Robin W., and David E. Wildasin. *Public Sector Economics.* 2d ed. Boston: Little, Brown, 1984.

Bodenheimer, Edgar. *Jurisprudence: The Philosophy and Method of the Law.* Rev. ed. Cambridge, Mass.: Harvard University Press, 1974.

Bottomly, Anthony. "The Effect of Common Ownership of Land upon Resource Allocation in Tripolitania." *Land Economics* 39 (February 1963): 91–95.

Boyle, James. *Critical Legal Studies.* New York: New York University Press, 1994.

Breimyer, Harold. "Government Intervention: A Deceptive Label." *Choices* 6 (Second Quarter, 1991): 3.

Breit, William. "The Development of Clarence Ayres's Theoretical Institutionalism." *Social Science Quarterly* 54 (September 1973): 244–57.

Brenner, Reuven. "Economics—An Imperialist Science?" *Journal of Legal Studies* 9 (January 1980): 179–88.

Bromley, Daniel W. *Economic Interests and Institutions.* New York: Basil Blackwell, 1989.

Bronfenbrenner, Martin. "Observations on the Chicago School(s)." *Journal of Political Economy* 60 (February 1962): 72–75.

Buchanan, James M. "Positive Economics, Welfare Economics, and Political Economy." *Journal of Law and Economics* 2 (October 1959): 124–38.

———. "Toward Analysis of Closed Behavioral Systems." In *Theory of Public Choice*, edited by James M. Buchanan and Robert D. Tollison, 11–23. Ann Arbor: University of Michigan Press, 1972.

———. "A Contractarian Paradigm for Applying Economic Theory." *American Economic Review* 65 (May 1975): 225–30.

———. "Why Does Government Grow?" In *Budgets and Bureaucrats: The Sources of Government Growth*, edited by Thomas Borcherding, 3–18. Durham, N.C.: Duke University Press, 1977.

———. "Rent Seeking and Profit Seeking." In *Toward a Theory of the Rent-Seeking Society*, edited by James M. Buchanan, Robert Tollison, and Gordon Tullock, 3–15. College Station: Texas A&M University Press, 1980.

———. *Liberty, Market and State.* Brighton, Sussex: Wheatshaft Books, 1986.

———. "The Economic Theory of Politics Reborn." *Challenge* 31 (March/April 1988): 4–10.

Buchanan, James M., Robert Tollison, and Gordon Tullock. *Toward a Theory of the Rent-Seeking Society.* College Station: Texas A&M University Press, 1980.

Buchanan, James M., and Gordon Tullock. *The Calculus of Consent.* Ann Arbor: University of Michigan Press, 1962.

Buckingham, Walter S. *Theoretical Economic Systems: A Comparative Analysis.* New York: Ronald Press Company, 1958.

Burrows, Paul, and Cento G. Veljanovski. "Introduction: The Economic Approach to Law." In *The Economic Approach to Law*, edited by Paul Burrows and Cento G. Veljanovski, 1–34. London: Butterworths, 1981.

Calabresi, Guido. "Some Thoughts on Risk Distribution and the Law of Torts." *Yale Law Journal* 70 (March 1961): 499–553.

————. *The Cost of Accidents: A Legal and Economic Analysis.* New Haven: Yale University Press, 1970.

————. "About Law and Economics: A Letter to Ronald Dworkin." *Hofstra Law Review* 8 (spring 1980): 553–62.

————. "The New Economic Analysis of Law: Scholarship, Sophistry, or Self-Indulgence." *Proceedings of the British Academy* 68 (1982): 85–108.

————. *Ideals, Beliefs, Attitudes, and the Law: Private Law Perspectives on a Public Law Problem.* Syracuse, N.Y.: Syracuse University Press, 1985.

————. "The Pointlessness of Pareto: Carrying Coase Further." *Yale Law Journal* 100 (March 1991): 1211–37.

Calabresi, Guido, and Jon T. Hirschoff. "Towards a Test for Strict Liability in Torts." *Yale Law Journal* 81 (May 1972): 1055–85.

Calabresi, Guido, and Alvin K. Klevorick. "Four Tests for Liability in Torts." *Journal of Legal Studies* 14 (December 1985): 585–627.

Calabresi, Guido, and A. Douglas Melamed. "Property Rules, Liability Rules, and Inalienability: One View of the Cathedral." *Harvard Law Review* 85 (April 1972): 1089–1128.

Carter, Michael R. "A Wisconsin Institutionalist Perspective on Microeconomic Theory of Institutions: The Insufficiency of Pareto Efficiency." *Journal of Economic Issues* 19 (September 1985): 797–813.

Cheung, Steven N. S. "Transaction Costs, Risk Aversion, and the Choice of Contractual Arrangements." *Journal of Law and Economics* 12 (April 1969): 23–42.

————. "The Structure of a Contract and the Theory of Non-exclusive Resource." *Journal of Law and Economics* 13 (April 1970): 49–70.

————. "On the New Institutional Economics." In *Contract Economics*, edited by Lars Werin and Hans Wijkander, 48–65. Cambridge, Mass.: Basil Blackwell, 1992.

Coase, Ronald H. "The Nature of the Firm." *Economica* 1, n.s. (November 1937): 386–405.

————. "The Problem of Social Cost." *Journal of Law and Economics* 3 (October 1960): 1–44.

————. "The New Institutional Economics." *Journal of Institutional and Theoretical Economics* 140 (March 1984): 229–31.

————. "Blackmail." *Virginia Law Review* 74 (May 1988): 655–76.

————. "The Institutional Structure of Production." *American Economic Review* 82 (September 1992a): 713–19.

————. "On the New Institutional Economics: Comments." In *Contract Economics*, edited by Lars Werin and Hans Wijkander, 72–75. Cambridge, Mass.: Basil Blackwell, 1992b.

————. "Law and Economics at Chicago." *Journal of Law and Economics* 36 (April 1993): 239–54.

Coats, A. W. "The Origins of the 'Chicago School(s)'?" *Journal of Political Economy* 61 (October 1963): 487–93.

Coleman, Jules. "Efficiency, Utility, and Wealth Maximization." *Hofstra Law Review* 8 (spring 1980): 509–51.

Commager, Henry Steele. *The American Mind.* New Haven: Yale University Press, 1950.

Commons, John R. *Proportional Representation.* 2d ed. 1907. Reprint, New York: Augustus M. Kelley, 1967.

———. *Legal Foundations of Capitalism.* 1924. Reprint, Clifton, N.J.: Augustus M. Kelley, 1974.

———. "Law and Economics." *Yale Law Journal* 34 (February 1925): 371–82.

———. *Institutional Economics.* New York: Macmillan, 1934.

Cooter, Robert. "The Cost of Coase." *Journal of Legal Studies* 11 (January 1982a): 1–33.

———. "Law and the Imperialism of Economics: An Introduction to the Economic Analysis of Law and a Review of the Major Books." *UCLA Law Review* 29 (June–August 1982b): 1260–69.

Cooter, Robert, and Thomas Ulen. *Law and Economics.* Glenview, Ill.: Scott, Foresman, 1988.

Cotterrell, Roger. *The Politics of Jurisprudence.* London: Butterworths, 1989.

Craswell, Richard, and Alan Schwartz. *Foundations of Contract Law.* New York: Oxford University Press, 1994.

Dales, John H. "Rights and Economics." In *Perspectives of Property*, edited by Gene Wunderlich and W. L. Gibson Jr., 149–55. University Park, Pa.: Institute for Research on Land and Water Resources, Pennsylvania State University, 1972.

Davis, Lance E., and Douglass C. North. *Institutional Change and American Economic Growth.* Cambridge: Cambridge University Press, 1971.

De Alessi, Louis. "The Economics of Property Rights: A Review of the Evidence." *Research in Law and Economics* 2 (1980): 1–47.

———. "Form, Substance, and Welfare Comparisons in the Analysis of Institutions." *Journal of Institutional and Theoretical Economics* 146, no. 1 (1990): 5–23.

De Alessi, Louis, and Robert J. Staaf. "Property Rights and Choice." In *Law and Economics*, edited by Nicholas Mercuro, 175–200. Boston: Kluwer, 1989.

Delgado, Richard. "The Ethereal Scholar: Does Critical Legal Studies Have What Minorities Want?" *Harvard Civil Rights-Civil Liberties Review* 22 (spring 1987): 301–22.

Demsetz, Harold. "The Exchange and Enforcement of Property Rights." *Journal of Law and Economics* 7 (October 1964): 11–26.

———. "Toward a Theory of Property Rights." *American Economic Review* 57 (May 1967): 347–59.

———. "Information and Efficiency: Another Viewpoint." *Journal of Law and Economics* 12 (April 1969): 1–22.

DeSerpa, Allan C. *Microeconomic Theory.* Boston: Allyn and Bacon, 1988.

Director, Aaron. "The Economics of Technocracy." In *Public Policy Pamphlet No. 2*, edited by Harry D. Gideonse. Chicago: University of Chicago Press, 1933.

Donohue, John J. "Law and Economics: The Road Not Taken." *Law and Society Review* 22, no. 5 (1988): 903–26.

Dorfman, Joseph. *The Economic Mind in American Civilization. Volumes IV and V: 1918–1933.* New York: Viking Press, 1959. Reissued by Augustus M. Kelley Publishers, 1969.

Downs, Anthony. *The Economic Theory of Democracy.* New York: Harper, 1957.

―――. *Inside Bureaucracy.* Boston: Little, Brown, 1967.

Duxbury, Neil. "Robert Hale and the Economy of Legal Force." *Modern Law Review* 53 (July 1990): 421–44.

―――. *Patterns of American Jurisprudence.* Oxford: Oxford University Press, 1995.

Dworkin, Ronald M. *Taking Rights Seriously.* Cambridge, Mass.: Harvard University Press, 1977.

―――. "Is Wealth a Value?" *Journal of Legal Studies* 9 (March 1980): 191–226.

―――. *Law's Empire.* Cambridge, Mass.: Belknap Press, 1986.

Easterbrook, Frank. "Ways of Criticizing the Court." *Harvard Law Review* 95 (February 1982): 802–32.

Eggertsson, Thráinn. *Economic Behavior and Institutions.* Cambridge: Cambridge University Press, 1990.

―――. "Institutions and Credible Commitment: Comment." *Journal of Institutional and Theoretical Economics* 149 (March 1993): 24–28.

Eisenberg, Melvin A. "An Overview of Law and Economics." Working Paper No. 90-9, School of Law, University of California, Berkeley, 1990.

Ellickson, Robert C. "Bringing Culture and Human Frailty to Rational Actors: A Critique of Classical Law and Economics." *Chicago-Kent Law Review* 65, no. 1 (1989): 23–55.

―――. *Order without Law: How Neighbors Settle Disputes.* Cambridge, Mass.: Harvard University Press, 1991.

Ely, Richard T. *Property and Contract in Their Relation to the Distribution of Wealth,* 2 vols. New York: Macmillan, 1914.

England, Izhak. *The Philosophy of Tort Law.* Aldershot: Dartmouth, 1993.

Epstein, Richard. "A Theory of Strict Liability." *Journal of Legal Studies* 2 (January 1973): 151–204.

―――. "The Static Conception of the Common Law." *Journal of Legal Studies* 9 (March 1980): 253–75.

―――. "Modern Republicanism—Or the Flight from Substance." *Yale Law Journal* 97 (July 1988): 1633–50.

Faith, Roger L., and Robert D. Tollison. "Voter Search for Efficient Representation." *Research in Law and Economics* 5 (1983): 211–24.

Fallon, Richard A. "What Is Republicanism and Is It Worth Reviving?" *Harvard Law Review* 102 (May 1989): 1695–1735.

Farber, Daniel A., and Philip P. Frickey. *Law and Public Choice.* Chicago: University of Chicago Press, 1991.

Feinman, Jay M., and Peter Gabel. "Contract Law as Ideology." In *The Politics of Law: A Progressive Critique,* edited by David Kairys, 373–86. New York: Pantheon Books, 1990.

Feldman, Allan M. *Welfare Economics and Social Choice Theory.* Boston: Martinus Nijhoff, 1980.

Field, Alexander J. "On the Explanation of Rules Using Rational Choice Models." *Journal of Economic Issues* 13 (March 1979): 49–72.

―――. "The Problem with Neoclassical Institutional Economics." *Explorations in Economic History* 18 (April 1981): 174–198.

Fisher, William W., Morton J. Horwitz, and Thomas A. Reed. *American Legal Realism.* New York: Oxford University Press, 1993.

Fiss, Owen M. "The Death of Law?" *Cornell Law Review* 72 (November 1986): 1–16.

———. "The Law Regained." *Cornell Law Review* 74 (January 1989): 245–55.

Fitts, Michael A. "Look before You Leap: Some Cautionary Notes on Civic Republicanism." *Yale Law Journal* 97 (July 1988): 1651–62.

Fox, Eleanor M. "The Battle for the Soul of Antitrust." *California Law Review* 75 (May 1987): 917–23.

Frank, Jerome. *Law and the Modern Mind.* New York: Brentano's, 1930.

Fraser, Andrew. "The Legal Theory We Need Now." *Socialist Review* 8 (July-October 1978): 147–87.

Fried, Charles. *Right and Wrong.* Cambridge, Mass.: Harvard University Press, 1978.

Friedman, Lawrence M. *A History of American Law.* New York: Simon and Schuster, 1973.

———. "The Law and Society Movement." *Stanford Law Review* 38 (February 1986): 763–80.

Furubotn, Eirik G., and Svetozar Pejovich. "Property Rights and Economic Theory: A Survey of the Literature." *Journal of Economic Literature* 10 (December 1972): 1137–62.

———. *The Economics of Property Rights.* Cambridge, Mass.: Ballinger Publishing, 1974.

Furubotn, Eirik G., and Rudolf Richter. "The New Institutional Economics: An Assessment." In *The New Institutional Economics,* edited by Eirik G. Furubotn and Rudolf Richter, 1–32. College Station: Texas A&M University Press, 1991.

Goetz, Charles J., and Robert E. Scott. "Liquidated Damages, Penalties, and the Just Compensation Principle: Some Notes on an Enforcement Model and a Theory of Efficient Breach." *Columbia Law Review* 77 (May 1977): 554–94.

———. "The Mitigation Principle: Toward a General Theory of Contractual Obligation." *Virginia Law Review* 69 (September 1983): 967–1024.

Goldberg, Victor. "Regulation and Administered Contracts." *Bell Journal of Economics* 7 (autumn 1976a): 426–48.

———. "Toward an Expanded Economic Theory of Contract." *Journal of Economic Issues* 10 (March 1976b): 45–61.

Goldberg, Victor, ed. *Readings in the Economics of Contract Law.* Cambridge: Cambridge University Press, 1989.

Goodman, John C. "An Economic Theory of the Evolution of Common Law." *Journal of Legal Studies* 7 (June 1978): 393–406.

Gordon, H. Scott. "The Economic Theory of a Common-Property Resource: The Fishery." *Journal of Political Economy* 62 (April 1954): 124–42.

Gordon, Robert A. *Institutional Economics.* Berkeley: University of California Press, 1964.

Gordon, Robert W. "New Developments in Legal Theory." In *The Politics of Law: A Progressive Critique,* edited by David Kairys, 413–25. New York: Pantheon, 1990.

Gould, John P. "The Economics of Legal Conflicts." *Journal of Legal Studies* 2 (January 1973): 279–300.

Gould, J. P., and C. E. Ferguson. *Microeconomic Theory.* 5th ed. Homewood, Ill.: Richard D. Irwin, 1980.

Gould, Lewis L., ed. *The Progressive Era.* Syracuse, N.Y.: Syracuse University Press, 1974.

Gouldner, Alvin W. *The Two Marxisms.* New York: Seabury Press, 1980.

Grey, Thomas C. "Langdell's Orthodoxy." *University of Pittsburgh Law Review* 45 (fall 1983): 1–53.

Griffin, Ronald. "The Welfare Analytics of Transaction Costs, Externalities and Institutional Choice." *American Journal of Agricultural Economics* 73 (August 1991): 601–14.

———. "On the Meaning of Economic Efficiency in Policy Analysis." *Land Economics* 71 (February 1995): 1–15.

Grossman, Sanford, and Oliver Hart. "The Costs and Benefits of Ownership: A Theory of Vertical and Lateral Integration." *Journal of Political Economy* 94 (August 1986): 691–719.

Gwartney, James D., and Richard Stroup. *Economics: Private and Public Choice.* New York: Harcourt Brace Jovanovich, 1980.

Gwartney, James D., and Richard E. Wagner. "Public Choice and the Conduct of Representative Government." In *Public Choice and Constitutional Economics*, edited by James D. Gwartney and Richard E. Wagner, 3–28. Greenwich, Conn.: JAI Press, 1988.

Hale, Robert Lee. "Economic Theory and the Statesman." In *The Trend of Economics*, edited by Rexford G. Tugwell. New York: Knopf, 1924.

———. "Economics and the Law." In *The Social Sciences and Their Interrelations*, edited by William F. Ogburn and Alexander A. Goldenweiser. Boston: Houghton Mifflin, 1927.

———. *Freedom through Law.* New York: Columbia University Press, 1952.

Hall, Margaret E., ed. *Selected Writings of Benjamin Nathan Cardozo.* New York: Fallon, 1947.

Hamilton, Walton H. "Property according to Locke." *Yale Law Journal* 41 (April 1932): 864–80.

Hardin, Garrett. "Tragedy of the Commons." *Science* 162 (December 13, 1968): 1243–48.

Hart, Oliver. "An Economist's Perspective on the Theory of the Firm." In *Organization Theory: From Chester Barnard to the Present and Beyond*, edited by Oliver E. Williamson, 154–71. New York: Oxford University Press, 1990.

Hayami, Yujiro, and Vernon W. Ruttan. "Toward a Theory of Induced Institutional Innovation." *Journal of Development Studies* 20 (July 1984): 203–23.

Hayek, Friedrich A. "The Use of Knowledge in Society." *American Economic Review* 35 (1945): 519–30.

———. *Law, Legislation and Liberty.* Chicago: University of Chicago Press, 1973.

Heller, Thomas C. "Structuralism and Critique." *Stanford Law Review* 36 (January 1984): 127–98.

Herman, Samuel. "Economic Predilection and the Law." *American Political Science Review* 31 (October 1937): 821–41.

Hicks, J. R. "The Foundations of Welfare Economics." *Economic Journal* 49 (December 1939): 696–712.

Hirsch, Werner Z. *Law and Economics: An Introductory Analysis.* 2d ed. Boston: Academic Press, 1988.

Hirshleifer, Jack, ed. *Evolutionary Models in Economics and Law, Research in Law and Economics* 4 (1982).

Hodgson, Geoffrey M. *Economics and Institutions.* Philadelphia: University of Pennsylvania Press, 1988.

Hodgson, Geoffrey M., Warren J. Samuels, and Mark R. Tool, eds. *The Elgar Companion to Institutional and Evolutionary Economics.* Aldershot: Edward Elgar, 1994.

Hoffman, Elizabeth, and Matthew L. Spitzer. "Willingness to Pay vs. Willingness to Accept: Legal and Economic Implications." *Washington University Law Quarterly* 71 (spring 1993): 59–114.

Hofstadter, Richard. *The Progressive Historians.* New York: Knopf, 1968.

Holdsworth, W. S. "A Neglected Aspect of the Relations between Economic and Legal History." *Economic History Review* 1 (January 1927–28): 114–23.

Holmes, Oliver Wendell, Jr. "The Path of Law." *Harvard Law Review* 10 (March 1897): 457–78.

———. *The Common Law.* Boston: Little Brown, 1923.

Horwitz, Morton. "The Emergence of an Instrumental Conception of American Law, 1780–1820." *Perspectives in American History* 5 (1971): 285–326.

———. *The Transformation of American Law: 1780–1860.* Cambridge, Mass.: Harvard University Press, 1977.

———. "Law and Economics: Science or Politics?" *Hofstra Law Review* 8 (summer 1980): 905–12.

Hovenkamp, Herbert. "Chicago and Its Alternatives." *Duke Law Journal* 6 (December 1986): 1014–29.

———. "Law and Economics in the United States: A Brief Historical Survey." *Cambridge Journal of Economics* 19 (April 1995): 331–52.

Hudson, Brad. "Horwitz: A Critical Look at Studying Law." *Harvard Law Record* 75 (1982): 5–14.

Hunt, Alan. "The Critique of Law: What Is 'Critical' about Critical Legal Studies?" *Journal of Law and Society* 14 (spring 1987): 5–19.

Hutchinson, Allan C. *Critical Legal Studies.* Landham, Md.: Rowman & Littlefield/ University Press of America, 1988.

Hutchinson, Allan C., and Patrick J. Monahan. "Law, Politics, and the Critical Legal Scholars: The Unfolding Drama of American Legal Thought." *Stanford Law Review* 36 (January 1984a): 199–245.

———. "The 'Rights' Stuff: Roberto Unger and Beyond." *Texas Law Review* 62 (May 1984b): 1477–1539.

Jensen, Michael C., and William H. Meckling. "Theory of the Firm: Managerial Behavior, Agency Costs and Ownership Structure." *Journal of Financial Economics* 3 (October 1976): 305–60.

Johnson, David B. *Public Choice: An Introduction to the New Political Economy.* Mountain View, Calif.: Bristlecone Books, 1991.

Johnson, Phillip E. "Do You Sincerely Want to Be Radical?" *Stanford Law Review* 36 (January 1984): 247–91.

Johnston, Jason Scott. "Law, Economics, and Post-Realist Explanation." *Law & Society Review* 24, no. 5 (1990): 1217–54.

Kahneman, Daniel, Jack L. Knetsch, and Richard Thaler. "Experimental Tests of the Endowment Effect and the Coase Theorem." *Journal of Political Economy* 98 (December 1990): 1325–48.

Kaldor, Nicholas. "Welfare Propositions in Economics." *Economic Journal* 49 (September 1939): 549–52.

Kanal, Don. "Institutional Economics: Perspectives on Economy and Society." *Journal of Economic Issues* 19 (September 1985): 815–28.

Kaplow, Louis, and Steven Shavell. "Do Liability Rules Facilitate Bargaining: A Reply to Ayres and Talley." *Yale Law Journal* 105 (October 1995): 221–33.

———. "Property Rules versus Liability Rules." Harvard Law School Discussion Paper No. 156 (March 1995b).

Katz, Avery W. "Positivism and the Separation of Law and Economics." *Michigan Law Review* 94 (June 1996): 2229–69.

Katz, Wilbur. "A Four-Year Program for Legal Education." *University of Chicago Law Review* 4 (June 1937): 527–36.

Kelman, Mark. "Choice and Utility." *Wisconsin Law Review* 3 (1979a): 769–97.

———. "Consumption Theory, Production Theory, and Ideology in the Coase Theorem." *Southern California Law Review* 52 (March 1979b): 669–98.

———. "Interpretive Construction in the Substantive Criminal Law." *Stanford Law Review* 33 (April 1981): 591–673.

———. *A Guide to Critical Legal Studies.* Cambridge, Mass.: Harvard University Press, 1987.

Kennedy, David. "Critical Theory, Structuralism and Contemporary Legal Scholarship." *New England Law Review* 21, no. 2 (1985–1986): 209–89.

Kennedy, Duncan. "Form and Substance in Private Law Adjudication." *Harvard Law Review* 89 (June 1976): 1685–1778.

———. "The Structure of Blackstone's Commentaries." *Buffalo Law Review* 28 (winter 1979): 209–382.

———. "Legal Education as Training for Hierarchy." In *The Politics of Law: A Progressive Critique*, edited by David Kairys, 38–58. New York: Pantheon, 1990.

Kennedy, Duncan, and Peter Gabel. "Roll over Beethoven." *Stanford Law Review* 36 (January 1984): 1–55.

Kitch, Edmund W. "The Fire of Truth: A Remembrance of Law and Economics at Chicago, 1932–1970." *Journal of Law and Economics* 26 (April 1983a): 163–233.

———. "The Intellectual Foundations of 'Law and Economics.'" *Journal of Legal Education* 33 (June 1983b): 184–96.

Klare, Karl. "Notes and Commentary: Law-Making as Praxis." *Telos* 40 (summer 1979): 123–35.

———. "Labor Law as Ideology: Toward a New Historiography of Collective Bargaining Law." *Industrial Relations Law Journal* 4 (summer 1981): 450–82.

Klein, Benjamin. "Self Enforcing Contracts." *Journal of Institutional and Theoretical Economics* 141 (December 1985): 594–600. Reprinted in *The New Institutional Economics*, edited by Eirik G. Furubotn and Rudolf Richter, 89–95. College Station: Texas A&M University Press, 1991.

———. "Contracts and Incentives: The Role of Contracting Terms in Assuring Performance." In *Contract Economics*, edited by Lars Werin and Hans Wijkander, 149–72. Cambridge, Mass.: Basil Blackwell, 1992.

Klein, Benjamin, Robert G. Crawford, and Armen A. Alchian. "Vertical Integration, Appropriable Rents, and the Competitive Contracting Process." *Journal of Law and Economics* 21 (October 1978): 297–326.

Kneese, Allen V. *Economics and the Environment*. New York: Penguin, 1977.

Komesar, Neil K. "In Search of a General Approach to Legal Analysis: A Comparative Institutional Alternative." *Michigan Law Review* 79 (June 1981): 1350–92.

———. "Injuries and Institutions: Tort Reform, Tort Theory, and Beyond." *New York University Law Review* 65 (April 1990): 23–77.

———. *Imperfect Alternatives: Choosing Institutions in Law, Economics, and Pubic Policy*. Chicago: University of Chicago Press, 1994.

Kornhauser, Lewis. "The Great Image of Authority." *Stanford Law Review* 36 (January 1984): 349–89.

———. "An Introduction to the Economic Analysis of Contract Remedies." *University of Chicago Law Review* 57 (summer 1986): 683–725.

Kreps, David M. *A Course in Microeconomic Theory*. Princeton: Princeton University Press, 1990.

Kronman, Anthony T. "Wealth Maximization as a Normative Principle." *Journal of Legal Studies* 9 (March 1980): 227–42.

———. *The Lost Lawyer: Failing Ideals of the Legal Profession*. Cambridge, Mass: Harvard University Press, 1993.

Kronman, Anthony T., and Richard A. Posner, eds. *The Economics of Contract Law*. Boston: Little, Brown, 1979.

Kuhn, Thomas S. *The Structure of Scientific Revolutions*. 2d ed. Chicago: University of Chicago Press, 1970.

Lancaster, K. J. "A New Approach to Consumer Theory." *Journal of Political Economy* 74 (April 1966): 132–57.

Landes, William M. "An Economic Analysis of the Courts." *Journal of Law and Economics* 14 (April 1971): 61–107.

Landes, William M., and Richard A. Posner. "Causation in Tort Law: An Economic Approach." *Journal of Legal Studies* 12 (January 1983): 109–34.

———. *The Economic Structure of Tort Law*. Cambridge, Mass.: Harvard University Press, 1987.

———. "The Influence of Economics on Law: A Quantitative Study." *Journal of Law and Economics* 36 (April 1993): 385–424.

Lang, Mahlon G. "Economic Efficiency and Policy Comparisons." *American Journal of Agricultural Economics* 62 (November 1980): 772–77.

Langdell, Christopher C. *A Selection of Cases on the Law of Contracts*. Boston: Little, Brown, 1871.

Leibenstein, Harvey. *Inside the Firm*. Cambridge, Mass.: Harvard University Press, 1987.

Levinson, Sanford. "On Critical Legal Studies." *Dissent* 36 (summer 1989): 360–65.

Libecap, Gary D. *Contracting for Property Rights*. Cambridge: Cambridge University Press, 1989a.

———. "Distributional Issues in Contracting for Property Rights." *Journal of Institutional and Theoretical Economics* 145, no. 1 (1989b): 6–24. Reprinted in *The New Institutional Economics*, edited by Eirik G. Furubotn and Rudolf Richter, 214–32. College Station: Texas A&M University Press, 1991.

Liebhafsky, H. H. "Law and Economics from Different Perspectives." *Journal of Economic Issues* 21 (December 1987): 1809–36.

Lindahl, Eric. "Just Taxation—A Positive Solution." 1919. In *Classics in the Theory of Public Finance*, edited by Richard A. Musgrave and Alan T. Peacock, 168–76. New York: St. Martin's Press, 1967.

Litchman, Mark M. "Economics, the Basis of Law." *American Law Review* 61 (May-June 1927): 357–87.

Llewellyn, Karl N. "The Effect of Legal Institutions upon Economics." *American Economic Review* 15 (December 1925): 655–83.

———. "What Price Contract? An Essay in Perspective." *Yale Law Journal* 40 (March 1931): 704–51.

———. "The Constitution as an Institution." *Columbia Law Review* 34 (January 1934): 1–40.

———. "Law and the Social Sciences, Especially Sociology." *Harvard Law Review* 62 (June 1949): 1286–1305.

Macneil, Ian R. "The Many Futures of Contracts." *Southern California Law Review* 47, no. 3 (1974): 691–816.

———. "Contracts: Adjustment of Long-Term Economic Relations under Classical, Neoclassical, and Relational Contract Law." *Northwestern University Law Review* 72 (January-February 1978): 854–905.

———. "Economic Analysis of Contractual Relations." In *The Economic Approach to Law*, edited by Paul Burrows and Cento G. Veljanovski, 61–92. London: Butterworths, 1981.

Marx, Karl. *On the Jewish Question.* Cincinnati: Hebrew Union College, 1958.

Mashaw, Jerry. "As if Republican Interpretation." *Yale Law Journal* 97 (July 1988): 1685–1723.

McLean, Iain. *Public Choice: An Introduction.* Oxford: Basil Blackwell, 1987.

Medema, Steven G. "Another Look at the Problem of Rent Seeking." *Journal of Economic Issues* 25 (December 1991): 1049–65.

———. *Ronald H. Coase.* London: Macmillan, 1994.

———. "The Coase Theorem." University of Colorado at Denver Center for Research on Economic and Social Policy Working Paper No. 9510, 1995.

Medema, Steven G., and Richard O. Zerbe Jr. "The Coase Theorem." In Boudewijn Bouckaert and Gerrit de Geest, eds., *The Encyclopedia of Law and Economics.* Aldershot: Edward Elgar, forthcoming.

Mensch, Elizabeth. "The History of Mainstream Legal Thought." In *The Politics of Law: A Progressive Critique*, edited by David Kairys, 13–37. New York: Pantheon, 1990.

Mercuro, Nicholas. "Toward a Comparative Institutional Approach to the Study of Law and Economics." In *Law and Economics*, edited by Nicholas Mercuro, 1–26. Boston: Kluwer, 1989.

Mercuro, Nicholas, and Steven G. Medema. "Schools of Thought in Law and Economics: A Kuhnian Competition." In *Law and Economics: New and Critical Perspectives*, edited by Robin Paul Malloy and Christopher K. Braun, 65–126. New York: Peter Lang, 1995.

Mercuro, Nicholas, and Timothy P. Ryan. "Property Rights and Welfare Economics: *Miller et al. v. Schoene* Revisited." *Land Economics* 56 (May 1980): 202–12.

———. *Law, Economics and Public Policy.* Greenwich, Conn.: JAI Press, 1984.

Merton, Robert K. "Three Fragments from a Sociologist's Notebooks." *Annual Review of Sociology* 13 (1987): 1–28.

Michelman, Frank I. "Norms and Normativity in the Economic Theory of Law." *Minnesota Law Review* 62 (July 1978): 1015–48.

———. "Politics and Values or What's Really Wrong with Rationality Review?" *Creighton Law Review* 13 (winter 1979): 487–511.

———. "Traces of Self-Government." *Harvard Law Review* 100 (November 1986): 4–77.

———. "Law's Republic." *Yale Law Journal* 97 (July 1988): 1493–1537.

Miller, H. Laurence, Jr. "On the 'Chicago School of Economics.'" *Journal of Political Economy* 70 (February 1962): 64–69.

Minow, Martha. "Law Turning Outward." *Telos* 73 (fall 1987): 79–100.

Mishan, Ezra. "The Futility of Pareto-Efficiency in Policy Analysis." *American Economic Review* 62 (December 1972): 971–76.

Mitchell, Wesley C. *Business Cycles: The Problem and Its Setting.* New York: National Bureau of Economic Research, 1927.

Mitchell, William C. "Textbook Public Choice: A Review Essay." *Public Choice* 38, no. 1 (1982): 97–112.

Monahan, John, and Laurens Walker. *Social Science in Law: Cases and Materials.* 2d ed. Westbury, N.Y.: Foundation Press, 1990.

Mueller, Dennis C. *Public Choice II.* Cambridge: Cambridge University Press, 1989.

Niskanen, William A. *Bureaucracy and Representative Government.* Chicago: Aldine, Atherton, 1971.

———. *Bureaucracy and Public Economics.* Aldershot: Edward Elgar, 1994.

North, Douglass C. "Sources of Productivity Change in Ocean Shipping 1600–1850." *Journal of Political Economy* 76 (September/October 1968): 953–70.

———. *Structure and Change in Economic History.* New York: Norton, 1981.

———. "Transaction Costs, Institutions, and Economic History." *Journal of Institutional and Theoretical Economics* 140, no. 1 (1984): 7–17. Reprinted in *The New Institutional Economics*, edited by Eirik G. Furubotn and Rudolf Richter, 203–13. College Station: Texas A&M University Press, 1991.

———. "A Transaction Cost Approach to the Historical Development of Polities and Economies." *Journal of Institutional and Theoretical Economics* 145 (December 1989): 661–68. Reprinted in *The New Institutional Economics*, edited by Eirik G. Furubotn and Rudolf Richter, 253–60. College Station: Texas A&M University Press, 1991.

———. "Institutions and a Transaction Cost Theory of Exchange." In *Perspectives on Positive Political Economy*, edited by James E. Alt and Kenneth A. Shepsle, 182–94. Cambridge: Cambridge University Press, 1990a.

———. *Institutions, Institutional Change, and Economic Performance.* Cambridge: Cambridge University Press, 1990b.

———. "Institutions and Credible Commitment." *Journal of Institutional and Theoretical Economics* 149 (March 1993a): 11–23.

———. "Institutions and Economic Performance." In *Rationality, Institutions and Economic Methodology*, edited by Uskali Maki, Bo Gustafsson, and Christian Knudsen, 242–61. London: Routledge, 1993b.

Note. "'Round and 'Round the Bramble Bush: From Legal Realism to Critical Legal Scholarship." *Harvard Law Review* 95 (May 1982): 1669–90.

Nozick, Robert. *Anarchy, State and Utopia.* New York: Basic Books, 1974.

Olsen, Frances. "The Sex of Law." In *The Politics of Law: A Progressive Critique,* edited by David Kairys, 453–67. New York: Pantheon, 1990.

Ostrom, Elinor. "A Method of Institutional Analysis." In *Guidance, Control and Evaluation in the Public Sector,* edited by Franz-Xarer Kaufman. Berlin: Walter de Gruyter, 1986.

Packer, Herbert L., and Thomas Erlich. *New Directions in Legal Education.* New York: McGraw-Hill, 1973.

Parrington, Vernon L. *Main Currents in American Thought.* New York: Harcourt, Brace, 1930.

Parsons, Kenneth H. "The Institutional Basis for an Agricultural Market Economy." *Journal of Economic Issues* 8 (December 1974): 737–57.

Pejovich, Svetozar. "Towards an Economic Theory of the Creation and Specification of Property Rights." *Review of Social Economy* 30 (September 1972): 309–25.

Peller, Gary. "The Metaphysics of American Law." *California Law Review* 73 (July 1985): 1152–1290.

Peltzman, Sam. "Toward a More General Theory of Regulation." *Journal of Law and Economics* 19 (August 1976): 211–40.

———. "The Growth of Government." *Journal of Law and Economics* 23 (October 1980): 209–88.

Pindyck, Robert S., and Daniel L. Rubinfeld. *Microeconomics.* 2d ed. New York: Macmillan, 1992.

Polinsky, A. Mitchell. "Controlling Externalities and Protecting Entitlements: Property Right, Liability, and Tax-Subsidy Approaches." *Journal of Legal Studies* 8 (January 1979): 1–48.

———. "Resolving Nuisance Disputes: The Simple Economics of Injunctive and Damage Remedies." *Stanford Law Review* 32 (July 1980): 1075–1112.

———. *An Introduction to Law and Economics.* 2d ed. Boston: Little, Brown, 1989.

Posner, Richard A. "A Theory of Negligence." *Journal of Legal Studies* 1 (January 1972a): 29–96.

———. *Economic Analysis of Law.* 1st ed. Boston: Little, Brown, 1972b.

———. "Strict Liability: A Comment." *Journal of Legal Studies* 2 (January 1973): 205–21.

———. "The Economic Approach to Law." *Texas Law Review* 53 (May 1975): 757–82.

———. *The Economics of Justice.* Cambridge, Mass.: Harvard University Press, 1983.

———. "The Decline of Law as an Autonomous Discipline: 1962–1987." *Harvard Law Review* 100 (February 1987a): 761–80.

———. "The Law and Economics Movement." *American Economic Review* 77 (May 1987b): 1–13.

———. *The Problems of Jurisprudence.* Cambridge, Mass.: Harvard University Press, 1990.

———. *Economic Analysis of Law.* 4th ed. Boston: Little, Brown, 1992.

———. "Gary Becker's Contributions to Law and Economics." *Journal of Legal Studies* 22 (June 1993a): 211–15.

———. "What Do Judges Maximize? (The Same Thing Everybody Else Does)." *Supreme Court Economic Review* 3 (1993b): 1–41.

———. *Overcoming Law*. Cambridge, Mass.: Harvard University Press, 1995.

Pound, Roscoe. "The Scope and Purpose of Sociological Jurisprudence, Part I." *Harvard Law Review* 24 (June 1911a): 591–619.

———. "The Scope and Purpose of Sociological Jurisprudence, Part II." *Harvard Law Review* 25 (December 1911b): 140–68.

———. "The Scope and Purpose of Sociological Jurisprudence, Part III." *Harvard Law Review* 25 (April 1912): 489–516.

———. *Introduction to the Philosophy of Law*. rev. ed. New Haven: Yale University Press, 1954.

Price, Catherine M. *Welfare Economics in Theory and Practice*. London: Macmillan, 1977.

Priest, George. "The Common Law Process and the Selection of Efficient Legal Rules." *Journal of Legal Studies* 6 (January 1977): 65–82.

Purcell, Edward A., Jr. "American Jurisprudence between the Wars: Legal Realism and the Crisis of Democratic Theory." In *American Law and the Constitutional Order*, edited by Lawrence M. Friedman and Harry N. Scheiber, 359–74. Cambridge, Mass.: Harvard University Press, 1988.

Rawls, John. *Theory of Justice*. Cambridge, Mass.: Harvard University Press, 1971.

Reder, Melvin W. "Chicago Economics: Permanence and Change." *Journal of Economic Literature* 20 (March 1982): 1–38.

Reisman, David. *The Political Economy of James Buchanan*. College Station: Texas A&M University Press, 1990.

Riker, William. *The Theory of Political Coalitions*. New Haven: Yale University Press, 1962.

Rizzo, Mario. "Law amid Flux: The Economics of Negligence and Strict Liability in Tort." *Journal of Legal Studies* 9 (March 1980): 291–318.

———. "Rules versus Cost-Benefit Analysis in the Common Law." *Cato Journal* 4 (winter 1985): 865–84.

Rose-Ackerman, Susan. "Law and Economics: Paradigm, Politics, or Philosophy?" In *Law and Economics*, edited by Nicholas Mercuro, 233–58. Boston: Kluwer, 1989.

———. *Rethinking the Progressive Agenda: The Reform of the American Regulatory State*. New York: Free Press, 1992.

Rosen, Harvey S. *Public Finance*. 4th ed. Homewood, Ill.: Richard D. Irwin, 1995.

Rowley, Charles K., and Alan T. Peacock. *Welfare Economics: A Liberal Restatement*. New York: John Wiley, 1975.

Rubin, Paul. "Why Is the Common Law Efficient?" *Journal of Legal Studies* 6 (January 1977): 51–63.

———. "Common Law and Statute Law." *Journal of Legal Studies* 11 (June 1982): 205–23.

Samuels, Warren J. *The Classical Theory of Economic Policy*. Cleveland: World, 1966.

———. "Interrelations between Legal and Economic Processes." *Journal of Law and Economics* 14 (October 1971): 435–50.

———. "Ecosystem Policy and the Problem of Power." *Environmental Affairs* 2 (winter 1972a): 580–96.

Samuels, Warren J. "Welfare Economics, Power, and Property." In *Perspectives of Property*, edited by Gene Wunderlich and W. L. Gibson Jr., 61–127. University Park, Pa.: Institute for Research on Land and Water Resources, Pennsylvania State University, 1972b.

———. "The Economy as a System of Power and Its Legal Bases: The Legal Economics of Robert Lee Hale." *University of Miami Law Review* 27 (spring/summer 1973): 261–371.

———. "Commentary: An Economic Perspective on the Compensation Problem." *Wayne Law Review* 21 (November 1974): 113–34.

———. "Approaches to Legal-Economic Policy and Related Problems of Research." In *Policy Studies and the Social Sciences*, edited by Stuart S. Nagel, 65–73. Lexington, Mass.: Lexington Books, 1975.

———, ed. *The Chicago School of Political Economy*. East Lansing, Mich.: Graduate School of Business, Michigan State University, 1976.

———. "Normative Premises in Regulatory Theory." *Journal of Post Keynesian Economics* 1 (fall 1978): 100–114.

———. "Maximization of Wealth as Justice: An Essay on Posnerian Law and Economics as Policy Analysis." *Texas Law Review* 60 (December 1981): 147–72.

———, ed. *Institutional Economics*. 3 vols. Aldershot: Edward Elgar, 1988.

———. "The Legal-Economic Nexus." *George Washington Law Review* 57 (August 1989a): 1556–78.

———. "The Methodology of Economics and the Case for Policy Diffidence and Restraint." *Review of Social Economy* 42 (summer 1989b): 113–33.

———. *Essays on the Economic Role of Government*. 2 vols. New York: New York University Press, 1992.

———. "Law and Economics: Some Early Journal Contributions." In *Economic Thought and Discourse in the Twentieth Century*, edited by Warren J. Samuels, Jeff Biddle, and Thomas W. Patchak-Schuster, 217–85. Aldershot: Edward Elgar, 1993.

———. "Reflections on the Intellectual Context and Significance of Thorstein Veblen." *Journal of Economic Issues* 29 (September 1995): 915–22.

Samuels, Warren J., and Nicholas Mercuro. "The Role and Resolution of the Compensation Principle in Society: Part One—The Role." *Research in Law and Economics* 1 (1979): 157–94.

———. 1980. "The Role and Resolution of the Compensation Principle in Society: Part Two—The Resolution." *Research in Law and Economics* 2 (1980): 103–28.

———. "A Critique of Rent-Seeking Theory." In *Neoclassical Political Economy: The Analysis of Rent-Seeking and DUP Activities*, edited by David C. Colander, 55–70. Cambridge, Mass.: Ballinger, 1984.

Samuels, Warren J., and A. Allan Schmid."Polluters' Profit and Political Response: The Dynamics of Rights Creation." *Public Choice* 28 (winter 1976): 99–105.

———. *Law and Economics: An Institutional Perspective*. Boston: Kluwer-Nijhoff, 1981.

Samuelson, Paul A. *Foundations of Economic Analysis*. Cambridge, Mass.: Harvard University Press, 1947.

———. "Diagramatic Exposition of a Theory of Public Expenditure." *Review of Economics and Statistics* 37 (November 1955): 350–56.

———. "Social Indifference Curves." *Quarterly Journal of Economics* 70 (February 1956): 1–22.

Sarat, Austin. "Critical Legal Studies outside of the Law School." *Focus on Law Studies* 4 (spring 1989): 1, 10, 11.

Saveth, Edward N. "Historical Understanding in Democratic America." In *Understanding the American Past*. 2d ed., edited by Edward N. Saveth, 1–54. Boston: Little, Brown, 1965.

Schlegel, John Henry. "Notes toward an Intimate, Opinionated, and Affectionate History of the Conference on Critical Legal Studies." *Stanford Law Review* 36 (January 1984): 391–411.

Schmid, A. Allan. "Biotechnology, Plant Variety Protection, and Changing Property Institutions in Agriculture." *North Central Journal of Agricultural Economics* 7 (July 1985): 129–38.

———. *Property, Power, and Public Choice: An Inquiry into Law and Economics*. 2d ed. New York: Praeger, 1987.

———. "Law and Economics: An Institutional Perspective." In *Law and Economics*, edited by Nicholas Mercuro, 57–85. Boston: Kluwer, 1989.

———. "Institutional Law and Economics." *European Journal of Law and Economics* 1 (March 1994): 33–51.

Schmidtchen, Dieter. "Time, Uncertainty, and Subjectivism: Giving More Body to Law and Economics." *International Review of Law and Economics* 13 (March 1993): 61–84.

Schön, Donald A. "Generative Metaphor: A Perspective on Problem-Setting in Social Policy." In *Metaphor and Thought*, edited by Andrew Ortony, 254–83. Cambridge: Cambridge University Press, 1979.

Schwartz, Alan. "The Case for Specific Performance." *Yale Law Journal* 2 (December 1979): 271–306.

Schwartz, Louis B. "With Gun and Camera through Darkest CLS-Land." *Stanford Law Review* 36 (January 1984): 413–64.

Schwartzstein, Linda A. "Austrian Economics and the Current Debate between Critical Legal Studies and Law and Economics." *Hofstra Law Review* 20 (summer 1992): 1105–37.

Scitovsky, Tibor. "A Note on Welfare Propositions in Economics." *Review of Economic Studies* 9 (November 1941–42): 77–88.

Seidman, Robert. "Contract Law, the Free Market, and State Intervention: A Jurisprudential Perspective." *Journal of Economic Issues* 7 (December 1973): 553–76.

Shavell, Steven. "Suit, Settlement, and Trial: A Theoretical Analysis under Alternative Methods for the Allocation of Legal Costs." *Journal of Legal Studies* 11 (January 1982): 55–82.

———. *Economic Analysis of Accident Law*. Cambridge, Mass.: Harvard University Press, 1987.

Shepsle, Kenneth A. "Prospects for Formal Models of Legislatures." *Legislative Studies Quarterly* 10 (February 1985): 5–19.

Shepsle, Kenneth A., and Barry Weingast. "Political Solutions to Market Problems." *American Political Science Review* 78 (June 1984): 417–34.

Shughart, William F., II, and Robert D. Tollison. "On the Growth of Government and the Political Economy of Legislation." *Research in Law and Economics* 9 (1986): 111–27.

Simon, Herbert A. *Administrative Behavior.* 2d ed. New York: Macmillan, 1961.

Smith, Adam. *An Inquiry into the Nature and Causes of the Wealth of Nations.* 1776. Reprint, New York: Modern Library, 1937.

Solo, Robert A. *Economic Organization and Social Systems.* New York: Bobbs-Merrill, 1967.

―――. *The Political Authority and the Market System.* Cincinnati: South-Western, 1974.

―――. *The Positive State.* Cincinnati: South-Western, 1982.

Sommerville, J. P. *Politics and Ideology in England 1603–1640.* London: Longmans, 1986.

Sparer, Ed. "Fundamental Human Rights, Legal Entitlements, and the Social Struggle: A Friendly Critique of the Critical Legal Studies Movement." *Stanford Law Review* 36 (January 1984): 509–74.

Spiegel, Henry W. *The Growth of Economic Thought.* Durham, N.C.: Duke University Press, 1971.

Srivastava, Sik. *History of Economic Thought.* Dehli: Atma Ram, 1965.

Stevens, Joe B. *The Economics of Collective Choice.* Boulder: Westview Press, 1993.

Stewart, Richard B. "Crisis in Tort Law? The Institutional Perspective." *University of Chicago Law Review* 54 (winter 1987): 184–99.

―――. "Controlling Environmental Risks through Economic Incentives." *Columbia Journal of Environmental Law* 13, no. 2 (1988): 153–69.

Stigler, George J. "The Economics of Information." *Journal of Political Economy* 69 (June 1961): 213–25.

―――. "The Theory of Economic Regulation." *Bell Journal of Economics and Management Science* 2 (spring 1971): 137–46.

―――. "The Sizes of Legislatures." *Journal of Legal Studies* 5 (January 1976): 17–34.

Stone, Julius. *The Province and Function of Law.* Cambridge, Mass.: Harvard University Press, 1950.

Summers, Robert S. "Pragmatic Instrumentalism in the Twentieth Century American Legal Thought—A Synthesis and Critique of Our Dominant General Theory about Law and Its Use." *Cornell Law Review* 66 (June 1981): 861–948.

Sunstein, Cass R. "Beyond the Republican Revival." *Yale Law Journal* 97 (July 1988): 1539–90.

―――. *After the Rights Revolution: Reconceiving the Regulatory State.* Cambridge, Mass.: Harvard University Press, 1990.

"Symposium on the Theory of Public Choice." *Virginia Law Review* 74 (March 1988).

"Symposium: The Republican Civic Tradition." *Yale Law Journal* 97 (July 1988).

Taub, Nadine, and Elizabeth M. Schneider. "Perspectives on Women's Subordination and the Role of Law." In *The Politics of Law: A Progressive Critique,* edited by David Kairys, 151–76. New York: Pantheon, 1990.

Telser, Lester. "A Theory of Self-Enforcing Agreements." *Journal of Business* 53 (February 1981): 27–44.

Tool, Marc R. *Evolutionary Economics*, 2 vols. Armonk, N.Y.: M. E. Sharpe, 1988.

Tool, Marc R., ed. *Institutional Economics: Theory, Method, Policy*. Boston: Kluwer, 1993.

Trebing, Harry M., ed. *New Dimensions in Public Utility Pricing*. East Lansing: Institute of Public Utilities, Michigan State University, 1976.

———. "Telecommunications Regulation—The Continuing Dilemma." In *Public Utility Regulation*, edited by K. Nowotym, D. B. Smith, and H. M. Trebing, 120–22. Boston: Kluwer, 1989.

Trebing, Harry M., and Maurice Estabrooks. "Telecommunications Policy in the Global Information Economy of the Nineties." In *International Perspectives on Telecommunications Policy*, edited by Rodney Stevenson, T. H. Oum, and H. Oniki, 17–37. Greenwich, Conn.: JAI Press, 1993.

Trubek, David M. "Where the Action Is: Critical Legal Studies and Empiricism." *Stanford Law Review* 36 (January 1984): 575–622.

Trubeck, David M., and Marc Galanter. "Scholars in Self-Estrangement: Some Reflections on the Crisis in Law and Development Studies in the United States." *Wisconsin Law Review* 4 (1974): 1062–1102.

Tullock, Gordon. *The Politics of Bureaucracy*. Washington: Public Affairs Press, 1965.

———. *Rent Seeking*. Aldershot: Edward Elgar, 1993.

Turner, Frederick Jackson. "The Significance of the Frontier in American History." In *The Frontier in American History*, 1–38. New York: Henry Holt, 1920.

Tushnet, Mark V. "Post-Realist Legal Scholarship." *Wisconsin Law Review* 6 (1980): 1383–1401.

———. "Perspectives on Critical Legal Studies." *George Washington Law Review* 52 (January 1984): 239–42.

———. "Critical Legal Studies: An Introduction to Its Origins and Underpinnings." *Journal of Legal Education* 36 (December 1986): 505–17.

Ulen, Thomas S. "Law and Economics: Settled Issues and Open Questions." In *Law and Economics*, edited by Nicholas Mercuro, 201–31. Boston: Kluwer, 1989.

Umbeck, John. "A Theory of Contract Choice and the California Gold Rush." *Journal of Law and Economics* 20 (October 1977): 421–37.

Unger, Roberto. "The Critical Legal Studies Movement." *Harvard Law Review* 96 (January 1983): 561–675.

Varian, Hal R. *Microeconomic Analysis*. 3d ed. New York: Norton, 1992.

———. *Intermediate Microeconomics: A Modern Approach*. 3d ed. New York: Norton, 1993.

Veblen, Thorstein B. *Theory of the Leisure Class*. New York: Macmillan, 1899.

———. *The Theory of Business Enterprise*. New York: Charles Scribner's Sons, 1904.

———. *Absentee Ownership and Business Enterprise in Recent Times*. New York: Huebsch, 1923.

Veljanovski, Cento G. *The New Law-and-Economics*. Oxford: Centre for Socio-Legal Studies, 1982.

Wallis, John J., and Douglass C. North. "Measuring the Transaction Sector in the American Economy, 1870–1970." In *Long-Term Factors in American Economic Growth*, edited by Stanley L. Engerman and Robert E. Gallman, 95–161. Chicago: University of Chicago Press, 1986.

Wandschneider, Philip. "Neoclassical and Institutionalist Explanations of Changes in Northwest Water Institutions." *Journal of Economic Issues* 20 (March 1986): 87–107.

Weingast, Barry R., and William J. Marshall. "The Industrial Organization of Congress: Or Why Legislatures, like Firms, Are Not Organized as Markets." *Journal of Political Economy* 96 (February 1988): 132–63.

Weinrib, Ernest J. *The Idea of Private Law.* Cambridge, Mass.: Harvard University Press, 1995.

Whalen, Charles J. "The Institutionalist Approach to Economics." In *Beyond Neoclassical Economics: Heterodox Approaches to Economic Theory,* edited by Fred Foldvary. Aldershot: Edward Elgar, 1996.

Wicksell, Knut. *Finanztheoretische Untersuchungen.* Jena: Gustav Fisher, 1896.

———. "A New Principle of Just Taxation." In *Classics in the Theory of Public Finance,* edited by Richard A. Musgrave and Alan T. Peacock, 72–118. New York: St. Martin's Press, 1967.

Williams, Robert A. "Taking Rights Aggressively: The Perils and Promise of Critical Legal Theory for Peoples of Color." *Law and Inequality* 5 (May 1987): 103–34.

Williamson, Oliver E. "Managerial Discretion and Business Behavior." *American Economic Review* 53 (December 1963): 1032–57.

———. *Markets and Hierarchies: Analysis and Antitrust Implications.* New York: Free Press, 1975.

———. "Credible Commitments: Using Hostages to Support Exchange." *American Economic Review* 73 (September 1983): 519–40.

———. "The Economics of Governance: Framework and Implications." *Journal of Institutional and Theoretical Economics* 140 (March 1984): 195–223. Reprinted in *The New Institutional Economics,* edited by Eirik G. Furubotn and Rudolf Richter, 54–82. College Station: Texas A&M University Press, 1991.

———. *The Economic Institutions of Capitalism: Firms, Markets, Relational Contracting.* New York: Free Press, 1985.

———. "The Economics of Governance: Framework and Implications." In *Economics as a Process: Essays in the New Institutional Economics,* edited by Richard Langlois, 171–202. Cambridge: Cambridge University Press, 1986.

———. "The Logic of Economic Organization." *Journal of Law, Economics, and Organization* 4 (spring 1988): 65–93.

———. "A Comparison of Alternative Approaches to Economic Organization." *Journal of Institutional and Theoretical Economics* 146, no. 1 (1990): 61–71. Reprinted in *The New Institutional Economics,* edited by Eirik G. Furubotn and Rudolf Richter, 104–14. College Station: Texas A&M University Press, 1991.

———. "Comparative Economic Organization: The Analysis of Discrete Structural Alternatives." *Administrative Science Quarterly* 36 (June 1991): 269–96.

———. "The Evolving Science of Organization." *Journal of Institutional and Theoretical Economics* 149 (March 1993a): 35–53.

———. "Transaction Cost Economics Meets Posnerian Law and Economics." *Journal of Institutional and Theoretical Economics* 149 (March 1993b): 99–118.

Wonnacott, Paul, and Ronald Wonnacott. *An Introduction to Microeconomics.* New York: McGraw-Hill, 1979.

Wood, Robert S. "History, Thought, and Images: The Development of International Law and Organization." *Virginia Journal of International Law* 12 (December 1971): 35–65.

Woodward, Calvin. "The Limits of Legal Realism: An Historical Perspective." *Virginia Law Review* 54 (May 1968): 689–739.

Zerbe, Richard O., Jr. "The Problem of Social Cost in Retrospect." *Research in Law and Economics* 2 (1980): 83–102.

Name Index

Subject Index